03354909

G000256648

EPSOM LIBRARY
www.surreycc.gov.uk/libraries
0300 200 1001

25. FEB. 1997

T₀ MARLOW LIB
BUCKINGHAMSHIRE.

From EWELL LIB.
SURREY.

App. 11/1018258

DIB. 5.2.99.

TO: ML10

FROM: EW

Oct 15

COUNTY
LIBRARIES
AND LEISURE
SERVICE

L21B

SUR
COUNTY

Charges will be payable at
the Adult rate if this item
is not returned by the
latest date stamped abov

B

JOHN WOOD
Architect of Obsession

The masonic symbol of a flaming sun in the triangle of the
Trinity circled by the serpent of eternity, from the Tyberton altar.

JOHN WOOD
Architect of Obsession

Tim Mowl and Brian Earnshaw

SURREY COUNTY LIBRARY

ART | 720.92
NOO

Millstream Books

88 442427

To Adam
who, in bleak February or tourist-teeming August,
cheerfully endured column and crescent,
condescending young ladies and impatient cognoscenti,
provided there was always the buggy to retire to
and some strict architectural appraisal of
Hamley's toyshop

First published 1988

This book has been set in Baskerville type by Character Graphics, Taunton
Printed in Great Britain by The Amadeus Press, Huddersfield
Jacket printed by The Matthews Wright Press, Chard

© Tim Mowl and Brian Earnshaw 1988

ISBN 094897513X

All rights reserved. No part of this publication may be reproduced, stored
in a retrieval system, or transmitted, in any form or by any means,
electronic, mechanical, photocopying, recording or otherwise without the
prior permission of Millstream Books.

Preface

The writing of architectural history can easily become a very solemn business, and it may be that the real reason why no one has published a life of John Wood the Elder until now is that all scholars with the wit to read have known the truth about his mind and motivation but no one has so far risked writing it down on account of its sometimes near-fictional quality.

One of us had the double fortune, first to study under Howard Colvin at Oxford, and then to serve for a time as Architectural Advisor to the Bath Preservation Trust. This led naturally to our following up one of those rare open-ended passages in Howard's indispensable *Biographical Dictionary of British Architects*. Under the entry 'John Wood (1704-1754)' it reads: 'What connection there may have been between Wood's antiquarian researches and his architectural projects is a subject that deserves investigation.'

Initially this appeared an invitation hard to resist. Here was a major architect, the creator of an enduring city, with several large question marks hanging over his career, yet not a single study of any substance had been published to explore the problems. Wood had himself written at length on the Classical Orders, on prehistoric antiquities and on the history of his home city, thus throwing much indirect light on his own nature and beliefs. As a result anyone who read his books knew exactly what he intended as he became a successful architect, town-planner and developer. The problem was certainly not one of Wood's obscurity, but it was, quite probably, one of the self-concept of the city he had created.

The name of Bath, originally a homely instance of Saxon plain speaking, has over the years become inseparable from a faintly precious association with 'Georgian elegance'. The place has developed an image, half-frivolous, half-valetudinarian, but always desperately refined, and any notion that John Wood, its second founder, was a typical half-baked intellectual product of the third decade of the 18th century, in a word a crackpot, has always disturbed the citizenry. It was never possible for them to sweep Wood's name under the carpet, his achievement was too lapidary and inspired. There has, however, been a consistent, unacknowledged tendency to sidestep the reality of the man, to joke about his druidic fixation, the monumental errors of his historical conclusions, then pass on quickly to safe Roman antecedents, to symmetry, balance, order and all the hackneyed concomitants of that 'Georgian elegance'.

The trouble with Wood was that he built brilliantly on theoretical foundations of some absurdity. That is why publishers have flinched from projecting him alongside fashionable coffee-table book subjects like William Kent and Robert Adam. Anyone who writes about the man risks being associated with his beliefs and may appear to countenance his eccentricity merely by chronicling it and admiring the great architecture which was its undoubted end product. More than most mortals John Wood did the right things for the wrong reasons; 'wrong' in the sense of inappropriate to 20th century concepts of religious values and period associations.

After that nervous disclaimer, the book has still seemed worth writing. There was a body of new material. Much also that was known and relevant had been wilfully ignored by earlier commentators. When all the facts were pulled together, a major early Palladian emerged as a romantic historicist. Finally it was time to do justice to an architect who had been seen as provincial simply because he did no work of consequence in London and remained singularly uninfluenced by contemporary building and town-planning on the Continent.

We wish to thank those scholars who were aware of the pitfalls and who have helped us generously over the last few years. Most of all our gratitude goes to Howard Colvin and to Trevor Fawcett, the Secretary of the History of Bath Research Group. They read our manuscript with critical austerity and cautious encouragement. Howard applied his famous rigour to our facts and directed us to archive sources of prime importance which we had missed. Trevor shared with us his unique background knowledge of 18th century Bath, advising where we had overstated a position or missed telling clues in contemporary journals. It was he who first directed us to the cogent analysis of Wood's mind and inspiration in Charles Edward Brownell's 1976 doctoral thesis on the Wood family. His thesis superseded all previous writing on the subject and was the groundbase for our own research. We wish to stress our debt to Dr Brownell's perception. More factually earth-bound but of equal value was Walter Ison's *The Georgian Buildings of Bath*.

Wendy Woodhouse-Mowl spent patient hours in the dark-room developing our photographs and never showed undue jealousy over her husband's obsessive affair with a city. Maureen and Reg Barton who typed and collated our manuscript were not simply immaculate in their standards but warmly interested in the unfolding narrative. To conclude our more personal debts, our publishers Tim Graham and Alan Summers stepped in with heartening speed after a London publisher had hesitated delicately for four months, thus proving that now, as then, Bath has a style and a confidence that often leave the capital standing.

In no other order than alphabetical, our thanks to the following who all helped to make the scholarly pursuit an easy and civilised pleasure: Victoria Barwell, Barbara Milner and Jill Knight at the Victoria Art Gallery, Bath, Dr Geoffrey Beard, William Bertram, Terry Bryant, Marion Carter, Major Anthony Crombie, James Elliott, Mrs E. M. Frayling, Andor Gomme, Philip and Ellie Gooden, John Hamill, Librarian and Curator of the United Grand Lodge of England, Pat Hayler, Charles Hind, Isabel Ide, Colin Johnston, Bath City Archivist, Mrs Joyce and her staff at Bath Reference Library, Francis Kelly, Nicholas Kingsley, Dr G. A. Knight, Jarl Kremeier, Phillip W. Kupper, Mr G. F. Laurence, Nicholas Lee and George Mayby of Bristol University Library, Janet Margrie, John and Rosamund Napier, Julian Orbach, Revd Paterson, Jean Pratt, Gordon Priest, Clive Quinnell, R. S. Redwood, Richard Riddell, Mary L. Robertson at the Huntington Library, Nicholas Savage, Julian and Helen Self, Mrs L. M. Shaw, Gillian and Paul Sladen, Janet Smith, Christopher J. Stark, Peter and Ann Stephenson-Wright, Arthur Tindall, Patrick Tobin, Roger White, John S. Williams and his staff at Bristol Record Office, Thomas Woodcock of the College of Arms, Mrs A. J. Woodruff.

Tim Mowl and Brian Earnshaw
Redland and Cotham, Spring 1988

Contents

Chapter One

The Enigma Years
of a
'Joyner' from Westminster

Nothing could be less appropriate to Wood than the geriatric title of 'John Wood the Elder' by which he is known. He was the Chatterton and the Mozart of English architects, projecting his new Imperial Bath when he was only 21 and completing half his best work before he was 30. This is what makes the obscurity of his early life so frustrating. His *Essay Towards a Description of Bath*, published in 1742-3 and thoroughly revised in 1749, is to all intents an autobiography, brimming with self-exposure and self-justification. Yet the baffling feature of all the writing is that the first 21 years of his life remain as if they never happened. It is this that allowed his native Bath to believe throughout the 19th century that he was born and bred a Yorkshireman.

In the summer of 1725 he emerges out of a mysterious blank, brash, confident and decisive, engaged in unstated activities in Yorkshire but already armed with a visionary scheme for a West Country spa town that would outrank anything built in contemporary London since Inigo Jones's Covent Garden of 80 years before. In scale and fantasy his plan for a *Royal Forum*, a *Grand Circus* and an *Imperial Gymnasium*[1] would have made more sense in 19th century Vienna than for a Somerset walled town of 9,000 inhabitants in the last years of George I. But what becomes clear from this conception and the constancy with which Wood followed it for the remainder of his life is that already in 1725 his mind had been shaped in a bizarre cultural cross-reference that was to be enduring.

Somewhere in the years before, he had developed three obsessions that were to interrelate and govern his architectural thinking and his town-planning. The first was a conventional enthusiasm for revived Palladian classicism. The second was a more esoteric, though by no means unique, interest in Celtic prehistory, limited in Wood's case by an intense regional patriotism. His third obsession was with Freemasonry and with the significance of the First Temple as built by Hiram for King Solomon at Jerusalem. Unexpectedly it was this last reverence for the sacred architecture of the Jews which supplied Wood with a theoretical framework for combining his first two obsessions. This theory was fanciful but satisfying: if all 'classical' architecture derived from the Jews then the glories of both Roman Bath and an imagined pre-Roman Celtic Bath of the Druids had a common ancestor. Thus, by recreating Bath in the forms of pure Palladianism, Wood could celebrate both Romans and Celts in the most appropriate cultural patriotism and with a biblical warranty.

---

1 *Essay*, 232. All references to Wood's *Essay* are taken from the 3rd, 1765 edition, reprinted in 1969 by Kingsmead Reprints, Bath, unless otherwise specified.

What was more extraordinary than the vision itself was the fact that Wood achieved a considerable part of it in stone, that successive architects followed his ideal for at least the next 70 years and that to the present day Bath is still roughly as Wood intended it. None of his contemporaries, Burlington, Kent, Campbell or Gibbs, have left anything so substantial or as enduring a template. Only Robert Adam's Edinburgh can be compared with John Wood's Bath. These are the only two British cities in the European league of urban design. Hence the extreme interest in whatever can be reasonably inferred from those formative years that he chose to conceal.

The meagre facts are that he was the son of George Wood, a local Bath builder who was still active in 1727, when he is mentioned briefly in the Chandos papers, but was otherwise without fame.[2] John was baptized on 24 August 1704 in St James's Church, Bath, and he had at least one other brother whom he later employed as a factotum and trouble-shooter in his business.[3]

Significantly, though John Wood delighted in shows of scholarship, was widely read and later styled himself as an antiquary as well as an architect, he never refers to his education or to an alma mater. A sermon preached at a Bath Charity Schools Benefit in May 1766 claimed 'the late Mr Wood, architect, of great skill and judgement' as an old pupil of the Blue Coat Charity School.[4] Most of Wood's family were still alive at that date and could have refuted the claim if it had been untrue, so it needs to be accepted. Wood will have worn a blue uniform with white stockings and bands. His curriculum would have been the limited one of reading, writing, arithmetic and reckoning, only varied with singing. It was usual on Charity Benefit Sundays for the 50 boys and 20 girls of the school to entertain the invited gentry with a holy cantata. One enduring effect of this education may have been the relish with which Wood records the specially composed hymn that opened his new chapel of the Blessed Virgin in Queen Square on Christmas Day, 1734.

He referred to the school in his *Essay*[5] but mentioned no personal link. His later use of source books is usually uncritical and his manipulation of data to support a preconceived notion suggests a self-educated man untrained in academic evaluation and debate. The Blue Coat School is unlikely to have fired his lively later interest in astronomy, geology, medicine, history, anthropology and primitive religion or to have set him reading on a wide, eccentric sweep of classical authors in English or French translations.

Somewhere on his travels Wood seems to have had the use of a good library and been directed to curious reading. He demonstrates a superficial knowledge of Virgil, Tacitus, Pliny, Polybius, Augustus Antoninus and Diodorus Siculus. These will have worked in his mind along with a rag-bag of books more appropriate to the previous century: travel, popu-

2 The Chandos Letterbooks in the Huntington Library, California; 6 April 1727: Chandos to Mrs Phillips.
3 Wood's brother is mentioned in the Tyberton papers, Hereford Record Office, A81/IV; letter of 3 April 1729: Wood to William Brydges.
4 Brigitte Mitchell and Hubert Penrose (eds.) *Letters from Bath 1766-7 by the Revd John Penrose*, 1983, 82-3.
5 *Essay*, 320-1.

lar science and theology. Lipton's *A Thousand Noble Things*, Greaves' *Pyramidographia* and *Traveller in the East*, Villalpanda's *Geographia Sacra Illustrata*, Harrington's version of *Orlando Furioso* and Toland's *History of the Druids* all surface in his own writing as reminders that the Age of Reason followed closely after an Age of Contentious Faith and a remoter epic romanticism.

It would be reasonable to look for the library and source of this reading in Bath if Wood had shown any sign of attachment or indebtedness to the local gentry, but in fact he is consistently barbed and hostile towards his fellow citizens and surveyed the parishes of Bathforum without a sign of interest in the squirearchy. Supposing, and it is pure supposition, that Wood remained at the Blue Coat School long enough to acquire the fine clear hand of his letters. He will have left school to take up an apprenticeship as a joiner, one peripherally related to his father's building business, when he was 12. He could have learnt the skills in Bath but something in his later cool detachment from the citizenry and his obvious ambition suggests that he served the apprenticeship in London. That certainly is where the first definite record of his existence since the baptismal registry appears.

Late in 1721, after Michaelmas, when he was still only 17, Wood is recorded as having leased a piece of land in a superior London residential development with the intention of building a house on it.[6] The plot was in the Broad Field, north of Oxford Street and part of the Cavendish estate. The owner was Edward Lord Harley, soon to become 2nd Earl of Oxford and Mortimer, a man with whom Wood was to remain on terms of polite friendship for the next 20 years, but as a fellow antiquary not as an architect.

What the steps were between charity school boy and adolescent building speculator can only be surmised, but the leap suggests that he had a little money, a remarkable self-confidence and a personable way with older men. Harley was not Wood's only early aristocratic contact. Robert Benson, 1st Lord Bingley, paid John Wood £3.11s.0d on 12 July 1722.[7] The services are unspecified in Bingley's accounts but they are recorded only eight days after a larger payment, £15, to Edward Shepherd who was just emerging as one of the most successful speculative builders in the West End.[8]

Shepherd's association with Wood was to continue intermittently to the end of the decade but another name, that of James Theobald, also appears in the Bingley account books against much larger sums of money. Theobald was a timber merchant with Baltic connections, a financier and financial advisor with a house on the riverside in Lambeth opposite the Temple.[9] All three aristocrats with whom Wood was associated had dealings with Theobald. He was to act after 1727 as banker between Wood and James Brydges, 1st Duke of Chandos, cashing money orders from the Duke and supplying timber for Wood's building operations in Bath and later at Tyberton. Wood used Theobald's house as a *poste restante* address

6 British Museum, Harley Estate Records, Add. MS. 18241, f.36.
7 Hoare's Bank, Account Book G.
8 Ibid.
9 Tyberton papers; letter of 16 November 1728: Wood to William Brydges.

11

Lord Harley, 2nd Earl of Oxford, Wood's first patron and lifetime correspondent on antiquities

on his frequent trips to London in the late 1720s and early 1730s. When he could put Wood in the way of a new commission, Theobald wrote accordingly, and whenever Wood was able to press the quality of Theobald's deals and planking on a client, he did so.

What is far more interesting than this profitable business relationship is the fact that James Theobald was not only a member of the influential Society of Antiquaries, but that in January 1727, after a year's interregnum, he was actually to succeed William Stukeley as Secretary to the Society.[10] Stukeley was the most influential antiquary of his day. In these early 1720s he was already lecturing on and researching into Celtic prehistory. The Druids were becoming an obsession with him and he was soon to be, probably without knowing it, John Wood's arch rival as an authority on stone circles.

10 Joan Evans, *A History of the Society of Antiquaries*, 1956, 78.

12

That, however, was for the future. Meanwhile it is reasonable to assume that, just as Shepherd was to link Wood with the latest Palladian design, so Theobald must have been the man who made an antiquary of Wood. Theobald had trading connections with the West Country and he could well have been responsible both for Wood's move to the capital and Wood's precocious building ventures. This would explain the very young man's contacts with Harley, Bingley and, later, with Chandos.

Another possibility needs cautiously to be mentioned. The Society of Antiquaries had cordial relations with the Freemasons who were, in effect, themselves a specialised branch of antiquarianism with Jewish interests. The Duke of Montague, F.S.A. 1725, was Grand Master in 1721, Lord Coleraine, F.S.A. 1717, was Grand Master of the Grand Lodge of England in 1727, Martin Folkes, F.S.A. 1720, was Deputy Grand Master of the same in 1724. Stukeley himself became a Freemason in 1721 and the master of a lodge in 1723. Both Freemasonry and antiquarian studies had experienced a revival after the Hanoverian succession, so their close relations developed naturally and it would have been a natural process for John Wood to have become both an antiquary and a Freemason during his early London years. This would go far to explain the obsessive confidence of a 21-year-old's plans for Bath as conceived in 1725.

He had first to undergo minor disasters and triumphs in the capital. London was still enjoying in these years the building boom which followed the Treaty of Utrecht, 1713, and the end of the long European war. Both Chandos and Bingley were Tory peers who had lost hope of office with the death of Queen Anne and the accession of George I and had now turned to improve their fortunes by various commercial ventures. By marriage Harley had acquired a sizeable estate immediately north of Oxford Street and was developing this along with a consortium of Tory peers which included Lord Bingley and the Duke of Chandos. The estate was laid out in a grid of regular streets around Cavendish Square. Just to the south Sir Richard Grosvenor was developing his Grosvenor estate in much the same way and at the same time, around Grosvenor Square.[11]

Wood seems initially to have worked his way into the building scene by practising his trade. He is referred to in the Harley papers as 'John Wood of the parish of St Anne Westminster in the County of Middlesex Joyner'.[12] Whether this implies the relatively polite craft of a furniture maker rather than the practical trade of a carpenter is not wholly clear. Wood refers in the Tyberton papers to 'joyners' when the panelling of a saloon is being put up. It was usual for a carpenter or a mason to lead any house-building team as they had mastered the principles of basic construction. Armed only with an awareness of design, Wood, nevertheless, used his contacts and tried his luck as a house builder.

Predictably this first venture failed. In 1723 Wood had to surrender the lease back to Lord Harley, but in a foretaste of his resilience and commercial dexterity he did not go bankrupt as so many of his fellow craftsmen did in these years. Harley not only paid him £5 for the surrender of the lease but allowed him, along with John Summers, William

11 See the *Survey of London*, volumes 39 and 40, on the Grosvenor Estate.
12 Harley Estate Records, Add. MS. 18241, f.36.

Jackling and William Wells to purchase another lease, No. 1 Oxford Street where, by the end of 1723, they had completed a house and found a tenant for it.[13]

This was not the end of the success story. Wood was in arrears of ground rent for that year of £1.7s.6d, as were his fellow entrepreneurs Summers and Jackling; only William Wells was paid up.[14] Next year Wood's arrears had risen to £5.10s.0d. and they remained at that figure through 1725 and 1726.[15] Yet in 1725 he paid £14.10s.0d towards the cost of common sewers on the property and is given as the original leaseholder not just of No. 1 but of 2, 3 and 4 Oxford Street in addition; and No. 3 is listed as having a substantial 58 foot frontage.[16]

Here clearly are the beginnings of a modest prosperity and perhaps an explanation for Wood's manifest incompetence over certain interior details of construction in his first work at Bath and, much later, in Bristol. He had achieved a reputation as a builder in London only because he was supported there by a team of other craftsmen. When he was alone he was liable to make errors from sheer lack of experience.

What must have happened was that Wood attempted his first house, on the Broad Field of the Cavendish estate, alone, carried on a wave of his habitual, brash self-confidence. Finding that he had over-reached himself he talked Lord Harley or his agent into giving him a second chance in a more conventional project. It was quite usual at this time for a group of craftsmen with complementary skills, usually led by a carpenter or a bricklayer, to acquire a 99 year lease on a piece of land at a low ground rent for the first two years. They would pool their labour to build a house, thus cutting costs, and then sell the completed property at a good profit before the ground rent rose to a level which would reward the original landowner.

Wood must have juggled his way dextrously along the construction of all four houses, increasing his profits each time, building up useful relations with timber merchants and suppliers and gaining the experience of surveying and handling labour which would carry him through much more ambitious schemes in Bath or perhaps at Bramham, Lord Bingley's seat in the West Riding. The Harley account books indicate the training of a young capitalist; what they do not reveal are the personal influences and the education by stylistic example to which the young John Wood must have been subject during his years in the capital.

Lord Bingley employed Wood in some capacity in 1724, 1725 and 1727.[17] There are payments or letters to prove this, and some of the work was done in London where Bingley was having a large town house built, partly to the dated baroque designs of Thomas Archer, on the west side of Cavendish Square. Another of the Cavendish estate consortium, the Duke of Chandos, consulted Wood about a house on the Square which Edward Shepherd had left unfinished.[18] This again was an old-fashioned design

13 Add. MS. 18241.
14 Ibid.
15 Ibid.
16 Add. MS. 18243.
17 Hoare's Bank, Account Books G and H.
18 Chandos Letterbooks; 13 June 1728 and 11 July 1728: Chandos to Wood.

and Wood never took up the offer to work on it. The consultant architect for the Cavendish estate was James Gibbs but the general standard of design on the estate was unadventurous. Cavendish Square was originally intended to be surrounded by separate grand houses, not by unified terraces, and the individual house elevations which Gibbs designed in Henrietta Place or approved for the side streets were modest affairs of bare brick with all the decoration reserved for the interiors.[19]

In the light of what he designed for Bath from 1727 onwards, Wood is far more likely to have been influenced by what was going on in the neighbouring Grosvenor estate. By nature John Wood was not inclined to close friendships with fellow architects; his instinct was always to surpass them. But he seems to have achieved at least a working relationship with Edward Shepherd, tolerating him later when Shepherd acted as Chandos's assessor, so Wood is likely to have been impressed and influenced by Shepherd's large-scale Grosvenor projects.

Shepherd was, like Wood, a craftsman; he was a plasterer, who rose by his own enterprise to create whole streets of houses. Shepherd's Market in Mayfair is his modest memorial. He seems to have had no very pronounced stylistic tastes. When left to his own devices he produced interiors of rich baroque stucco and marble, as at 66 Brook Street, but 12 North Audley Street, which in 1730 he built for Lord Ligonier, has a sophisticated Palladian interior.[20] Shepherd was an associate of Colen Campbell, the archpriest in Britain of the Palladian revival, and indeed Shepherd lived next door but one to Campbell in Brook Street. Until 1725 the design of individual house elevations on the Grosvenor estate had been quite uncontrolled but in that year Campbell produced a palatial Palladian design for 'Seven New intended Houses on the East Side of Grosvenor Square'.[21] These were absolutely uniform, with half-engaged columns on a rusticated base and must, if they had ever been built, have transformed the Square and exercised a powerful influence on all future development in the area.

Campbell's design never in fact left the drawing board but it was the first attempt to apply the Palladianism of a country house like Campbell's Wanstead to a unified group of city houses and it was in 1725, the year when Campbell produced it, that John Wood, working so he claimed in Yorkshire, first conceived his grandiose scheme of two great squares and a round Circus for his native Bath. The date may be a coincidence but Wood was to clash bitterly with Campbell in 1728 over an inquiry into the stone for Greenwich Palace and he would boast openly in his *Essay* that at Prior Park he had surpassed Wanstead.[22] Rivalry, on Wood's part at least, certainly existed and rivalry can be the strongest kind of positive influence.

Wood knew Shepherd well and it must have come as a sharp spur to his competitive instinct to learn what Shepherd was intending to build on the north side of Grosvenor Square early in 1728. This was nothing less

19 Henrietta Place is illustrated in Terry Friedman, *James Gibbs*, 1984, plate 231.
20 Shepherd's interior for 12 North Audley Steet is illustrated in *The Survey of London*, volume 39, plate 11.
21 The ground plan and front elevation for the east side of Grosvenor Square as proposed by Campbell in 1725 are illustrated in the *Survey of London*, vol. 39, plate 4b.
22 *Essay*, 426 and 432 respectively.

To the RIGHT HONORABLE   EARL GROSVENOR &c
THIS VIEW OF   GROSVENOR SQUARE.

A late 18th century view of Grosvenor Square showing Shepherd's mutilated scheme for the North Side

than a unified palace elevation for all the houses with a great temple pediment at each end, hexastyle Corinthian on an arched rusticated base. If Shepherd had been able to control the leases of every house on that side of the Square the effect would have been at least as splendid as Wood's north side of Queen Square in Bath, but in the event only three houses at the west end of the range were built to this grand design and looked, consequently, faintly absurd in isolation. Knowing Shepherd's relative neutrality in matters of design it is more than likely that this scheme was roughed out for him by Colen Campbell. 'The modell plann or forme and elevation' of it were in existence by 6 April 1728 when Shepherd drew up an agreement with a bricklayer who was to work on the houses.[23] Wood's elevation for the north side of Queen Square, which features a great hexastyle Corinthian central portico on a rusticated base, is dated 1728.

Even if Wood never knew Campbell socially, he lived in London in the 1720s, Campbell's triumphant decade. Eventually Wood himself

23 P.R.O. C105/32/1, agreement of 6 April 1728, E. Shepherd and F. Drewitt.

16

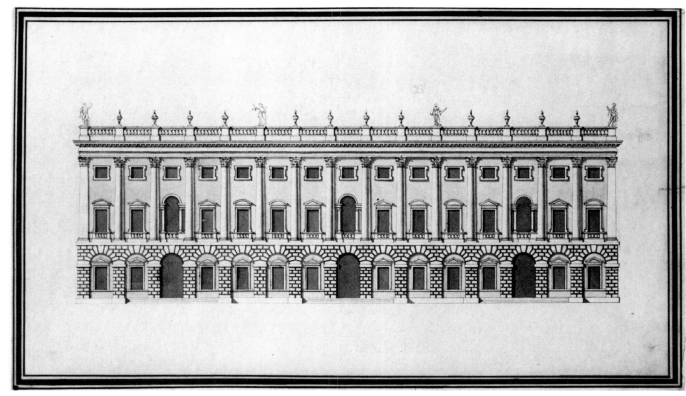

bought the three volumes of Campbell's *Vitruvius Britannicus*, to which all three of his patrons, Harley, Bingley and Chandos, had subscribed. The first two volumes are heavy with old-fashioned houses like Drumlanrig Castle and buildings by Wren, Talman or Archer. Most of the pure Palladian designs are only unbuilt schemes 'of my invention' put out by Campbell as a bait for potential clients. The third volume, which came out in 1725, the year of Wood's projection of an Imperial Bath, was very different. Not only did it include town houses by Campbell, like the Rolls in Chancery Lane and Plumptre House, Nottingham which were not unlike some of the houses Wood later built on the St John's Hospital site in Bath, but it featured a succession of Palladian country palaces which Campbell had actually built or was building. There were Mereworth, Wanstead, Stourhead, Houghton, Baldersby and Ebberston, and in addition the London town houses of Lord Burlington, Lord Herbert and General Wade.

This was the evidence of real achievement, indigestible to one of Wood's temper, but also proof conclusive that the pure Palladian was the style which an ambitious architect would have to master. It was not Campbell's new designs 'in the theatrical style' which were taken up from the second volume.[24] These with their heavy overlay of Mannerist decoration remained mere pages in a book; the aristocracy opted for plain surfaces and austere fenestration when it came to the realities of brick and stone. This would not have been lost on Wood, nor would one notable absentee from the third volume of Campbell's collection: he did not include his rejected design for the east side of Grosvenor Square. If Wood was a

24 *Vitruvius Britannicus*, volume 2 (1717), plates 42 and 90.

Colen Campbell's unexecuted design of 1725 for Grosvenor Square, East Side

17

young man in a hurry then there was still one quick way to an architectural first on the grandest scale by linking a number of town houses together behind a palatial façade.

Another factor which may have pressed Wood into trying his fortune away from London was his limited success with aristocratic patrons. In a recent, perceptive article, John Harris has projected Lord Harley as an early 18th century Maecenas, equal to Lord Burlington in his love of the arts.[25] However, the lumbering brick bulk of Wimpole Hall, where he employed James Gibbs, suggests that the pleasures of literature far outweighed his taste in architecture; 'indolence, good nature and want of worldly wisdom' were his characteristics.[26] The Duke of Chandos had also passed the peak of his fortunes when Wood met him. His greater building ventures were behind him and he was to lead Wood into much trouble with minimal profit.

Robert Benson, the first Baron Bingley, was in a different league and Wood's relationship with him was more interesting. Bingley's bank accounts reveal further payments to Mr Wood of £15 in the summer of 1724 and of £47 the next summer.[27] These are small amounts but they are unlikely to be all that passed between them as Wood was still working for Bingley early in 1727 when Chandos had to request him twice to release Wood so that Wood could travel to Bath for the St John's Hospital venture.[28] In a letter of 6 February 1727, to his lawyer Marchant, the Duke refers to Wood as 'an architect here in London' so Wood is likely to have been assisting Edward Wilcox on Bingley's new town house at that time.[29] Much later, in a letter to James Theobald of 5 April 1728, the gossipy Chandos implied that Wood was Bingley's protégé.[30]

What makes the relationship interesting is that if Bingley's earlier architectural preferences are anything to go by, he and the young Wood should have been sharply opposed. While still plain Robert Benson and the son of a rich Yorkshire attorney, he had made an extensive Grand Tour, spending as much time in France as in Italy. The house, Bramham Park, which he had built between 1699 and 1710 has been variously attributed to Archer, Gibbs and Leoni but is probably the creation of its owner.[31] It is a building of distinction and a refined individuality, its main elevation producing an impression of richness with a minimum of decorative detail or spatial massing, a creation oddly apart from stylistic fashions, neither baroque nor Palladian but 'classical' in the almost abstract sense of that word.

At some time between 1722 and 1727 John Wood was working at Bramham and on the left-hand side of the forecourt to Bingley's serene main house a stable block has been dropped like a gesture of brash Palladian modishness. The date of its construction is not known, but the higher

25 'Harley, the Patriot Collector' in *Apollo*, September 1985, 198-203.
26 See the Dictionary of National Biography.
27 Hoare's Bank, Account Books G and H.
28 Chandos Letterbooks; 5 February 1727: Chandos to Bingley.
29 Quoted in C.H.C. and M. I. Baker, *The Life and Circumstances of James Brydges, First Duke of Chandos*, 1949, 301.
30 Ibid., 300-302.
31 See Arthur Oswald in the first of a series of four articles on Bramham in *Country Life*, 20 February 1958.

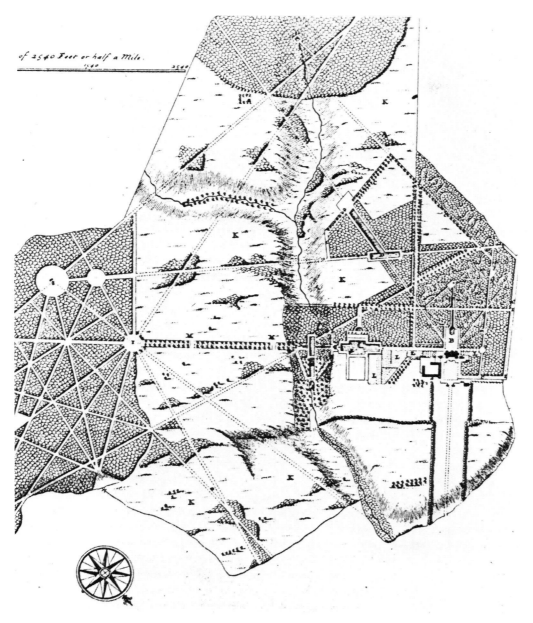

of 2540 Feet or half a Mile.
2540   2540

wings to either side in the style of James Paine are later additions of
c.1741, built by the 2nd Lord Bingley.

There is no proof that Wood designed this cheerful affront, but it is
not shown on an estate map which can be dated to between 1710 and 1713
and it does appear on the map of the park which Wood himself drew and
which was printed in 1731.[32] The stable has been attributed to Wood[33]

Bramham Park Estate Map by
Wood, published in 1731

32 Both maps are in the Estate Office at Bramham. The first is titled 'A Map of Bramham
    Parke the Seat of the Rt. Honble Robert Benson Esqre.' Benson would have been the
    'Rt. Honble' after August 1710 when he was made a Lord of the Treasury in Harley's
    administration (Robert Harley, 1st Earl of Oxford). After July 1713 Benson would
    have been Lord Bingley.
33 By James Lees-Milne in *English Country Houses: Baroque 1685-1715*, 1970, 204-5; Ar-
    thur Oswald in *Country Life* suggests that Wood built the stable block to a design by
    James Gibbs.

19

The stable block at Bramham Park – Wood's first Palladian design; the wings are later additions

and this may then be his first important building. Its arched recesses with inset windows recall a design for a stable block in a volume of Wood's drawings in Bath Reference Library,[34] and its door with keystones rising up into the pediment is an Inigo Jones device which Wood used for houses on the west side of Queen Square. As a composition the stable is busy rather than decisive and it descends a fairly steep slope by an elevation designed for level ground. It could easily be the work of an inexperienced Palladian determined to achieve a statutory temple pediment but unsure of general proportions or the relation of cornice levels.

What is so interesting about this block is the *volte-face* it represents in Bingley's own taste. He was considered an architectural expert, mentioned as such alongside Burlington and Pembroke. His town house was described as having the appearance of a Parisian mansion and Bramham has the same air, yet against his established preference and perhaps his better judgement he allowed someone to build this stable in a visually strategic position. But Bingley was an important Freemason, Grand Master of the Grand Lodge of York as early as 1707, and by the 1720s the Palladian style of architecture was becoming virtually an orthodoxy in Masonic circles. In *The Constitutions of the Free-Masons*, published in 1723, James Anderson writes: 'many Erections of the Roman Style may be reviewed in Mr Campbell the Architect's ingenious book call'd VITRUVIUS BRITANNICUS: and if the Disposition for true ancient Masonry prevails, for some time, with Noblemen, Gentlemen, and learned men (as it is likely it will) this ISLAND will become the MISTRESS of the Earth, for Designing, Drawing and Conducting and capable to in-

34 'Architectural Drawings in Somersetshire', presented by A. N. Page to the Library in 1923. The volume, containing drawings by both the Elder and the Younger Wood, is discussed in Chapter 11.

20

struct all other Nations in all things relating to the Royal Art'.[35] Anderson uses the term 'the Augustan style' and speaks of 'our great Master-Mason Inigo Jones'.[36] When Bingley first became a Mason, fashions in architecture were less partisan, Sir Christopher Wren being Grand Master, but Wood may well have been able to persuade Bingley that times had changed and that it was incumbent on him to demonstrate this 'Roman Style' of Campbell on his estate. Whether it was Bingley who actually introduced Wood into a Masonic lodge and the mysteries of the Craft is not known, but Wood, his protégé, retained a life-long, almost religious, devotion to the Masonic theory that the proportions of classical architecture had come down, via the First Temple of Solomon, from the divinely ordained dimensions of Moses' Tabernacle. So if Wood introduced Bingley to Palladian manners it is likely that the older man introduced Wood to the seductive notion that God was the founder of correct architecture and that this Palladianism, to be valid, must find parallels in the Jewish Temple.

What influence the park and gardens of Bramham had on the man who worked in them is more debatable, though the survival of these geometric groves to the present day makes arguments for their impact more potent. With their ruler-straight rides slashing at acute angles through beech woods, their rigid rectangles of parterre and their compass exact rond-points, they testify to a time when nature was seen as order and man the master of that harmony. But, in the close planted thickets near the house, the map which John Wood drew shows the winding asymmetrical paths of a picturesque wilderness. These in their way are as much a manifestation of new visual thinking as the stable block was of a new classical vocabulary. There are paths like these in Pope's Twickenham garden and they are a sign that the wilder and more casual beauties of Nature were beginning to be enjoyed alongside the formal groves.

This aesthetic dualism illuminates, and may even be the source of Wood's own later pleasure in the contrast between the magisterial order of his Grand Parade in Bath and the wildness of the prospect it commanded:

> the building of this Parade, consisting of twelve houses, with the country before it, reflect a Beauty to each other, which has the Power of charming and delighting the Eye of almost every Beholder! For Solsbury Hill, at the distance of two miles, faces the Walk; and though Triangular at the top, appears like the Frustrum of a Conical Mountain rising up among Hills of Vast Magnitude.[37]

Evidently Wood relished the opposition of man's order and Nature's wildness but moderated the conflict by formalizing the natural objects in his mind's eye into geometrical forms, triangles and cones, much like the rigid shapes to which Nature was reduced on his Bramham map. He described the Beechen Cliff south of Bath as 'a stupendous Cliff above in the Shape of a large Cressant'.[38] Thus the crescents and circles into which he

35 James Anderson, *The Constitutions of the Free-Masons, Containing the History, Charges, Regulations, etc., of that Most Ancient ... Fraternity*, 1723, 48.
36 Ibid., 41, 43 and 39 respectively.
37 *Essay*, 351.
38 Ibid., 52.

shaped Bath's new housing were reflections of the geometricity which he, like the gardeners of his day, perceived as inherent within the outward ruggedness of wooded hills and slopes.

However deeply the 'Natural' order of Bramham may have worked in Wood's mind (and it is possible to look at his map through half-closed eyes and see the long line of Gay Street lancing uphill to spear the Circus), his only response, apart from the map, which survives is the drawing of an aqueduct preserved in Bath Reference Library. Lord Harley, who was bored by gardens, had visited Bramham and glimpsed 'a great penury of water'[39] in the stepped cascade when he looked through a window, so Wood's design was probably intended to remedy this. It was not built and that cascade has gone.

If Wood had any hand in the construction of the T-shaped canal which was dug *c*.1727 it might explain why he approached his work on the new navigation channel for the Avon in the same year with such confidence in his knowledge of 'the real use of the Spade'.[40] With this kind of assurance mountains are moved and enduring cities founded.

He may, as he claimed, have conceived his extraordinarily ambitious scheme for Bath up there in Yorkshire in his leisure hours, going down to London to fire Mr Gay with his enthusiasm 'on the last day of December 1725'.[41] The new Bath which he envisaged borrowed something from schemes which his rivals had failed to launch in London and something from the scale and the response to Nature of the layout at Bramham. In addition he must have been directed by a shrewd developer's instinct that the London building boom was flagging just as Bath, propelled by fashion, health and commerce, was taking off.

There was one other factor working at this time which could, given Wood's competitive nature and his loyalty to Bath, have influenced the grandiose projection which he made and his subsequent return to his city.

In 1724 William Stukeley brought out the first volume of his eminently readable *Itinerarium Curiosum*, illustrated with his own views and maps. It ranged over most of the historic towns and ancient sites of England and arrived, on page 128, at Bath with a finely drawn map and a town view from the Beechen Cliff. But in tone it was unusually acid, delivering the oddly conflicting judgement:

> The small compass of the city has made the inhabitants croud up the streets to an unseemly and inconvenient narrowness. 'tis handsomely built, mostly of new stone, which is very white and good, a disgrace to the architects they have there.

Remembering that Wood's father was a Bath builder, and supposing that Wood read the passage (not an unreasonable supposition considering that both Wood and James Theobald knew Bath and that Theobald was Stukeley's fellow Antiquary) it is probable that Wood took the curious attack personally. He will have been the more irritated by his awareness of the truth of the comment on the rather blowsy baroque style of building still favoured at that late date by Bath's native architects.

39 *Country Life*, 12 June 1958.
40 *Essay*, 241.
41 Ibid., 232.

After remarking on the Abbey square 'lately deformed with houses encroaching', and 'the negligence of the magistracy ... who suffer idle servants to throw all manner of dirt and ashes into the streets',[42] Stukeley aimed a shrewd thrust at a cherished Bath folk hero, one whom Wood was to defend with a wealth of spurious scholarship. This was King Bladud, the city's legendary founder. Stukeley wrote of 'the fanciful image of K. Bladud, with a silly account of his finding out these springs, more reasonably attributed to the Romans'.

The scornful antiquary went on to visit the prehistoric stone circles at nearby Stanton Drew in the company of John Strachey, F.R.S. and promised a full account of 'this memorable curiosity upon another occasion'.[43]

There was much here to stimulate both Wood's anger and his imagination. He will have recognised the truth in the slighting remarks and possibly the sense in applying that stone 'very white and good' to a fashionable Palladian rebuilding programme.

For the full account of Stanton Drew, nine evocative pages with three views of the stones, one dated 23 July 1723, the general public had to wait for the publication of the second volume of *Itinerarium Curiosum* in 1776 after Stukeley's death.[44] But the similarities between that account and Wood's own description of the stones in a letter to Lord Harley of 1740

1723 view of the Stanton Drew stone circles from Stukeley's *Itinerarium*

42 *Itinerarium Curiosum: Centuria I*, 1724, 128.
43 Ibid., 128.
44 *Itinerarium Curiosum: Centuria II*, 1776, 169-77.

suggest that Wood had been able to read Stukeley's manuscript through James Theobald's agency.[45]

To appreciate Wood's probable reaction to the admirable writing, it is necessary to recall what he will have heard about Stukeley's professional integrity from James Theobald, who succeeded Stukeley as secretary to the Antiquaries.

As well as being the most active and contentious member of the Society, Stukeley was a jealous and selfish accumulator of other men's research. He refused members any access to the Society's minutes and kept the transcripts of earlier lectures hidden away for his own use. Finally, early in 1726, he was ordered, after a heated debate, to make the minutes and transcripts available to all members. As a direct result he retired as Secretary, retreated to Grantham, and for the next few decades played a diminished role in the Society's affairs.

It was at this time that Theobald could, in the Society's new spirit of openness, have shown Wood a transcript of Stukeley's account. This poached on what Wood may have regarded as his native ground with a lyrical appraisal of the works of the Celtic 'Druids' and a clear anticipation of what was to be a theme of Wood's own writing: that the Druids' temples were equal or even superior to those of the Greeks and Romans.

Stukeley's delighted reaction to what he called, from its five concentric circles, 'the Planetary temple' at Stanton Drew is worth quoting. It is an instance, with its outrageously insular comparison between the aesthetics of prehistoric and classical constructions, of how strongly the patriotic current was flowing at that time in antiquarian research. Referring to the circles, Stukeley wrote:

> upon moving towards them or sideways, they must have created the same beautiful and surprising appearance to the eye as the more learned architects have endeavoured by the multiplicity of columns in their porticoes, forums and the like of which Vitruvius speaks: yet I think in my judgement, this circular work must needs have exceeded, in this particular, those most celebrated works of the Greeks and Romans.[46]

Such a passage puts the wild enthusiasm and over-writing of Wood's own account of the prehistory of Bath into perspective. It is essential for the modern reader to empathize with the scholarly condition of the time and not to view the past through the eyes of the present. An insular trium-

45 For Wood's letter to Lord Harley, see Chapter Twelve.
Wood's claim to be the first to describe the Stanton Drew circles was clearly wishful thinking. Aubrey had mentioned them and William Musgrave had published an account of two of the three circles with a careful plan of them in his *Antiquitates Britanno-Belgicae* (1719). Musgrave concluded that they were Belgic funerary monuments. It was Stukeley who first saw them as a primitive planetarium and made the Pythagorean connections. Wood followed him, only varying the individual attributions, to produce a more ingenious Pythagorean model. Musgrave found only three porticoes at the smallest circle. Stukeley detected five and again Wood followed his lead. Both Stukeley and Wood mentioned the possibility that Stanton Drew derived from the name of a local family not from 'stone town of the Druids', only to reject it. Both offered an etymology for the place name 'Pensford'. Both attempted a romantic evocation of the religious processions which they believed had wound about the site.
46 *Itinerarium Curiosum: Centuria II*, 1776, 172.

phalism had followed the victories of Marlborough and the Hanoverian succession. That mood led Britain to opt for a revived Palladianism against the continental stylistic drift through baroque to rococo. Stukeley's, and later Wood's, notion that a native pre-Roman culture had excelled the civilization which the Romans imposed was merely a part of this island self-confidence. Similarly there was nothing fantastic in a Protestant Christian state (which took for granted the fact that the Bible was literally the word of God) believing that Solomon's architecture predated all that of ancient Egypt and was the source spring from which the Parthenon rose. In that period of its revival the faiths of Freemasonry were little removed from orthodoxy. Only the biblical scholarship of the 19th century and the accumulation of archaeological research has left it seeming isolated and extreme. Stukeley reported after a discussion in 1720 with Sir Isaac Newton on Solomon's Temple, 'He says it is older than any great heathen temples'[47] and Newton's colleague William Whiston had prepared models of the Temple and Moses' Tabernacle which Whiston used when lecturing in Bath and London in 1726. So in the context of his time there was nothing eccentric in Newton's expressed conviction any more than in his move from pure science to biblical exegesis.

This chapter was written in an effort to account for the singular self-assurance of John Wood in 1725-7 at the threshold of his career and for the sheer presumption of his ambitions. The Stukeley-Theobald-Wood connection points to an explanation. It certainly explains why Stukeley and his friend Roger Gale were later to regard Wood as a contemptible plagiarist. 'The best things in my book' [on Stonehenge], Stukeley complained of Wood's *Choir Gaure*, an account of Stonehenge, 'he has pillaged from me', and ended

> ... this *wooden* performance is no more than the fermented dregs
> and settlement of the dullest, and most inveterate mixture of
> ignorance, malice and malevolence.[48]

Stukeley loved the range of the English language almost as much as he loved his 'Druids', but the originality of Wood's scholarship is not being judged, only the intensity of its conviction.

With a characteristic perceptive warmth, Sir John Summerson moved straight to the source of Wood's inspiration when he suggested 'that nothing would have surprised the architect less than to meet a centurion in Gay Street or to find a toga hanging in his front hall'.[49] This is not idle musing but a sympathetic appraisal of a very unusual mind. One side of Wood's nature was as practical and prosaic as the mind of an architect-developer needed to be. The other side was a Romantic visionary, a poet who could write of the God Apollo 'attending the Grand Festival at the End of every Cycle of Years with his Harp; and spending his whole Nights, from the Vernal Equinox, in March, to the Rising of the Pleiades,

47 Surtees Society, vol. 76: 'Letters and Extracts from Diaries of the Rev. William Stukeley' (1883), 62.
48 Ibid., vol. 80 (1885), 276.
49 John Summerson, 'John Wood and the English Town-Planning Tradition' in *Heavenly Mansions*, 1949, 87-110; 94.

about the latter End of *July* in playing upon that Instrument; and in sing-ing and dancing to it', which reads like an account of real events and of a living deity.[50] For Wood, the Past was almost the Present; Summerson calls it an 'amiable vagueness as to historic fact'.[51] That vagueness com-bined with a sharp business sense recreated Bath, which is essentially a realized fantasy rather than an organically developed city.

As clear witness to this link between antiquarian fantasy and realized stone there is a passage in Wood's *Essay*:

> ... as we ascend the Hill now bearing the Name of *Lansdown*, there
> are three large Stones lying upon the Ground, in a little Field by
> the Side of the Road, known by the Name of *Sols Rocks*, with a
> Foundation just behind them, shaped into a Circular Form ...
> These three Stones, when erect and perfect, seem to have made a
> stupendous Altar; and the circular Foundation behind them seems
> to have borne other erect Stones, which, in all Probability, were
> set up by King Bladud for a Temple in honour of the Sun.[52]

At one level this is a pathetic flight of pseudo-antiquarianism, an attempt to match Stukeley's Stanton Drew circles of the Druids with a home-grown specimen based on a few rocks on Lansdown, up the hill just north of the low-lying old city. Then the truth dawns of what this fantasiz-ing was actually to create on lower Lansdown. It was the King's Circus – a sun-shaped roundel of houses to recall a temple to *Bel-Apollo* that never really existed: a prodigy of modern Bath to be ritually circled by the tourist coaches throughout the long, profitable season.

In the same long chapter, Wood contrived a similar prehistoric an-tecedent for the Royal Crescent which he proposed and which his son, John, was actually to build. After some devious anthropological shuffling, Wood managed to identify the Sul-Minerva goddess worshipped at Bath with the Phoenician moon goddess Onca. He ignored the fact that the lat-ter was a Virgin Goddess and the former the Mother of the Gods. Then, by an even less plausible analysis of 'a mere Labyrinth of Holes, Ditches, Banks and Barrows' up on Lansdown, he declared that 'In the Intrench-ment therefore that now appears on the Summit of that Part of the Moun-tain, we may suppose *Bladud* to have placed the Priests destined to watch for *Onca's* first Appearance'.[53] So he had devised a temple of the moon goddess Onca in her first or crescent phase to the west of the circular sun temple of *Apollo-Belenus-Bel* on the same northern slope above the city. The Royal Crescent lies, of course, west of the King's Circus.

This is as fair an indication as any that an understanding of the ar-chitect John Wood the Elder should be based on a sympathetic reading of a young man's stolen antiquarian dreams.

50 *Essay*, 116.
51 Summerson, 99.
52 *Essay*, 119.
53 Ibid., 128-9.

Chapter Two

'So slovingly and knavishly performed'
A Ducal Comment
on the Inadequacies of a Surveyor.

According to the printed account, in the early spring of 1727, John Wood returned to the West Country like a young, conquering Alexander falling upon Asia. Urbane, confident and highly trained, he moved easily among doctors and dukes, the richest landowners of Bath, projecting generous schemes to the City Corporation for re-ordering the streets, and to the charity trustees for a new hospital and bathing facilities. He had been only in his twenty-first year when, on the last day of 1725 'I imparted my first Design to Mr Gay, an eminent Surgeon, in Hatton Garden, and Proprietor of the Land',[1] this land being the Barton Fields on Bath's immediate north-western outskirts. Within the space of the next four years he had built Bath's second set of Assembly Rooms in the fashionable quarter near the Abbey, raised four large houses in the latest classical fashion for the Duke of Chandos, rebuilding as he did so St John's Hospital, an almshouse of ancient foundation, briskly supervised the canalization of a strategic section of the River Avon and designed a town house façade of concentrated richness for Ralph Allen, the quarry owner and dominant figure in Bath politics. Add to these a speculative development of his own on the west wide of Barton Street and humbler ventures like the creation of two settlements for quarry workers and a design for the Widcombe Poor House and it appears, by his own narrative, that Wood bestrode his home town like a colossus, revitalising its fabric and directing its style.

There is one important reservation to this triumphalist chain of credits. The principal and often the only authority for them is John Wood's own *Essay towards a Description of Bath*, a work of careful self-recommendation published years later in 1742-3. Almost the only substantial contemporary sources for Wood's character, ability and working methods are the letterbooks of James Brydges, first Duke of Chandos, who used Wood as his architect and his builder in Bath between 1727 and 1730.[2] These letters are valuable simply by their number, 108 to Wood alone and many more to agents and clients of the Duke who were associated with Wood. Two cautions must, however, be made before they are considered as fair evidence.

As they were written to Wood and copied for reference by the Duke's secretary, very few of Wood's replies survive and the correspondence represents, therefore, only one half of a relationship. The second reservation involves the personality of James Brydges. He was hyperactive and emo-

1 *Essay*, 232.
2 Chandos Letterbooks.

James Brydges, 1st Duke of
Chandos

tionally unpredictable. Enormously rich, he had lost money in the South
Sea Bubble and was actively seeking safe areas of investment within the
bounds of Hanoverian Britain. Though keenly conscious of aristocratic
privilege, he had little sense of conventional aristocratic dignity. When
one of his landladies rejected the second-hand bedding which the Duke
and his Duchess had collected for her to use, on the ground that it might
harbour bed-bugs, Chandos's response was not one of noble pique, but of
amusement at her ignorance for not realizing that a bed-bug could not

28

possibly survive the naturally sulphurous atmosphere of Bath. 'Can she imagine', the Duke wrote, 'that if Bath was a place where bugs could live, it would not have swarmed with them long ago seeing that people of all sorts flock there.'[3] His wide experience of builders and building included the hiring, and almost as often, the sacking, of architects like James Gibbs, William Talman, John James and William Kent, so his opinions on the young Wood cannot be wholly discounted. He was, however, by fits and starts, gossipy, ingratiating, abusive, threatening and devious.

With these reservations in mind, the correspondence is still valuable if it is balanced against writing from the other side of the same relationship. On Chandos's recommendation Wood worked between 1728 and 1734 for Chandos's second cousin, William Brydges, a lawyer and landowner at Tyberton in Herefordshire. In this instance it is Wood's letters and not the client's that survive.[4] These will be considered in a later chapter; meanwhile it is fair to say that Wood could hardly have chosen a client more informed, opinionated or determined to meddle than Chandos.

Mutual acquaintances who may have introduced the two men included Lord Bingley, Wood's patron; Edward Shepherd, Wood's nearest approach to a professional friend; and James Theobald. But Wood was not Chandos's first choice to develop the St John's Hospital site. Shepherd, involved in London schemes, had turned the job down and John Strahan, an up and coming Bristol architect, Wood's natural rival, had surveyed the site and shaped a plan late in 1726 before Chandos had found him wanting.[5] Wood had been badgering Chandos ever since May of 1726 to join in his grand schemes for the regeneration of Bath[6] so the Duke is likely to have turned to Wood as someone available, malleable and cheap. For his part, Wood will have seen Chandos's request to build an extensive set of lodging rooms onto old foundations as an ideal opportunity to earn money and reputation while he re-established himself socially in his native city and fostered his own far more ambitious projects.

The architectural significance of what Wood managed to erect for the Duke in the face of carping and counter plot will be most profitably assessed in the next chapter against the work of Wood's Bath contemporaries. There were four buildings: Mrs Phillips's lodgings over and on the foundation walls of the St John's almshouse, begun in February 1727; Mrs Degge's lodging house on the Borough Walls, begun in May 1728; Mr Carey's small tavern built in the spring of 1729; and finally Mrs Robertson's lodging house, begun in May 1729.

Lodging houses and a tavern have an unimpressive ring but the Phillips house, which still stands relatively unchanged facing the Cross Bath to the east and the Hospital courtyard to the west, appears to have cost the Duke £2,000, the price of a small country house.[7] The Duke was to sell it for more than £3,500 in 1734, a pointer to why so many Londoners and, of course, John Wood were hurrying to invest in Bath's boom-town prop-

3 Chandos Letterbooks; Chandos to Fergusson: 1 March 1737.
4 Tyberton Papers, Hereford Record Office, A81/IV.
5 He was dismissed on 12 January 1727.
6 Chandos Letterbooks; Chandos to Wood: 17 October 1726, 'I return you the plan and elevation you sent me 17th May last ... I had so much of that work on my hands already I did not care to engage in any more'.
7 Chandos Letterbooks; Chandos to Wood: 19 August 1727.

This doorcase led into the alms womens' quarters at St John's Hospital

erty market.[8] The Degge lodging at a first estimate was to cost £1,600 and was intended to be rented at £350 a year.[9] It survived until a fire in 1935 and was indeed a substantial property. Carey's tavern was of no importance, but the last Wood building for the Duke, the Robertson house, was what is now the handsome Chapel Court House or Horace Walpole

8 It was bought by an old servant of the Duke, John Leaves, who had prospered in the paymaster's office.
9 Chandos Letterbooks; Chandos to Wood: 8 July 1728.

30

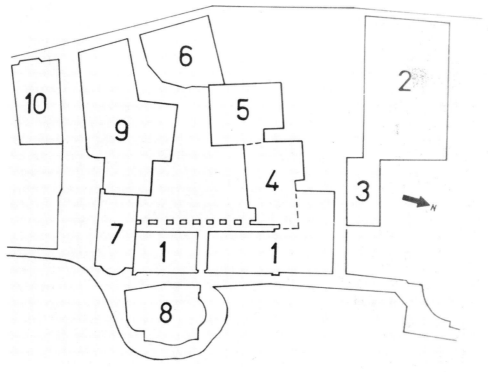

Plan of the buildings at St John's Hospital
1 Hospital on the ground floor; Phillips house above
2 Degge house
3 Carey tavern
4 Robertson house
5 House of Wood's mother-in-law
6 Wood's 1740 development
7 Chapel
8 Cross Bath
9 Master's house
10 Abbey Church House

House facing south into the Hospital courtyard at right-angles to the main block on its eight arches.

At this point it should be stressed that the exact identification of these four properties is a matter for debate. Chandos had bought a whole drift of small cottages around St John's. He, himself, was often vague about their exact locations and changed his rebuilding plans abruptly. At one point the correspondence as to development on the Degge and the Robertson sites closed down while Wood hurried up to London to argue his case. The eventual decision on the schemes was oral and never precisely written down. C.H.C. and M. I. Baker in the scholarly and entertaining *The Life and Circumstances of James Brydges, First Duke of Chandos* confess openly that the identifications they make are based largely on reasoned guesswork.[10] On plain stylistic evidence they seem to be in error when they name the present Surveyor's Office on the west side of the courtyard as the Robertson house, the last of Wood's four. The blocked surrounds to its windows and its moulded string course mark the Surveyor's Office clearly as a pre-Wood building, earlier in style than the four houses which he built on the site. One half of it at least was the property of Wood's mother-in-law Mrs Chivers, who also owned that large garden

10 The authors are quite frank about the problem of identification – 'Few of the clues are precise; most of them are allusive. But if, straining the reader's patience, we try to fit mere bits of evidence into our topographical puzzle, it may in time work out' (303). At this distance in time no firm solution to the problem exists but the Bakers, while admirably persistent in their unravelling, paid little attention to stylistic evidence. They may, also, have become fixated on a Mrs Jones who occupied a small property on the site where the Robertson house was built, and who disappeared from the scene when her house was pulled down. In earlier letters the Duke refers to 'plans for Mrs Jones's house', but the final tenant, who offered the rent the Duke required, was Mrs Robertson. Hence some confusion.

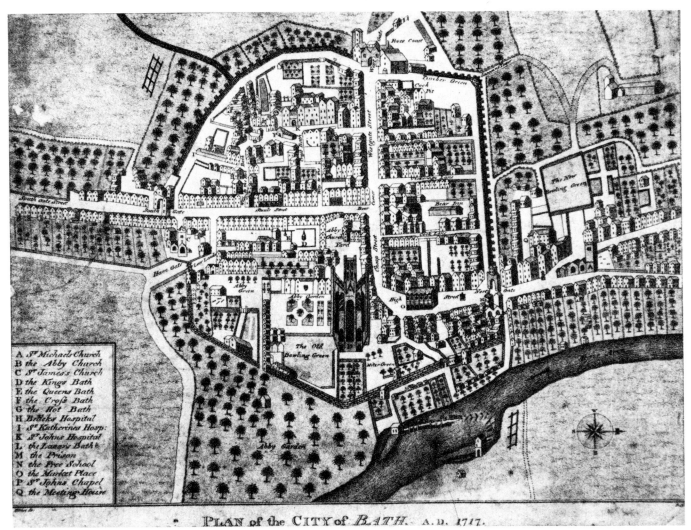

Key on map:

A St Michaels Church
B the Abby Church
C St James's Church
D the Kings Bath
E the Queens Bath
F the Cross Bath
G the Hot Bath
H Belletts Hospital
I St Katherines Hosp:
K St Johns Hospital
L the Lazers Bath
M the Prison
N the Free School
O the Market Place
P St Johns Chapel
Q the Meeting House

PLAN of the CITY of *BATH*. A.D. 1717.

Plan of the City of Bath, 1717

running west of it to the Borough Walls which the Duke so clumsily ang-led after for several years. In the event it was Wood, himself, who, about 1740, eventually built on this covetable green the large square house which still stands with 'Chandos Buildings' misleadingly carved onto its side wall.

What is ultimately important in this context is what was actually built and what was written during that building. Then the interesting questions are: did the Duke trust Wood to design the houses himself, were they built efficiently, and did Wood acquit himself with integrity? To which the re-spective answers must be: reluctantly 'yes', definitely 'no' and probably 'no'.

As it was one of the city's historic institutions, an illustration of what he had built at the St John's Hospital might be expected to feature in Wood's *Essay* on Bath. It does not. He was never satisfied with it and, though he 'provided Masons from Yorkshire, Carpenters, Joiners and Plasterers'[11] from London to raise the standard of its construction, he re-fused to take responsibility for its design. His rival Strahan had been there

11 *Essay*, 242.

32

before him, 'that Structure was plan'd by another Hand, who, through Carelessness or Incapacity, took such a false Survey of the Land, that there is scarce a Right Angle in the whole Building'.[12] Because of this incompetent preparatory work the area finally covered by the first house exceeded by '337 Square feet and half' what had been stipulated in the contract Wood had signed with the Duke on 23 January 1727.[13] He was not allowed to advance the three central bays of the courtyard elevation nor raise on them the pediment which he had designed. As a final bitter stroke he had to suffer Strahan as its assessor.

The next house should have been built on Mrs Phillips's garden, where the Chapel Court House eventually went up. In January 1728 Wood sent the Duke a design for this. The Duke promptly riposted with: 'I am getting another made which I believe will be more convenient'.[14] A curious poker-game followed with design countering design, concessions followed by abandonments. But in July the much larger Degge house was going up on a quite different site on the Borough Walls. Its scale and the Duke's silence suggest that Wood had won. On 16 July the Duke made a second capitulation: 'I approve very well the design you made' for the house that was to be built the following year in the old Phillips garden, the Robertson house, now called Chapel Court House. It was to these last two designs that Wood was referring when he proudly described his Fifth Rate houses 'some plain and some dress'd with Ornaments proper to the Ionick Order'.[15] As these went up Wood was feeling his way towards the standard elevations that he was to build on the main streets of the city.

A vital battle had been won; but every other victory was to go to the Duke, and indeed when all allowances have been made for Chandos's irascibility and for the spite of Mrs Phillips, Wood does seem to have been either coolly indifferent or woefully incompetent in his handling of the workforce. Every house except the little Carey tavern was plagued with delays and disasters. The completion of the Phillips house was promised for August 1727; it was not handed over until March 1728. Then the rooms were so noisy that every partition wall had to be brick lined. By that time Mrs Phillips had come to despise the builder so much that she was 'by no means inclined to let Mr Wood have anything to do with the Repairs'.[16] The Duke told Wood 'I cannot blame her for desiring to have nothing more to do with you. It was the Resolution I had once taken myself... You have used me very unhandsomely'. The complaints went on: 'I will employ some other Workmen and you shall not receive any more money from me'.[17]

It seems likely that Mrs Phillips thoroughly enjoyed her position as trouble-stirrer in ordinary to the Duke. Even he wearied of her behaviour at times: 'it is uncomfortable to receive almost every post nothing but letters filled with complaints'.[18] At other times, however, he rose like a fat trout to the bait of her allegations. On 5 July 1729, as a result of one of her

12 Ibid., 304.
13 Ibid., 241.
14 Chandos Letterbooks; Chandos to Wood: 12 January 1728.
15 *Essay*, 243.
16 Chandos Letterbooks; Chandos to Phillips: 23 November 1729.
17 Ibid., Chandos to Wood: 23 November 1729 and 16 December 1729.
18 Ibid., Chandos to Phillips: 1 May 1729.

letters, the Duke wrote furiously to Wood complaining that 'the pipe which carrys down the dirty water from the water closets and comes down through one of the alms women's houses, instead of being lead according to your articles, is nothing but boards nailed together'. Obviously the boards were simply a cover to the lead pipe behind them, and on the two occasions when the Duke accused Wood of building little houses for himself in the ducal gardens, he was reacting to a twisted Phillips story concocted around a temporary estate office which Wood had put up. It is significant that not one of the Duke's many rages with Wood was the result of first-hand evidence but always from a complaint at second-hand.

The verdict on Wood's last two Chandos houses was even more severe:

> It is the opinion of almost everyone who has seen them, and especially who have lodged in them, that no two Houses have been worse finished and in a less workmanlike manner by anyone who pretended to be an Architect and that had any regard for his own Reputation or the interest of the Person who was his Benefactor and imployed him.[19]

A particular grievance was 'your abominable performance of your Work about Mrs Robertson's House with regard to the Tiling'. This was what had been 'so slovingly and knavishly performed ... there came down no less than 25 or 30 Tiles with one Blast of Wind and not one which had been pin'd'.[20]

Overriding all the dismay over partitions, tiling, flying staircases and uncleared rubbish was the Duke's obsessive fixation with water closets. This was met head on by Wood's total and admitted inability to make water closets work. Doubts had begun to surface as early as 27 April 1727:

> My Lord Duke desires to know whether you don't prepare to fit up the ten Water Closets ... with all manner of Conveniences such as Scots Marble Basons Lead Pipes to let in and out the water for £45, being the Sum charged on the Expense of that Article in the Estimate you have sent his Grace.

But the real trouble came when Wood succumbed to pressure and actually installed these ill-named conveniences. 'Cou'd I have imagined that I had been used in so vile & shameful a manner by you', the Duke declaimed, '& that the tenth part of what Mrs Phillips & others have wrote had been true, you shou'd never have been employed by me again.'[21] Wood's troubles were compounded in that Chandos was far from being technically illiterate. 'The abominable smell', he explained, 'is a sure sign that it is the effect of your ignorance, and had they been contrived with cesspools just above the drain (which is the manner of building them everywhere else) they wou'd not have been subject to this inconvenience which is so great now that I must be forct to have them stopt up.'[22]

19 Ibid., Chandos to Wood: 29 August 1730.
20 Ibid., Chandos to Wood: 6 November 1730.
21 Ibid., Chandos to Wood: 24 September 1728.
22 Ibid.

Unfortunately even this despairing resort was not to be a complete cure. Wood had made such a direct connection with the main town sewer that 'the abominable smells' continued. And the Duke never learnt. At each house a new attempt was made and dreadful overflows were the result. Ingeniously the Duke suggested 'as this smell comes from the Town Vault I should think it might be easy to prevent it ... if you do but dig a Well ... and let the Pipes from the W.C.s carry all down into it, it would do every Whit as well and be an Age before it filled'.[23] Always the end was the same: close stools in the rooms and 'necessaries' out in the yard. The Duke was only able to modify the social crudity of Wood's arrangements by insisting on separate cubicles each with a door to give a modicum of privacy to lodgers who were strangers to one another.

Late in 1729 the Duke's secretary wrote to Wood's last assessor, Mr Fergusson:

> that Mr. Wood deserves the names you gave him my Lord does not at all question, but as his Grace had had the misfortune to employ him and that he is come so near the end of his work, he had better let him go on to finish, than make use of fresh Workmen.[24]

These are obviously not the usual first steps of a great city builder, but behind the Jonsonian slapstick of the four building operations there are contradictions and there are questions to be asked, the first being the mystery of how Wood survived so long. This may possibly be explained by the use he made of Mrs Chivers, his mother-in-law.

When he had arrived in Bath in May 1727 Wood had lodged with a Mr Silcock in a house at the south-east corner of the Cross Bath, almost next door to Mrs Chivers.[25] He can have lost no time in marrying her daughter Jane because his son and namesake was baptized in Bath Abbey on 25 February 1728.[26] Throughout the Duke's correspondence, alternating with the angry recriminations, runs the cajolery: 'The purchase of these two pieces of Ground will be a very acceptable Service to me and you may be sure I will not be wanting to make you a handsome Reward for it'.[27] At one point Chandos was offering £400 for the garden plot. As late as November 1729 he was suggesting 'occasionally talk with Mrs Chivers again concerning her garden, without seeming to have any Design'.[28] Clearly Chandos saw Wood as the key to a deal and equally clearly Wood was reserving that deal for himself.

It is, of course, just possible that the letters are part of an aristocrat's temperamental self-indulgence. Baker and Baker suggest that the Duke's troubles arose from his driving too hard a bargain on Wood's contracts. In fact he seems to have been reasonably generous. In addition to the £2,000 for the Phillips rebuilding he paid out at least another £4,904 in October 1730 with probably many more payments in between. That makes over £7,000 for three lodging houses and a very small tavern. It sounds as if a

23 Ibid., Chandos to Wood: 26 January 1729.
24 Ibid., Chandos to Fergusson: 10 December 1729.
25 *Essay*, 265
26 Walter Ison, *The Georgian Buildings of Bath*, 2nd revised edition, 1980, 234.
27 Chandos Letterbooks; Chandos to Wood: 20 January 1728.
28 Ibid., Chandos to Wood: 6 November 1729.

East facade of St John's Hospital built of crude rubble masonry

fool and his money were being soon parted. Yet in April 1728 the Duke described Wood as 'an able and honest man' to William Brydges, writing that Wood had 'agreed to carry up another range of Building at the Bath ... & I hope it will turn me to as good account as the last has done'.[29] The £350 yearly rent of the Degge house was, after all, a reasonable return on an investment that could hardly have exceeded £2,500. Another indication of the Duke's satisfaction is the fact that in 1735 Chandos was still prepared to pay three guineas for the privilege of standing godfather to one of Wood's daughters, though two years later he did firmly refuse to subscribe to Wood's first book.[30]

The most intriguing question of all is how Wood himself responded to this three year psychic battering of abuse over his highly dramatized inadequacies. It would be remarkable if the period did not in some way shape his self-awareness and suggest future alternative ways of handling the harsh practicalities of the building trade. Whatever antipathy he may have grown to feel towards the Duke, he can hardly have failed to absorb some impression of the Duke's high standards for Bath lodging houses. This is important because a very high proportion of the houses behind the fine façades which Wood was to erect were intended to accommodate lodgers in the season. Wood had a lady and her maid lodging at his own house in Queen Square, South Side in 1731. In the Preface to his *Essay* Wood boasted of the huge advance in the standard of lodging between 1727 and 1742: 'the best Chambers for Gentlemen were then just what the Garrets for Servants now are'.[31] He did not mention that it was Chandos who pioneered the way to bedrooms with en suite dressing rooms and who fought in the teeth of Wood's own incompetence to have decent toilet facilities on every floor and soundproof partitions between rooms.

Overall, this first Brydges correspondence should be reviewed in the light of the second Brydges interchange, that over the work at Tyberton in Herefordshire, where the reserved tones of Wood himself are recorded and the petulant anger of the client is not heard, yet the course of events was still significantly similar.

In the meantime the Duke's last words are worth noting as they are part of the testimonial which he wrote on 10 October 1730 to serve Wood as an introduction to the Bishop of Llandaff:

> The outside work is very well performed but as for the inside it is generally agreed ... that no work can be worse done ... but I don't attribute this to either his want of capacity, or understanding his business, or to his want of honesty, but purely to a want of due care in making his agreement.[32]

So, primed with this measured commendation, the support of a duke for the enlistment of a bishop, John Wood moved on.

In the rough comedy of manners which the Chandos letters present — the greedy, bad-tempered lord, the spying landlady, the young builder

29 Hereford Record Office, A81/IV; Chandos to William Brydges: 12 April 1728.
30 Chandos Letterbooks; Chandos to Wood: 25 January 1735.
31 *Essay*, Preface, 6.
32 Chandos Letterbooks; Chandos to the Bishop of Llandaff: 10 October 1730.

Ashlar masonry of the Hospital's inner courtyard; the Robertson house is on the left

who can only build exterior walls – certain traits of Wood's character are already becoming established. He appears less interested in the technical skills of his trade and the functional utility of a building than in the outward show of an elevation. To achieve this last he will cut corners and ignore criticism, but indifference and haste will, as a result, leave him careless over the fine print of an initial contract. There remains an impression that he enjoyed enemies as ordinary men enjoy friends, an architect for confrontation, impatient of restraint.

Chapter Three

The Dark Years of the Piraticals

Viewed dispassionately, Wood's surviving buildings at St John's Hospital are not impressive. At best they have the air of a badly planned Oxford college, Trinity perhaps or Pembroke. The Degge house which was, for all its plain uncompromising elevations, a key building in the evolution of Wood's style, was burnt in 1935, though it is still possible to get an impression of it from the mis-named Chandos Buildings. That has very similar fenestration but was not built by Wood until 1740, when his mother-in-law finally permitted her garden to be used for speculative development. Carey's tavern was pulled down long ago so only the east and north sides to the courtyard survive of Wood's work.

To appreciate the significance of these faintly lack-lustre remnants of a ducal investment it is useful to remember Beau Brummel. What he did for male evening dress in the 19th century is close to what Wood did in the 18th century for the domestic architecture of Bath city streets. Black and white tails are not the most exciting costume but they saved gentlemen with an indifferent sense of colour and a poor eye for lace from having to make embarrassing choices and they ensured that men would look soberly elegant *en masse*.

In the same way, these plain handsome façades, first developed here and then applied wholesale to the advancing streets of Bath, set up an acceptable standard elevation which saved later builders from making foolish experiments in style. At the same time, they gave the city that aesthetic unity which remains its most memorable feature. Even now a lapse in architectural taste is more disturbing in Bath than in any other British city simply because of the polite uniformity of the buildings that stand about any strident intruder.

Obviously the St John's houses are no foretaste of Wood's town planning. They were random developments on an irregular site. But as he built them Wood was working out how to produce a grand impression on a limited budget, which sets him at the opposite economic pole to Vanbrugh. The point suggested is a fine one. Is a great architect one who designs great buildings at great expense or one who makes fine architecture available to all? By the end of his life Wood had qualified on both counts.

To walk through the dark passageway that connects the clumsy rubble wall on the east side of St John's Hospital with the smooth ashlar of its west elevation overlooking the courtyard is to trace the first, and certainly the most significant, battle which Wood fought with old Bath in his drive to build a new city. The ashlar is the key. Though marred by a dribble of modern drainpipes, the façade to the court is regular and it has a fine finish of well-laid ashlar stonework to conceal its rubble core. It is plain but it still survives as architecture. In contrast, the east front looking out onto the Cross Bath is uncouth, surfaced like the wall of a farmyard and a reproach to a visually strategic point in the cityscape.

'Chandos Buildings' – Wood's speculative development of 1740

As Wood planned his return to Bath he realized that the kind of city he meant to build would require a minor technological revolution. The change he intended was from the ornate, highly individual, grossly expensive baroque town houses which had been going up in the city since the turn of the century, to the simple dignity of this new pared-down Palladian which he was evolving in the houses he built for the Duke. The Palladian elevations would obviously be more economical to build but the two fronts, east and west, of the Hospital proved that good quality ashlar was essential. The plainer the façade the more the eye lingered on the finish to the masonry. That was why Wood wrote that the success of his scheme depended 'in a great Measure upon a Collection of Experienced Workmen, such as by their Facility would make Building come upon the most reasonable Terms';[1] and that was why he brought with him a small army of masons from Yorkshire.

To introduce north country stone masons to a Somerset city with a long and proud tradition in the same craft seems needlessly provocative. It would flout local opinion and unite the opposition of the local building trade to a threatening newcomer. But by reading between the lines in Wood's *Essay* it is apparent that he was making a carefully planned attack and had hedged his bets.

He had spent 1726 in securing the support of Robert Gay, Humphry Thayer and Chandos, calculating that the projections of at least one of these would come to something, giving him a foothold in the building trade and time to mature his major schemes for an Augustan city of unprecedented grandeur. What he must also have done at the same time was to contact Ralph Allen, one of the richest and most influential men in local Bath politics, and convince him that the two of them could work together to their great mutual benefit. As a shareholder in the Avon Navigation Company, Allen probably secured Wood a share in the digging of the Twerton cut. A contract for that, 16 February 1726[2], gave Wood a relatively lucrative excuse to return to Bath. Following this, Allen commissioned 'Designs, as well as a Model' from Wood for a lavish addition to his town house in Lilliput Alley before Wood returned to Bath, 'while I was in London in the Spring of the Year 1727'.[3] It is unlikely that Wood could have persuaded a whole group of experienced Yorkshire masons down to the potentially hostile territory of Somerset without the job guarantees of someone wealthy and interested. Allen at that time was both.

He had made a fortune by organizing the Cross Posts, a system whereby provincial mail was rerouted swiftly to other provincial addresses without having to pass through London. Thereafter his shrewdness, his philanthropy and his genius for friendship with men like Alexander Pope

1 *Essay* 241. On the next page Wood makes it quite clear that local Bath masons were not only ill-organised, but actually under-skilled in all the basic crafts and trades necessary for house building: 'I likewise provided Masons in *Yorkshire*, Carpenters, Joiners, and Plaisterers in *London* and other Places .... and it was then, and not till then, that the Lever, the Pulley, and the Windlass, were introduced ... in the upper part of *Somersetshire*'. It should be remembered that when Wood first wrote this passage in 1742 there were many alive to contradict him if he had been boasting idly. Allen did not simply offer local masons a secure job. He used Wood's Yorkshiremen to break a corrupt local monopoly.
2 British Transport Historical Records, London: An/1/1A. Minutes, 18 February 1726.
3 *Essay*, 244.

Wood is standing on the right of this portrait group with, from the left, Richard Jones, Ralph Allen and Robert Gay

and Henry Fielding were to make him a well-known figure in the West Country. Wood contacted him just as Allen was moving into the Bath stone trade, buying up Pitcher's and Greenway's freestone quarries on Combe Down in order to create a monopoly for himself.

Until Allen stepped into it, the stone industry was in the grip of two groups of masons which, by Wood's account, had sewn up the whole production process to create expensive, poor quality goods at a maximum level of employment. Writing years later in 1742, Wood was still angry as he recalled their demarcation system. Upon the hill the freestone was handled 'by Men who stile themselves Free Masons i.e. Masons whose Province it is to work Free Stone'.[4] Wood was careful to define the term, being himself a Freemason of another and socially very superior kind. The stone was then carted down the hill, 'by which Means the sharp Edges and Corners of the Stones are generally broke'.[5] There it was worked in yards by men of another guild 'who call themselves Rough Masons'.[6] Thus,

4 Ibid., 339. Wood goes into a detailed explanation of the terms 'Free Mason' and 'Rough Mason' at this point because the terms as used in Bath implied almost the exact opposite of what was understood by them in London and Bristol. It was the sheer proximity of the quarries in Bath which must have given rise to the custom of shaping the stone at the quarry instead of carrying it in large blocks to be shaped on site.
5 Ibid.
6 Ibid.

Wood bitterly complained, 'the Works in Bath lose that Neatness in the Joints between the Stones, and that Sharpness in the Edges of the Mouldings which they ought to have; and which People, accustomed to good Work in other Places, first look for here'.[7]

Ralph Allen, for all his genial reputation as the godly 'Squire Allworthy', was determined with Wood's help to smash this cosy, inefficient, anachronistic set-up and drag the protesting work force into the methods of the 18th century 'with a View of reducing the Price of the Material to encourage the Consumption of it'.[8] This was the very purest kind of capitalism. Wood needed cheap, well-cut stone. Allen wanted an expanding local market for his goods. Only the masons stood in the way.

What happened next was ruthless but logical. The bland account of it in Wood's *Essay* skates easily over what must at the time have been an episode of much local anger and disruption. Allen, he records,

> embarked in the domestic Masons Trade of Bath, and proposed to lower the Rates for all manner of Workmanship not only by a Saving to the Workmen of all the Time they lost in going between their Habitations in and about the City, and the Quarries in the external Brow of Camalodunum; but by finding them constant Employ, and Paying them their Wages regularly every Week.[9]

What really happened was that Allen threw out all the old independent masons who refused to co-operate with his new order. Using a nucleus of scab labour which Wood had brought down from Yorkshire he settled his labour force into tied cottages which Wood designed for him in 'two small Towns to receive the two Sets of People thus to be employed'.[10] One of these settlements was up at the quarries, the other was down by that section of the Avon which Wood was just canalizing. 'By Working Masons entering into his Service under these Advantages', Wood complacently concluded, 'Workmanship by the Piece, and Measure was considerably reduced; and the Prices of Free Stone Work, for the Home Consumption, was lowered about a tenth part.'[11] What the labouring masons thought of this was not recorded but clearly a new way of life was being built on the destruction of an old.

In fairness it must be said that the accommodation which Allen offered to his artisans of this new order was so generous and the elevations which Wood devised for his 'two small Towns' were so distinguished that

7 Ibid.

8 Ibid., 425.

9 Ibid. Local resentment at the consequent reduction in the masons' living standards is expressed in the detailed memoirs of Richard Jones, Allen's Clerk of Works (see Chapter 7, footnote 3). He was born in 1703, and in 1718 was apprenticed to a 'freemason' in the unreformed system. He records on folio 1 of the account of his life, 'and it was at that time a very good trade, and had good prices for their work'.

10 Ibid. Wood does not make it clear, but it is to be assumed, that the upper 'Town' was for the quarrymen who hewed out the large blocks and the lower 'Town' was for the 'artificers' who cut the stone ornament and ashlar to order. Bath builders like Strahan would have their own 'rough' and 'free' masons, but would buy the large blocks from Allen at the riverside quay. This was certainly the arrangement in 1741 when Wood was building the Exchange in Bristol.

11 Ibid., 426.

Model village for Ralph Allen's
stonemasons on Combe Down

both 'Towns' have survived to the present as impressive instances of early
industrial housing. Each 'Town' is actually no more than a terrace of ten
houses, two miles apart, but thematically related. The one is urban, front-
ing immediately onto a street leading to the Quay, the other is rural behind gardens. The lower terrace, Ralph Allen's Cottages, composes between distinctive end units, its eight middle houses linked by shared
porches and a pilaster strip. Up on the hill by the quarries, the second terrace of double-fronted, two-storey houses has a central pediment over
The Dial House which was originally the foreman's home with a small
chapel or prayer room at the rear. In their pleasant understated rhythms
both terraces could be seen as social statements by their architect that
there should be harmony everywhere, but a harmony within degrees.

The plan went smoothly. 'Proper Models ... of the Roads and Carriages in the North' were sent down to Bath and 'a Person whose natural
Genius for Mechanicks enabled him to improve upon the Original',[12]
John Padmore of Bristol, connected the quarries to the quays by rails at
the side of the road. As a result there was less damage to the sharp edges
and mouldings of the blocked stones. It is harder to estimate the social
damage which Wood suffered in his relations with fellow Bath masons
and building workers while all this took place. His frequent distraction
from practical supervision of the Chandos houses becomes easier to excuse.

The sweetener which Allen offered Wood as an introduction to this
partnership was a bizarre one in view of Wood's aim of introducing plain
Palladian façades of high quality stonework to the streets of the city. But
then throughout their relationship Allen and Wood seemed to bring out

12 Ibid., 425.

44

Allen's town house as originally built – a 19th century watercolour by Henry Venn Lansdown '

in each other a wonderfully positive vulgarity. There are stories of the Post Master bringing out coffer after coffer of guineas from his vaults merely to dazzle the young architect with the extent of his resources. Certainly Wood never committed anything again quite as outrageous as the pocket-sized, back garden palazzo for the house in Lilliput Alley.

Clamped away now in the shadow of later housing, its pale golden stone is still alight in the darkest weather with a concentration of decorative devices that would comfortably have served an elevation four times as long. It was essentially a prestige project, a business base as well as a home. Allen would have wanted something to surpass the complex baroque houses of fellow notables on the City Corporation, and Wood replied to the challenge with an elevation where Palladian motifs make wholly baroque connections. In essence it is a pedimental central feature that has never sprouted its supporting bays, one so narrow that the Venetian window on the first floor has had to be rationed out into three bays, and even so is squeezed breathlessly between a giant order of four engaged Corinthian columns. Shamelessly ostentatious, it is a reminder of the brash cultural ambience which Wood had just entered, a foreshadowing of Prior Park, that extraordinary realization of the grossest kind of Palladian villa which Wood was soon to poise for Allen on the brink of a vertiginous Arcadian valley.

45

The rich Palladian detail of Ralph Allen's town house

46

An example of Bath's early 18th century bucolic baroque – The Grapes, Westgate Street

It is unfortunate that, while the Allen town house still stands, so few of the baroque façades which it was built to outshine have survived. They would have put Wood's atypical design into perspective and illustrated the kind of opposition which he had to face in those precarious years, 1727-9, before his Queen Square project had got under way. Some idea of their individual character and decorative overkill can be gained from General Wolfe's House in Trim Street, No 14 Green Street or The Grapes in Westgate Street, with its bucolic parade of the three classical orders 'over

47

Prince of Orange House Orange Grove Bath Earl of Burlington Architect

Pre-Wood Bath – Nassau House, Orange Grove (demolished)

one another, an Order to every Story of Building'[13] as Wood admiringly described another of the same type in Cheap Street. But the most over-weening examples must be hunted out in old photographs. There was Nassau House in the Orange Grove, a lost temple of ingenious solecisms that might have been designed as a parody of the Allen façade, and Weymouth House which rose with the same assertive tower-like effect on a relatively narrow base, pediment above pediment, pilaster perched upon pilaster, massively moulded string courses and boldly projecting architraves to every window. All these houses, lost or surviving, have a common baroque feature of the interconnection of detail. Every element of their façades links up with another and there is a fretful horror of vacant space. Smooth ashlar may have been at a premium in pre-Wood Bath but there had been a thriving school of stone carvers. As Wood reported respectfully: 'Ornaments of a larger Kind, such as Chimney Pieces, Door Cases, Window Cases, Pedestals, Peers, Obelisks, Ballustrades and the like, are commonly made by the same Artificers and sent abroad to a great Distance from Bath'.[14] These 'Artificers' had been inherited by Allen when he bought up his quarries, so Wood had to preserve a delicate

13 Ibid., 332.
14 Ibid., 424.

48

Dr Bave's House, Lower Borough Walls (demolished)

balancing act. On the one hand he had to favour correct simplicity so that large numbers of cheap plain houses would be built using up a vast amount of freestone, on the other hand there would be pressure from Allen to popularize the virtuosity of the skilled carvers in his employ. The town house in Lilliput Alley will have been deliberately designed as a showcase for the kind of detail that might have been more appropriate on Nassau or Weymouth House's hyperactive elevations.

It is not immediately apparent where Wood's private inclinations lay in this dilemma of aesthetics and economy. When he attacked the architecture of his Bath rivals as 'Piratical' he could have been deploring their designs as pirated, that is as stolen, or as ruffianly exotic and crude. Throughout his own designing career he seems to have turned out long elevations of unrelieved severity and flowery excess with equal satisfaction provided that they were, by his standards, correct. Such analytical criticism as he delivers on fellow Bath architects needs to be valued inversely. The longer his prose attack the more he felt threatened by the man he is discussing.

Wood names four chief competitors in his *Essay*: John Harvey, William Killigrew, Thomas Greenway and John Strahan, and he honours

49

John Harvey's Pump Room of 1705–6, admired by Wood

only one of them, Strahan, with the title of architect . In Wood's eyes Harvey was a 'Stone Cutter',[15] Greenway a mason and Killigrew 'a Joiner who laid his Apron aside about the Year 1719'.[16]

John Harvey is a tantalizingly obscure figure, possibly a father and a son of the same name, though Wood treats him as one person. Unlike the other three he seems to have lacked financial backing but the Pump Room which he designed and built at the early date of 1705-6 was a near Palladian structure of some elegance, almost as far in advance of architectural fashion as Dean Aldrich's 1706 design for Peckwater Quad at Christ Church, Oxford. It stood in its original form with five Corinthian columns to the north and four Doric to the south, like two pages from the first of Palladio's four books realized in stone: a pleasure pavilion in the heart of the city and a flat negative to Wood's claim to have been first with the style in Bath. Wood desperately wanted to pull this down as part of his grand

15 Walter Ison, *The Georgian Buildings of Bath*, states that three generations of masons bearing the name of Harvey worked in Bath. However, in his *Essay*, Wood categorically refers to John Harvey, 'the second of that Name' as being responsible for the Pump House of 1706 (p. 269), the Lansdown Memorial of 1720 (p. 231) and St Michael-extra-Muros (p. 308).
16 *Essay*, 318.

50

Thomas Greenway's palace for Beau Nash; now part of the Theatre Royal

scheme for redeveloping the King's Bath precinct. The only ground on which he could attack it was that of convenience: 'too hot in Summer, and too cold in Winter', but he allowed that it was 'one of the best Pieces of Architecture the City could boast of, even for ten or fifteen Years after the Room was erected'.[17]

Years later in 1734 when Harvey, or his son, defeated Wood in the competition to build St Michael-extra-Muros, Wood related the story that horses had to be hood-blinded before they would pass it as they were 'so frighted at the odd Appearance of the Church'.[18] This heavy and ungenerous jocularity is one of Wood's less engaging traits.

Killigrew and Greenway escaped with only mild mockery. Theirs was the provincial linear baroque of Weymouth House, by Killigrew, and Greenway's St John's Court. Killigrew had built a large new ballroom for Thomas Harrison's Assembly House in 1720. This had the dismal aspect of a Dissenting Tabernacle but Wood offered no criticism of it apart from suggesting that the roof was unsound.[19] Possibly he was conscious that the Assembly House which he himself had built across the way for Dame Lindsey, 1728-30, was architecturally even less reputable. About Greenway's five house speculative scheme in St John's Court, Sawclose, not to be confused with St John's Hospital, Wood is ambivalent. He worked alongside Greenway at Tyberton in 1728 and continued later to employ Greenway's sons. This may have restrained his criticism but he does describe the first of these five houses, the one first occupied by Beau Nash, as 'so profuse in Ornament, that none but a Mason, to shew his Art, would have gone to the Expense of those Inrichments'.[20]

17 Ibid., 269.
18 Ibid., 308. This misleading anecdote does not appear in the 1742-3 edition of the *Essay*.
19 Ibid., 319.
20 Ibid., 338.

Greenway's house was no more 'inriched' than Wood's town house for Ralph Allen but the rich linear fret of its two surviving elevations makes no overt reference to the classical orders and was in no way correct by Wood's standards. Only one element of Greenway's local linear baroque seems to have been acceptable to Wood and that was the broad double platband which makes such a pronounced emphasis of the internal structure on Wood's exterior elevations. Colen Campbell employed these bands to relieve plain façades but never with quite such a heavy hand as Wood.

It was John Strahan who presented the only real threat to the vision of a greater Bath planned out and dominated by John Wood. Strahan was ambitious, architecturally sophisticated and had a rich developer as his friend. Across the years, when the threat of his competition had passed away, Wood still remembered him balefully:

> While I was entering into these Engagements, and making these Preparations, [Wood is carefully vague about the exact year because he wished to portray Strahan as his practical imitator and follower, never as his precursor. The most likely date is 1727] one John Strahan came to Bristol; and, by printed Bills, offering his Service to the Publick, as a Land Surveyor and Architect, Mr Hobbs, the Deal Merchant, thereupon took him under his Patronage, and employed him in laying out some Meadow and Garden Ground on the West Side of the Body of the City of Bath into Streets for Building.[21]

The threat was acute, the competition was direct. Hobbs had initiated the Avon Navigation scheme back in 1710 and was potentially as influential a figure in Bath business as Ralph Allen. The Duke of Beaufort supported him and the land which he commissioned Strahan to develop bordered the Barton Fields of Robert Gay which were vital to Wood's plans. Bath was a property ripe for the plucking and Wood and Allen were not the only sharp-eyed business men to have noticed the fact.

1727 was set to be Wood's year of triumph; it marked, in fact, the nadir of his fortunes when all his schemes went awry and all his backers failed him. First to collapse was the Barton Street scheme.

This was to have been a 'Street of one thousand and twenty five Feet in Length', though only a precursor to 'the grand Part of the Design'.[22] Back in November 1726 the landowner Robert Gay had impowered Wood, to use his own suspiciously vague phrase, 'to engage with any Body that I could bring into the Scheme'.[23] But in the political uncertainty which followed George I's death on 12 June 1727, Gay, who was an absentee Londoner, backed out. In a near panic measure Wood 'at the Instance of some Friends' thrust a plan for rebuilding the whole town before a Cor-

---

21 Ibid., 242. The earliest rate records for Strahan's building projects are for 1736 (Somerset R.O., D/P/Wal. SW 4/1/1). At that time there were no houses in his Avon Street, only three in Beaufort Street, five in King's Mead Square and seventeen in King's Mead Street. By that time Wood had Queen Square virtually complete.
22 Ibid., 240-1. Wood hoped to 'restore' the street plan of a supposed legionary camp.
23 Ibid., 240.

poration 'so far as it related to the Estates under their Guardianship'.[24] Wood had not been acting in recent months in such a way as to win local friends or influence local people, so not surprisingly his plan was thrown out: 'they thought proper to treat all my Schemes as Chimerical'.[25]

By his own account Wood claimed that he thereupon 'determined instantly to become an absolute Contractor ... for Ground sufficient to compleat the fourth Part of an open Area which we agreed should bear the Name of Queen Square'.[26] Brave words, but the reality was that for more than a year he was to be on his own, whistling for new support.

The second backer on whom he had depended was the apothecary, Humphry Thayer, and his projects had looked particularly promising early in the year. Though another Londoner, Thayer was treasurer to a charity subscription which had opened in 1723 with the aim of building a General Hospital. There is little doubt that this, on land adjacent to the King's Bath, was what Wood had in mind with his 'Imperial Gymnasium': a health centre with healing waters and royal tennis courts attached. Thayer's instructions to Wood were 'to provide a Piece of Ground for the Building, to prepare proper Draughts for the Structure, and to use my utmost Endeavours to bring the Work into Execution'.[27] By 26 May 1727, after a whirl of efficient action, Wood had found an ideal site near the King's Bath and was pressing the trustees. Bath's establishment responded with the alacrity of a pudding. Eleven years later Wood was still pressing them with different draughts for a different site.

Even Allen deserted him and employed another builder to make the additions to his town house following Wood's designs and model. In another promising opening Thayer had employed Wood 'to contrive such an Assembly House for the famous Dame Lindsey, as could be turned to other Uses for a small Expense' and 'to make a Plan for covering the Bowling Green and Abbey Orchard ... with Houses'.[28] On 16 May 1727 Wood had 'found Dame Lindsey so zealously bent upon a House, that a great Part of my Time was at first employed upon her Designs'.[29]

Once again inaction followed. No ground was cut for Lindsey's Assembly House until September 1728 and what she had made Wood design was a row of four houses which could serve as lodgings, gaming rooms and polite bordello; the Dame, as Wood discovered, had an unsavoury reputation. At the end of the little terrace was the curious façade of the ballroom, for all the world like a 1920s cinema, with blind panelling

24 Ibid., 243.
25 Ibid.
26 Ibid.
27 Ibid., 242. At this distance in time it is not possible to be certain about Humphry Thayer's character, but it may be that he was less anxious to lay out the money, £273, which had been collected in 1723 to build a Hospital, than Wood seems to have imagined. It is a fact that until Thayer died in 1737 no real progress was made in selecting a site, by which time the £273 had increased to £379.
28 Ibid., 242.
29 Ibid. Wood never mentions that he was still engaged in building ventures on the Harley Estate in London at this time and remained involved there until at least 1732 (Harley Add. MS. 18,240). He had leased a frontage of 80 feet in Edward Street on 12 December 1728 and frontages of 17 feet, 36 feet and 20 feet in Edward Street and Margaret Street in 1730 so not all his projects were in Bath. This helps to account for his frequent distraction from local work.

Lindsey's and Harrison's
Assembly Houses on Terrace
Walk viewed from North Parade

on its ground floor windows, recessed panels above and three circular attic windows with shutters. It was not the elevation of which a strict Palladian could boast.

In the meantime Wood depended precariously upon his work for the Duke of Chandos with all its humiliations and his contract to act as foreman to a gang of Cockney navvies digging out the Avon at the New Quay. In his usual indomitable Toad of Toad Hall manner Wood put a brave face even on this last humble achievement: 'till which time the real Use of the Space was unknown in, or about the City, and the Removal of Earth was then reduced to a third Part of what it formerly Cost'.[30] Even that contract ended when he was paid off, 15 July 1727, after a disagreement with the main contractor.

In these reduced and clouded circumstances it is hardly surprising that Wood made many visits to London and, when William Brydges asked him to advise on certain constructions which he had in hand, snatched eagerly at the chance of a respite from hostile Bath in the rural calm of Herefordshire. What he could not have guessed was that this country idyll would afford posterity the only first-hand insight into his business methods, his practical building expertise and his manner with the gentry.

30 Ibid., 241.

Chapter Four

An Altar up the Wye

Tyberton is in the very rural deeps of western Herefordshire over against Wales and in the lee of the Black Mountains. In Wood's time the area was virtually impassable in winter because of the sticky red clay into which its lanes were cut. The errant and unreliable Wye was its best line of communication with the east and Sugwas, the port for Tyberton, was subject to summer shallows and sudden floods. It was not a river which a barge captain undertook without substantial financial inducement. Later in life it was said of Wood 'he is not one that chooses to be much put out of his way'[1] but at this stage of his fortunes he was clearly ready to be put very far out of his way and to catch at any commission.

What possessed the Duke of Chandos to recommend John Wood to a second cousin struggling with the complexities of building a sizeable country house cannot be known. He had a rough sense of humour but it is more probable that in his usual breezy way he had dropped a casual commendation hoping to do a favour to both cousin and architect. By late 1727, which is when Wood seems first to have visited Tyberton, the Duke should have been well aware of Wood's shortcomings.[2] It is possible, however, that Wood had worked his own way into the good graces of the lesser branch of the Brydges family.

The silent voice in the Tyberton correspondence is that of William Brydges, the man who received the letters and carefully filed them away. Building upon known facts of his life and speculating around the gaps and questions in Wood's own letters, a much milder character than the Duke emerges. He stood as godfather to Wood's first son John, baptized on 25 February 1728.[3] Employing, probably, no secretary but writing his own letters in the midst of much other legal business, he was often tardy in his replies. He seems to have been bemused by, rather than intolerant of delays, slow to settle accounts but never as chiding and devious as James his cousin.

His first wife Jane had died suddenly in 1718 and in March 1719 he began to rebuild Tyberton church, using a local mason and a Gloucester carver. The dates hint at a religious sadness. The church, a very modest brick building, was complete by 1720[4] and in 1723 William Brydges mar-

1 Reported by Sarah Clayton writing from Bath to an influential friend in Liverpool when she suggested that the town council should employ Wood to build the Exchange (now Town Hall); see S. A. Harris, 'Sarah Clayton's Letter and John Wood of Bath' in *Trans. Historic Soc. of Lancs. and Cheshire*, c (1948).

2 By this time Mrs Phillips had begun to create friction between the Duke and his architect at St John's Hospital.

3 Tyberton papers; Wood to Brydges: 3 May 1735 – 'Yr. Godson begs his humble Duty'.

4 Bruce A. Bailey, in 'William Brydges and the Rebuilding of Tyberton Church' in *Transactions of the Woolhope Naturalists' Field Club*, vol. xxxvii, part 2 (1962), 210-21, records that the building began about March 1719 and that by November the structure was complete. He also states that the finishing touches to the interior were completed in March 1722 and quotes a letter to support the statement. However, the memorial to William Brydges in the church states that the church was begun and completed in 1720.

ried again, a Catherine Rice whose parents lived in Bath.

This second marriage inspired Brydges to rebuild Tyberton Court. As early as 10 April 1724 he was pricing Peak marble fireplaces.[5] Thomas Rogers of London sent in bills for flooring boards, nails, guttering and centring for vaults in April 1726, and by 26 August 1727 Brydges' father, Francis, was writing of 'the happy progress also of the building'. A few days later Francis wrote, 'I am sorry you will not begin covering your house this five or six weeks and wish the weather may not retard you longer. I fear you have had some ill accidents by workmen'.[6] The letter is certain proof that Wood was not, as some authorities have claimed, involved in the basic design.[7]

At that point, with the house already up to roof level, Wood may have been consulted. William Brydges had been in Bath that August taking the waters for his gout. They did him no good and thereafter he relied on chalybeate Holt Water from Wiltshire posted on to him by Wood, his jack-of-all-trades and agent. Francis Brydges died that September. Father and son had been on close and affectionate terms; the old man's last letters show that he approached death confidently and his memorial in Tyberton described him as 'a true member of that pure part of the Catholick Church The Church of England' an unusual phrase which suggests High Church convictions.

For a second time a death was followed by church building. This time William Brydges decided to enrich the existing church with a new sanctuary and he chose Wood for the work, bringing him in at the same time in an advisory capacity to help with the house. Wood must have been at Tyberton late in 1727 as he had sent 'Draughts of the Hall and Drawing Room' by 27 January 1728 and was promising 'Draughts of the Green House, Terrass Walls and Common Parlour' very shortly.

Tyberton Court was pulled down, unlamented, in 1952. It was a plain brick block, seven bays by five, with canted bays on one of the elevations and a Bath stone cornice and balustrade worked by Thomas Greenway who also supplied much of the labour. Wood should never have had this uninspired design attributed to him though he certainly took over the task of fitting out the interior. Because his actual visits to the site were rare his letters to William Brydges often read like a manual for 'do-it-yourself' tasks. They are interesting as a revelation of Wood as a practical joiner having to give advice as a surveyor and concentrating, therefore, on those aspects of the building which he understood. But they reveal no particular stylistic insights or innovations. It is the work on the 'altar' as he calls it, really the reredos, which is uniquely interesting. This raises the level of the whole Tyberton involvement from mere hack work undertaken to fill in a bleak period of underemployment, to something of much deeper significance.

Up to this point Wood has appeared brash, thrusting, ruthless even, and capable of projecting building schemes on an ambitious scale. But there has been nothing in the young speculative builder, dilatory surveyor and union smasher to suggest spiritual qualities. Yet these are what the

5 Tyberton papers; Higgins Harris to Brydges: 10 April 1724.
6 Ibid., Francis Brydges to William Brydges: 9 September 1727.
7 Bailey, 'William Brydges ... Tyberton Church', 216.

Tyberton altar demonstrates and the intriguing question is: whose spirituality, that of William Brydges or of John Wood? The obvious answer, and the one that has previously been accepted,[8] is that Brydges contributed the symbolism and Wood the design; but that is not what the correspondence or Wood's later activities confirm. Wood frequently re-draughted the design and was still using the symbols 26 years later.

It would be foolish to claim the work as a masterpiece of English ecclesiastical art, but it has been finely conceived within a fake plaster apse that gives spatial quality to the square east end. Carved in coarse, bold relief in oak are four festoons descending from a band of cherub heads. The carving has none of the virtuosity of the lime or pear wood altarpieces that Grinling Gibbons and his imitators carved in and around London, but what is so impressive, and indeed moving about the reredos, is that all the trophies on the festoons have a clear meaning. Typical London work of the kind may feature a conventional pelican in her piety but the rest will be garlands of fruit and flowers, equally appropriate to a domestic chimney piece. Here at Tyberton the iconography is that of the Anglican church in

8 Ibid., 217: 'the symbolism must have been thought out by William Brydges, the artistic aspects of the design being entrusted to Wood'.

(*left*) Detail from the Tyberton
Altar showing the severed ear
(*right*) Symbols of the Deity from
the Tyberton Altar

its Laudian prime, that 'pure part of the Catholick Church The Church of
England' which Francis Brydges' memorial recalled. It also suggests that
Caroline age of Wood's hero architect Inigo Jones.

On each of the four festoons of entwined cord are three trophies.
These are composed in the conventional, cross-set style of classical
trophies like the metopes on the Inigo Jones-Webb designs for Whitehall
Palace.[9] The individual trophies are those of Christ's Passion and the
Christian Church triumphant with an admixture of those mystical symbols popular in 17th century Emblem books: burning hearts, the serpent
of eternity, the clenched arm of power and the flaming brand. The left-
hand festoon features the Passion most directly with Cross, ladder, pin-
cers, spear, sword and crown of thorns with crossed palms and brands. On
each side of the altar (it is notable that Wood never uses the correct Protestant term of 'communion table') the symbols are more triumphalist and
esoteric. Prominent among them is the Freemasons' symbol of a flaming
sun in the triangle of the Trinity circled by the serpent of eternity. Also
represented are St Peter's cockerel, a sword with the ear of the High

9 Edited by William Kent and published in 1727 as *The Designs of Inigo Jones consisting of
Plans and Elevations for Public and Private Buildings, with some Additional Designs*; see Plates
11 and 24.

58

Priest's servant still stuck to it, the axes and fasces of power, a communion chalice set upon palms, the coroneted T cross, more brands and the Lamb of God. The right-hand festoon is exactly the same as the left-hand one, so the Passion is forcefully impressed upon a worshipper kneeling to take Communion. The cherubs' heads on the band are carved in splendid relief and divided by burning hearts, more serpents, tablets of the law and the Holy Ghost in Glory upon palms.

This is 17th century iconography in the wrong age. John Donne, Francis Quarles, George Wither, and surely the ecstatic Crashaw, with his poetry to 'The Flaming Heart' of the 'Seraphical Saint Teresa', would have responded to it; and the community of Little Gidding would have been happy with it in their own chapel. As an isolated episode in Wood's creative life it might be of minor importance; something produced to please an old-fashioned country squire. It is, however, the first clear sign of that confident architect's Christianity which hereafter runs like a thread through his writing and his design. To a Freemason the details of the Tabernacle which Moses set up in the Wilderness and the dimensions of the Temple of Solomon were, and remain, a practical revelation by the Almighty. John Wood saw these everywhere, in prehistoric stone circles and even in the choir of 16th century Bath Abbey. He wrote about them at length and he believed that they gave an almost sacred importance to the Classical, but to him Jewish, style in which he designed. He was a 'born again' architect and if the notion is difficult for a modern mind to assimilate it should be remembered that such concepts are not dead and that a living, fashionable English architect like Quinlan Terry was not ashamed to publish in the *Architectural Review* of October 1983 a statement of faith identical to that held by Wood 250 years before.[10]

With this particular version of Christianity, shaped to be relevant to one profession more than any other, we have the driving force and the creative exhilaration otherwise notably lacking in Wood's career. On 14 September 1730, while the altar was still half finished and the commonplace cares of room partitions and toilet plumbing still beset him, Wood set off confidently to see the Bishop of Llandaff and begin the construction of the inner court of Solomon's Temple in a ruined Welsh cathedral. And in the early spring of 1754, almost from his death bed, he was to lay the foundations of his long-postponed masterpiece in Bath, the King's Circus, around the Doric frieze of which reappear, multiplied many times over, flaming hearts, circling serpents, fire brands and arms of power, all the strange symbols which he had first set up so many years before in Tyberton.

It would be pleasant to be able to report that up there, in rural Herefordshire, Wood became a changed man and coupled spiritual expression with efficiency and promptitude. But it would be untrue. The record of the Tyberton letters is very much that of the Chandos papers.

10 Entitled 'Origins of the Orders', Terry wrote: 'Privilege and discipline are anathema to this age as indeed are faith and worship; but I can only explain the phenomenon of Classical orders as a direct consequence of the fact that first and foremost they were ordained to contain the visible manifestation of human worship of the only true God. It does not take a fanatical believer to see this – any intelligent man who has worked in and understood Classical principles of architecture will sooner or later admit the sense of wonder that surrounds them'.

Symbol from the Tyberton Altar suggestive of Roman power

As far as the house was concerned Wood probably inherited chaos – the 'ill accidents by workmen' that Francis Brydges referred to, weeks before his death. Wood began with one of those introductory flourishes to show his technical expertise that he had enjoyed in Bath. There, it will be recalled, 'the Lever, the Pulley, and the Windlass were introduced among the Artificers in the upper Part of Somersetshire' for the first time by his agency.[11] His reception at Tyberton had not been welcoming: 'the workmen ... seem'd to be very uneasy at a Surveyors coming amongst them and tho one Man said a Surveyor wou'd be very serviceable to the Country yet there was ten that said Surveyors were all Roagues and good for nothing but to make mischief between Gent. and their Workmen'.[12] After blinding them with his science Wood was shortly after able to write to Brydges: 'I am glad I am so much in favour with the Bricklayers as to have their prayers. I am sure what they are about will teach 'em to use their plumb Rules with more exactness than any work they have hitherto been employ'd in.'[13] He was on confident joking terms with his employer at this point.

Apart from these infrequent visits, often ingeniously postponed, Wood's chief service was to liaise with London dealers like Theobald, whom he knew of old, to supply deals, glass, balusters, window frames, even celestial and terrestrial globes for the new house. Watch repairs and regular bottles of Holt Water were also part of the service. A typical letter reads: 'been with Mr Theobald and he has a Parcell of Deals in his Yard exceeding good and such as you shall want. I believe these Prizes to be as low as can be'.[14] Then a bill would arrive for Brydges from Theobald 'with great respect tho' unknown ... for Christianna dry deals £105..5 the double deals being Mr Woods he will acct. with you for them'.[15]

Wood's most grievous chores concerned transport. On 3 April 1729 he reported:

> The Ship wherein was your Glass and Marble, my Deals and Lead to near the value of 500 Pound was run on ground near Biddiford Bay in Devonshire ... the Captain of this Ship is a very proud, idle and ill natured Fellow, he lay in the Downs near 3 weeks the same at the Island of Scilly whilst other ships proceeded on their voyages and got safe home.

That was the occasion when Wood sent his brother down to sort matters out. Later Wood left a load of deals all night by the first lock on the Avon at Keynsham and then had to hear the lock-keeper's tale next day about a high tide washing them all out to sea. How William Brydges reacted to this extraordinary episode is not known.

In addition to his agency for building materials Wood supplied labour when it was required, drawing up and witnessing the workers' contracts with Brydges (see Appendix 2) and determining justice 'if any dis-

11 *Essay*, 242.
12 Tyberton papers; Wood to Brydges: 21 May 1728.
13 Ibid., Wood to Brydges: 10 August 1728.
14 Ibid., Wood to Brydges: 14 March 1728.
15 Ibid., James Theobald to Brydges: 30 July 1728.

pute shou'd arrise'. It often did arise and Wood was learning how to act tactfully as intermediary between gentleman and workman: 'Michael Bray [a joiner] is come hither and makes sad complaints but no notice is taken of them till I hear from you how he behaved himself. I am Sr Your most obet hum' Servant John Wood'.[16] Simply to read Wood's gently sloping copperplate may have soothed the angry Brydges. There were even demonstrations of thoughtful charity as when he ordered his foreman to give the wife of an absconded worker: 'a small matter more for the Poor Woman has three small children and is ready to lie in with another'.[17]

There are signs too that Wood was learning how to distance himself from hard work and responsibility by paying others as in a letter of 29 July 1728:

> I have sent you one Man and will send you two more on Wednesday to carry on the Carpentry work. The Agreement I have made is with my Carpenter who sends these Men to work under him and he himself will come over with me to direct the Roof, Partitions and Flooring in the House. He has agreed upon the same terms you offered George Wall.

Another device to avoid the turmoil of a muddy building site was a long detailed letter setting out exactly the panelling of a room, the projection of its mouldings, the beading on the doors, the number and height of stair balusters, rise of stair treads, even the method whereby panels were to be fixed to the walls and 'painted twice in Oyle as soon as it is fasten'd up against the Walls, for this Maxim must ever be observed'; much further sound advice on shrinkage followed (see Appendix 3). This letter was dated 19 March 1729 when letters relevant to the house were growing fewer, though the altar still caused trouble. By that time Wood's affairs in Bath were beginning to prosper again and he was extricating himself from what must have been a very dull and unrewarding task. If the rooms he describes were built to his instructions they would have been indistinguishable from thousands of other plain panelled interiors up and down the country.

The long and lingering history of the altar's design and construction is worth a summary because of its intrinsic importance and as an instance of Wood's stewardship in a matter of real concern to his patron.

'The foundation is already laid and part of it raised to the levell of the Floor', Wood wrote cheerfully on 21 May 1728, within months of starting his work. But a week later from London, 'the Italian Plaisterer has done nothing towards the Modell of the Altar',[18] a model which Wood himself had apparently made. In July the Italians were demanding £40 for a plaster reredos so, 'I took the Draught from them and when I come to Tibberton I will make you a Modell of it in Clay and believe it will be no great difficulty to get other people to do the work'.[19] The original 'Modell' must, then, have been only a drawing.

16 Ibid., Wood to Brydges: 3 April 1729.
17 Ibid., Wood to Brydges: 3 November 1728.
18 Ibid., Wood to Brydges: 28 May 1728.
19 Ibid., Wood to Brydges: 6 July 1728.

The next real move came in February 1729. Brydges seems to have been pressing for a stone altar and Wood was tactfully urging that 'Wood is much Cheaper and beautifull than stone. I saw Mr Wilson who seemed to desire to do something for you'.[20] In April 'I saw Mr Wilson in London and shewed him the Draught of the Alter which he will not undertake to execute for less than 50 pound I also shewed it to Mr Artari an Italian Plais' and to Mr Serini', who also stuck out for £50.[21] In August 1729 Wood had three alternative draughts for the altar, one at least 'to be performed in Wood',[22] so Brydges was still thinking of stone or plaster.

December passed with Wood stalling, 'I am not sure whether you did not say you wou'd have 3 large crosses finneared with Mahogggany in the 3 Pannels',[23] and considering a Bristol craftsman. Then suddenly on 16 January 1730, along with 'a great many happy new Years', 'the Alter is portable for Carridge' and 'The Festoons are done and laid on a Floor ... on purpose to shew Mrs Rice'. She was Brydges' mother-in-law and tended to pay Wood's bills. In May, Wood wrote tentatively: 'I believe all the Alter is done but the Circular Mouldings'.[24] But in August there was a new burst of unconvincing optimism: 'I have at last got your Alter as good as done ... I was forced to get it done here' (he wrote from Bath) 'both Joyner work and carving, the carving is a little backwards'. He had 'accidentally heard of the Carver', which seems to rule Paty of Bristol out, and paid the man on account £15.14s.8d.[25]

In October the festoons were still not done but, 'I have given the Carver a severe reprimand and he has promised to finish 'em next week'.[26] In November, Wood warned Brydges that Bradley the bargeman wanted £10 to carry the altar up to Sugwas. Then on 19 December 1730 Wood exploded into written rage:

> The whole Affair concerning this Alter has been quite perplext to me and if it had not been purely to oblige you I would not have meddled with it upon any acco' after all the Lyes and disappointments I receiv'd from the Bristol People.

His real grievance seems to be the £15.14s.8d which Mrs. Rice had not been directed to pay him. On 28 February 1731 things really seemed to be moving fast at last and he would send the altar 'in 3 weeks or a month'.

A year later, 5 February 1732, the altar was finally on its way 'entirely good as it came out of the Workman's Hand so be pleased to take particular notice how it comes out of the Barge'. The five year saga was over.

It is possible that the work had been completed by Thomas Omer, a carpenter who features mysteriously in this correspondence, always on

20 Ibid., Wood to Brydges: 7 February 1729.
21 Ibid., Wood to Brydges: 3 April 1729.
22 Ibid., Wood to Brydges: 16 August 1729.
23 Ibid., Wood to Brydges: 24 December 1729.
24 Ibid., Wood to Brydges: 22 May 1730.
25 Ibid., Wood to Brydges: 22 August 1730. Bailey in the article above suggested that the Bristol wood-carver James Paty (the elder) may have done the work on the strength of his carving for the Bristol Library in King Street. There is little similarity.
26 Ibid., Wood to Brydges: 17 October 1730.

the point of leaving for America and having to be tempted back by obscure proposals for his advancement. He was to continue as one of Wood's most valued workmen, even, perhaps, in later years, a personal friend.

Unexpectedly the conclusion to the Tyberton letters was mellow. Writing on 3 May 1735 from Bath, where he had almost completed Queen Square and could afford to take a more philosophical view of debts outstanding, Wood had been overlooking his account books. He confessed benignly that he was at a loss what bill he should send in, 'therefore I must intreat the favour of you to fix the Sum that will be agreeable to you and I dare say It will be the same to me'. Tyberton Court was still incomplete and Wood was willing as ever to order chimneys and frames for it. Hoping for 'an answer by the return of the Post' he concluded by sending the young John Wood's humble duty to his godfather.

It is to be hoped that William Brydges did not keep him waiting as long for his money as he had kept Brydges waiting for his altar.

Chapter Five

Queen Square
and the
Architect as Social Illusionist

The building history of Queen Square is complex but its significance is direct and simple. When it was achieved, at the end of seven years' contriving, Bath had demonstrated to England the lesson which London should have delivered long before: that the aesthetics and the economics of real estate development can be complementary.

Time has not been altogether kind to the Square, but there are rare sunsets in winter, with the overgrown trees leafless and the traffic briefly still, when the great North Side still appears as Wood described it: in 'all the Advantage possible of Light and Shadow from the Sun to make it Picturesque. Besides this', he continued, 'it stands upon rising Ground; faces those who come from the City into the Square; and soars above the other Buildings with a Sprightliness, which gives it the Elegance and Grandeur of the Body of a stately Palace.'[1]

In his lifetime Wood completed none of the three projects, the *Royal Forum*, the *Grand Circus* or the *Imperial Gymnasium*, which he had returned to Bath to build. But with Queen Square he engineered a triumphant compromise between vision and profitability; it was a flawed design but one visibly grand and apparently uniform. Once achieved it would never be ignored and it was a model for all the city's later development, for the splendid monotony of its standard streets and the sudden columned grandeur of its focal features.

It was in keeping with Wood's robust sense of self-satisfaction that he should have made his home in No. 9, the central house of the plain south side. There he could enjoy, on an axial line, his Egyptian obelisk and the 23-bay palace of the north side. This last he had legally contracted with five sub-leaseholders to build to his own design. The difference between what he paid Robert Gay for the 99 year lease of the land and what Mrs Pearce and Messrs Emes, Greenway, Collins and Chilly paid Wood for their 98 year leases of the seven houses was his profit. The elevation itself, with engaged Corinthian three-quarter columns to the central and end pavilions and corresponding pilasters to the wings, was his permanent artistic satisfaction.

In its scale and its style this north side should be judged in the context of the time. It was first designed, so Wood claims, in 1728, and by 1736 it was outwardly complete with one leaseholder, Mrs Pearce, already resident and paying rates of 3s.9d for her house under the central pediment.[2] Later than Wanstead (*c.* 1714-20), roughly contemporary with Houghton,

1 *Essay*, 345-6.
2 Information on the rating of houses in Queen Square is taken from the Walcot Parish Vestry records in Somerset County Record Office, D/P/Wal.SW, 4/1/1.

The palatial elevation of Queen Square, North Side

but earlier than Holkham or Wentworth Woodhouse, it was for a short time the most ambitious Palladian elevation to have been built in Britain. When Wood called it a 'Palace' it was no more than a factual description. It brought the style and the grandeur of an aristocrat's country home to the urban housing of the middle classes and, perhaps more remarkably, to the boarding house hotels of fashionable visitors. Wood himself took lodgers and the first 27 residents of the Square numbered only one earl, one baronet, two esquires and a Madam Long. The remainder were plain Mr or Mrs, and the best house in the Square, at the west end of the north side, was occupied by Samuel Emes, the contractor for the rough masonry of all the buildings.

What distinguished the careers of both the Woods, father and son, was scale and boldness of concept rather than originality of design or detail. If Wood had, as he claimed, designed the central palace feature of the north side as early as 1728, he could have been influenced by any of four contemporary English projects.

Dean Aldrich's Peckwater Quad at Christ Church, Oxford was easily the earliest of these, begun in 1706 and complete by 1714. Colen Campbell omitted to illustrate it in *Vitruvius Britannicus* perhaps because it was the real source of the Palladian revival in this country. It has hexastyle porticoes, Ionic not Corinthian, alternate segmental and triangular pedimented 'tabernacles' to the windows of its *piano nobile* and a rusticated basement with keystones that reach and appear to support a platband. Being three-sided it needed no end pavilions, otherwise it was remarkably similar to the north side of Queen Square. A pedigree has been drawn up

66

for Dean Aldrich's confident composition, linking it with Palladian Vicentine examples at Lisiera, Quinto and Bertesina and with the cortile façades of the Thiene palace.[3] But in essence it followed Inigo Jones's example, extracting the sturdy classical elements from Palladio's designs and rejecting any of the Mannerist excess of ornament present in his town houses.

Shepherd's botched scheme for the north side of Grosvenor Square is often suggested as Wood's source,[4] but it was exactly contemporary and notably inferior, as was a project for an Assembly Room with houses on each side which John Price, another from the Chandos stable of architects, began but never completed at Headley, near Epsom.[5]

There remains Wanstead in Essex, the prodigy Palladian house of its time, built by Colen Campbell for the immensely wealthy Sir Richard Child. This was begun in about 1714 and was externally complete in 1720. By the three designs, Wanstead 1, 2 and 3, which Campbell produced for his patron and published in *Vitruvius*, Wanstead became the most celebrated house of the 1720s. Sir Richard Child has never been given the kind of credit for its building that Beckford has received for Fonthill, though he was an exacting and fastidious employer who pressed Campbell to excel himself for several years before he was satisfied and began building the Wanstead 2 design.

In the Spring of 1728 Wood clashed verbally with Campbell during an enquiry over whether to use Bath or Portland stone for the new work at

Peckwater Quad, Christ Church College, Oxford – designed in 1706 by Dean Aldrich

3 By Howard E. Stutchbury in *The Architecture of Colen Campbell*, 1967, 16.
4 First put forward by Summerson; *Heavenly Mansions*, 91.
5 For Price's scheme see *Vitruvius Britannicus*, iv (1739), plates 96-7.

67

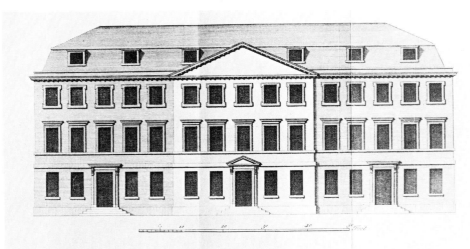

The ELEVATION, to the South, of one of the Side BUILDINGS of QUEEN-SQUARE in BATH, as designed by John Wood, Architect, A.D. 1728.

P. Fourdrinier Sculp.

The original design from the *Essay* for houses in Wood Street, now much altered

Greenwich Hospital.[6] Later in his *Essay* he boasted that his design for Prior Park gave it 'a juster Hexastyle Porticoe' than Wanstead 1, on which it was otherwise closely modelled.[7] Both architects claimed to be Inigo Jones enthusiasts so it is likely that Wood, in his perverse way, admired Campbell.

With its correct but conventional detail the elevation of the north side of Queen Square could be mistaken for an actual Campbell design if it were not, perhaps, quite so predictably sumptuous in its unfolding and so frightened of blank wall spaces. It is, therefore, curious that more has not been made of the fact that Richard Child, raised by that time to the British peerage as Earl Tylney, was sub-leaseholder for no less than three of Wood's houses in and around the Square. The first was the central pedimented unit of a block of four at the corner of Wood Street and the east side of the Square, or Barton Street as it was then numbered. These were Wood's earliest ventures in the area, begun in December 1728 and illustrated with pride in the *Essay* as 'a Sample for uniting several Houses so as to have the outside Appearance of one magnificent Structure'.[8] Though relatively plain the group represents a step in Wood's growing confidence, a mid-point between his Chandos houses and the north side.

Around the corner on the east side of the Square proper, Tylney was later to build two five-bay houses which were to remain among the highest rated in the Square. He was thus Wood's major backer in those first precarious years when there was insufficient capital even to level the site as Wood had originally intended and when it seemed that the development might peter out half way along Wood Street. These facts have to be gathered from the vestry records of Walcot parish as Wood never mentions his august sub-leaseholder. Tylney's connection with a second grandiose Palladian façade could be a coincidence but Chandos was his brother-in-law and could well have effected an introduction. Tylney's house on Barton Street would have commanded a fine glancing view of

6 *Essay*, 426-7.
7 Ibid., 432.
8 Ibid., 345.

68

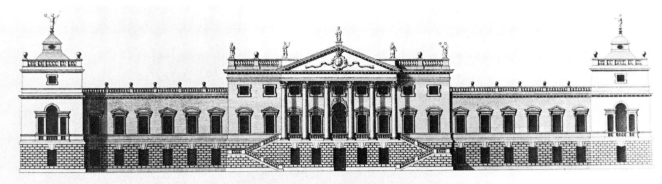

The West front of Wanstead in Essex with the four new Towers, the Seat of the Right Honble the Lord Viscount Castlemain. designd by Colen Campbell 1713

a scale of 60 feet
5 10 20 30 40 50 60

the north side when it was built and, by another coincidence, the north side has 23 bays, exactly the same number as the grandest of Campbell's designs, Wanstead 3, which did not get beyond the drawing board. Tylney could well have given Wood substantial encouragement to build the north side so that he could enjoy from the windows of his Bath town house the view of a substitute for the Wanstead 3 which he never built himself.

Earl Tylney's presence makes it hard to accept Wood's statement that the scheme was 'one begun by People of moderate Circumstances',[9] though it is true that many of the first sub-leaseholders were speculative builders, men like the carpenter William Greenway and the stone mason, Samuel Emes, who took no less than three houses in the north side. Wood's London friend James Theobald only bought into the Square when the investment began to look safer. By 1740 Theobald had purchased seven houses in all, four houses from one original developer, Mr John Burch. The professions of some sub-leaseholders indicate that Wood was content, after his experiences at St John's Hospital, to leave the practicalities of construction work to experienced craftsmen. If the internal layout and fittings of houses were made the responsibility of the people who intended to live in them, then they would only have themselves to blame if the plumbing proved to be less than adequate.

It is hard to resist the suspicion that when the first three Wood Street houses with their return house in Barton Street were going up in 1729 the whole design of Queen Square as it later developed was only a wisp of an idea at the back of Wood's mind. Why else should he have begun with three substantial houses that had only a narrow return façade facing into the main body of the square, leaving Earl Tylney's first house looking out over some back gardens on the south side of Wood Street? If he intended it at that time, then Queen Square was still very much secondary in Wood's interest to the residential Circus which he was hoping to build much nearer to the fashionable heart of Bath. There, next to the two Assembly Houses on the marshy Abbey Orchard site, he was planning a grand circle of houses much in the style and on the scale of the eventual King's Circus. Sited on the Avon and linked to the opposite bank by a bridge, it would have been dramatic and monumental, altering the whole social geography

Colen Campbell's third design for Wanstead House from *Vitruvius Britannicus*

9 Ibid., 344.

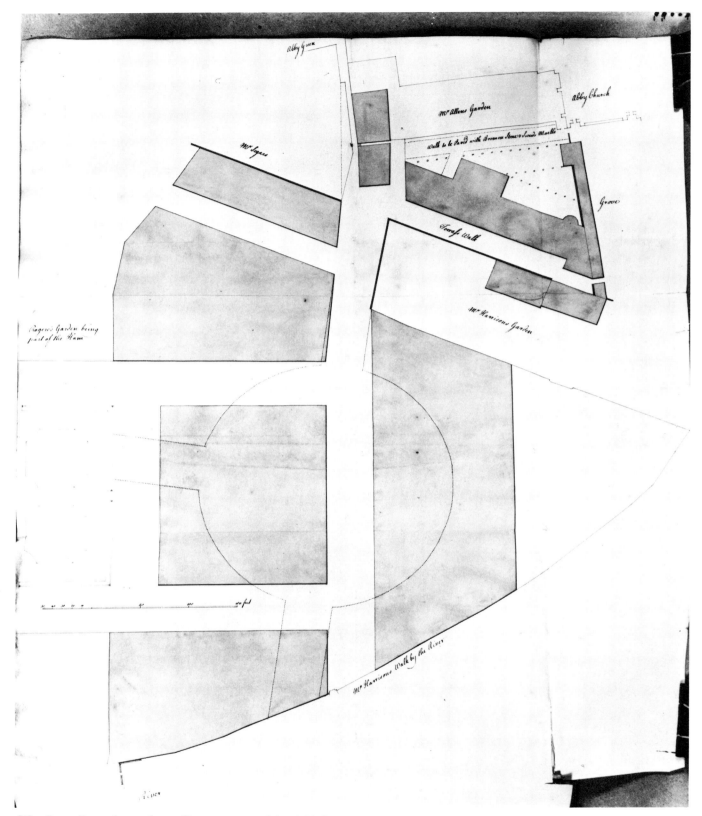

Wood's earliest scheme for a Circus, prepared in 1730 for the Abbey Orchard

of the city. Wood was so confident of its success that he displayed plans of it at the breakfast and ball which Humphry Thayer gave on 6-7 April 1730 to launch Dame Lindsey's faintly raffish Assembly House. The plan, or a copy of it in Wood's hand, survives in a collection of legal papers put together in chronological order by the executors of the will of Evelyn, Duke of Kingston, who had just died leaving his son and heir under age.[10] It is not a detailed plan but it shows that the Circus was to be 260 feet in diameter, roughly 58 feet less than the King's Circus which Wood was to build 24 years later. Three roads led into it but, unlike the layout of the later Circus, one road, that entering from the direction of Abbey Green, was axially aligned with a second, the road leading to a proposed bridge across the Avon. If it had been built, this Circus would have lain partly across the present gardens of the St James' Triangle and partly over the North Parade. There is no evidence that Wood proposed any formal elevations to front the river. Only the inward face of the Circus is indicated by a dotted line so the rear elevations would have been left to individual owners, resulting in a picturesque chaos such as faces the Avon now at the back of Duke Street. Wood's greatest fault as a town-planner was this indifference to the rear elevations of his great projects.

A few weeks after the plan had been 'shewn and approved of'[11] it was 'transmitted to a Person at that Time in London, with Instructions to fix upon the proper Method ..... of carrying it into execution, and laying it open to the Country by means of a Bridge'.[12] But then, inexplicably, the scheme collapsed, according to Wood on account of 'Resolutions taken in London'.[13] In fact, the executors' papers reveal that before Thomas Cromp, the old Duke's steward, left London on 5 May 1730, 'A Lycence for Mr Thayer to Build on the Leased Lands he holds at Bath of his Grace was signed by both the Guardians pursuant to his Proposals and in Obedience to the Orders of the Court of Chancery'.[14] So there was no legal reason for the abandonment of the Circus. Wood remarked that 'Mr Thayer, to the Day of his Death, which happened on the 9th of December 1737, would not enter into the Treaty again with the Zeal of one determined to come to the Point'.[15] Thayer must personally have blocked the project because soon after his death Wood was able to lease the land himself and build the parades. Thayer's death also seems to have opened the way to building the Mineral Water Hospital.

Whatever personal disagreements may have arisen (and it is worth noting that the Circus as proposed would have blocked the view from Ralph Allen's town house) when Thayer pulled out he left Wood desperate for a major success.

He claimed in the *Essay* that he had swung immediately into action on the Queen Square project, leasing more land on 17 June.[16] In fact on that date he only bought a few strips five yards wide to make pavements for Wood Street.

10 Lincolnshire Archives Office, Monson MSS XLIII, f. 21.
11 *Essay*, 245.
12 Ibid., 246.
13 Ibid.
14 Monson MSS, f.10.
15 *Essay*, 246.
16 Ibid.

In this return elevation to Gay Street the original proportions of Wood's fenestration survive

Two factors were probably confusing him at the time. The Wood Street area was far out on the fields of Barton Farm, an expensive fare for chairmen carrying late revellers. The piece of land which he had leased in September 1728 only extended 100 feet, less than half way across the present south side of the square, and in 1730 those sites were not selling. Wood Street was little more than a name with just the block of three, the Tylney house in the centre, standing at the east end of the street and facing south, the wrong way. Then there was the mysterious scheme which Wood had put before the City Council and which they had dismissed as 'Chimerical'.[17] Wood never revealed the details of this but the antiquarian sections of his *Essay* hint at its nature.

He believed, quite mistakenly, that Bath had been a legionary camp and, basing his speculations on his readings of Polybius, he confidently

17 Ibid., 243.

72

laid out a plan of the legion's streets and barracks as they must have existed. Central to this was a T shape of streets. The cross bar of the T was 'The Street called the *Principia*, and containing one hundred Feet in Breadth'. The down stroke was 'The Street, of fifty Feet in Breadth, that divided the two Legions'.[18] As part of his plan to revive the Roman glories of Bath, Wood seems to have wanted to relay these two streets with Wood Street as the cross bar 'one hundred Feet in Breadth' and Barton Street the narrower down stroke. As well as being Roman in scale they would have served to link the rather isolated plots, which he had leased, to the main part of the town, and he intended the 100-foot-wide Wood Street 'to have made a grand Place of Parade'.[19] As usual he was frustrated by the conservatism of interested parties:

> These two Grand Avenues I had a View of making, tho' not so much for my own Advantage, as for the Ornament and publick Utility of the City; but the Parties interested in the Land had other Designs, which prevented Mine from taking Place; and drove me to the Necessity of reducing the Street on the South Side of the Square from one Hundred to fifty Feet in Breadth.[20]

If this T shape of streets rather than a square was his original project it explains why his first houses with their 'outside Appearance of one magnificent Structure' were outside the Square on what was to have been a 100-foot-wide Wood Street looking down the line of 50-foot-wide Barton Street. It may incidentally explain Earl Tylney's later move round the corner to front an even grander scheme. But with Wood Street confined in width, his residential Circus lost before a stone had been laid and his other design for a circular hospital endlessly delayed by the devious man-oeuvres of the hospital committee, it was time for a bold and imaginative move.

Self-criticism and introspective doubt rarely feature in Wood's writings and it is engaging to observe the child-like confidence with which he projected schemes of the purest self-interest as public benefactions. In the 20th century it is possible to raise the house prices of a new estate almost overnight if a council decides to build a leisure centre near it or simply a municipal lido. The genteel equivalent of a leisure centre in the 18th century was a new church, preferably a proprietary chapel where the pew rents would guarantee a certain class of congregation. There would be the likelihood of music concerts, long sermons, bible study and social occasions.

With all this in mind Wood announced his intention of terminating Wood Street at its western end with an edifice 'inscribed with the Name of the blessed Virgin *Mary*'.[21] This would serve the spiritual needs of the Queen Square residents who, at that time, probably numbered no more than four households.

18 Ibid., 168. The influence of this supposed legionary camp on Wood's town-planning is discussed by William Bertram in 'The Origins and Building of Queen Square, Bath'. (Architectural Association thesis, 1963).
19 Ibid., 346.
20 Ibid., 344.
21 Ibid., 312.

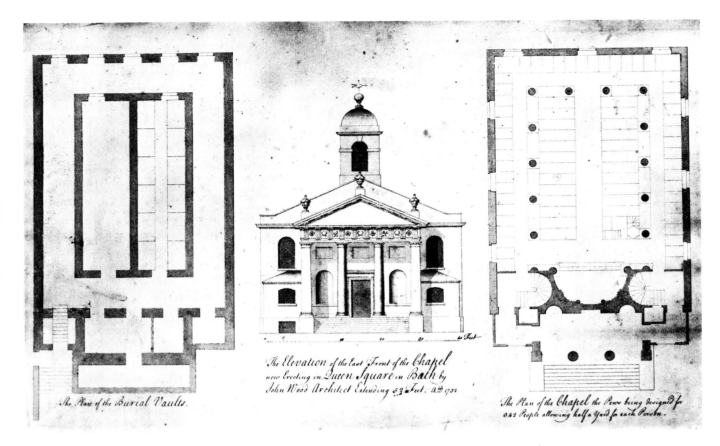

The Plan of the Burial Vaults.

The Elevation of the East Front of the Chapel
now erecting in Queen Square in Bath by
John Wood Architect Extending 63 Feet. a.D. 1732

The Plan of the Chapel the Pews being designed for
342 People allowing half a Yard for each Person.

Wood's design for St Mary's
Chapel, Queen Square

As usual the Bath establishment set about frustrating his scheme.
The Rector of Bath proposed that St Michael's should be rebuilt to accommodate the additional worshippers. Wood submitted a design for the new St Michael's which was promptly rejected in favour of one by John Harvey.[22] Undeterred, Wood pressured the Rector, Archdeacon Hunt, and was allowed to declare 'publickly my Resolution of erecting a handsome Chapel by Queen Square, which raised such a Spirit in People to build near the Place where the Chapel was to stand that I had an immediate Application made to me for ground for no less than seventeen Houses!'[23]

This was on 3 February 1731. Rather than risk the enthusiasm cooling, Wood signed up the eager 17 would-be householders on 26 February in a 'conditional Contract' for houses on land which he had not yet leased.[24] On 8 March he hurriedly leased from Mr Gay 'as much land as was necessary to supply this great Demand, as well as to build a Chapel upon'.[25] Gay still hesitated over legal details for a year. Wood had been pressing Gay too zealously on an entirely different matter, the building of a circular hospital, and Gay tended to react to pressure with nervous withdrawal, simply not answering letters. The tangled episode is an interesting instance of Wood the salesman pushing too many schemes at the same time too fast.

22 Ibid. St Michael's was eventually financed eight years later by General Wade.
23 Ibid.
24 Ibid.
25 Ibid.

What had happened was that in the previous November of 1730 Wood had cornered the hapless Gay and talked him into 'a noble and generous Resolution' of making a free gift of a piece of land, Broad's Garden in the Ambrey field just south-west of the city wall, as a site for the new hospital.[26] This was to be nothing less than Wood's *Imperial Gymnasium* for the practice of medicinal exercises. It was to be a circular structure with a 70 foot diameter and a small portico. There would be ward room for 60 patients and hot or, by the time it was piped there, lukewarm water from the King's Bath for the treatment of ailments. Everything was going well but then Sir Joseph Jekyll, a prominent committee member, suddenly insisted, probably at Wood's prompting, that the hospital building should be enlarged to a diameter of 100 feet and made capable of taking 150 patients. That meant that Mr Gay's free gift of land would have to become even more generous. Not surprisingly Gay went into one of his retirements and on 29 April 1731 Wood hastily returned to his 70 foot design, anxious to keep Gay positive for his other scheme of the Chapel.

It was too late; a corrupt trustee of the hospital charity made a hurried purchase of land to block the scheme. Gay retracted his offer and out of pique kept Wood waiting until 25 March 1732 before he allowed him to lay the foundation stone of the Chapel. Such were the realities of small town politics and charitable good works. But even then Wood had moved too fast and with too little tact. He had not thought to consult the Bishop of Bath and Wells about this new addition to the diocese. This omission was remedied on 31 March, and on 4 September following Wood was able to open his subscription for 11 Proprietors, in addition to himself, to buy shares and build the Chapel. The 11 soon came forward and, at a cost of £2,000 the Chapel was opened with a 'Concert of Vocal and Instrumental Musick' on Christmas Day 1734.[27]

As the choir sang to Mr Chilcot's music:

> O how pleasant is thy Dwelling
> Thou Lord of Hosts!
> My Soul hath a Desire and Longing To Enter
> Into the Courts of the Lord

Wood may have been tempted to join in the 'Chorus with Trumpets':

> O sing Praises, sing Praises unto our God!
> O sing Praises, sing Praises unto our King![28]

because it marked the completion of a singularly neat piece of business. Thanks to the impetus of the Chapel there were now 15 substantial houses in Wood Street, nine of them forming the south side of Queen Square and another nine houses and a tenement, all of a lower rating, going up in Chapel Row. As a bonus Wood was shortly to sell his proprietary share in the Chapel at a reasonable profit.

26 Ibid., 285.
27 Ibid., 314.
28 Ibid., 314-5.

St Mary's Chapel as built -- a
19th century view by H. V.
Lansdown

What should in fairness be stressed is that this essentially capitalistic method of building a church had only been pioneered as recently as 1730 in the Mayfair Chapel in London.[29] Wood had proved himself a very smart operator, quick to appreciate a new idea and highly efficient at putting it over to the public. The episode of the Blessed Virgin's Chapel proves again that Wood's real strength was in planning, financing and projecting at least as much as in designing and rather more than in actual building.

To be honest the Chapel of St Mary was a very pedestrian piece of design. The Doric pediment was too small for the unrelieved bulk of the main building and the bell turret, if it was ever built, was conversely over-scaled.[30] Wood was already building his short-lived cathedral at Llandaff, based on certain dimensions of the Temple of Solomon at Jerusalem, and he would later, in his role as antiquary, detect the dimensions of Noah's Ark, Moses' Tabernacle and Solomon's Temple in Bath Abbey. But he did

29 For the Grosvenor Chapel, South Audley Street, see *The Survey of London*, volume 39, 118-19.
30 Henry Venn Lansdown's *c*.1855 watercolour of the chapel shows it without the turret.

not take the opportunity to indulge these esoteric interests when he designed his Queen Square chapel. This suggests that in 1730 he was still, where the Square was concerned, in his Augustan, Roman frame of mind and had not yet become deeply involved in Jewish and Druidical obsessions. St Paul's, Covent Garden, designed by Inigo Jones with similar deep Tuscan eaves and Doric portico at the east end, was the obvious influence on Wood's design.

If it was an architectural opportunity missed, then at least St Mary's chapel gave a green light for Wood to create a square on what had previously been an uncertain suburban crossroad. Reading Wood's description of his palace-square: its north side centre-piece 200 feet long, with two intervals of 50 feet and then two wings each 100 feet in length, a 500 foot spread in all, it is easy to forget that what came first was the relatively plain south side, that the 50 foot intervals are simply gaps and that neither the east nor the west sides of the Square, for all their Ionic trim, ever looked like wings subordinate to the Corinthian north side. The east side was built over an extended period and looks exactly like what it is: five plain handsome houses side by side, climbing a gentle slope and breaking forward in two understated wings. They are unified by a dentil cornice, in contrast to the far richer modillion cornice of the north side, all their attic windows have eared-and-shouldered architraves, their first floor windows have flat cornices. These are the tried elevations of the Chandos houses and of the nine south side houses.

As Wood ruefully admitted, 'I found myself under a Necessity of dispensing with an uniform Building for the West Side of the Square',[31] but the actual result of his enforced improvisation was satisfying and imaginative. Basically what he devised to please two strong-willed sub-leaseholders, Sir John Buckworth and Esquire Greville, were three Palladian country 'villas' – he actually uses the term himself[32] – ingeniously sub-

31 *Essay*, 346.
32 Ibid., 347.

Thomas Malton's watercolour of Queen Square showing the west side as it was first built

divided not into five houses, as is often stated, but into eight.[33] Three in each end unit, two in the middle one.

Two of these villas happily survive, one at each end of the west side, or Little Prince's Street as it was first named. The middle villa, actually a semi-detached, shared between Buckworth and Greville, was pulled down and replaced in 1830 by John Pinch's heavy-handed infilling in Greek Revival style. The original composition, preserved in Thomas Malton's watercolour, provided a spatial release to the Square with the three villas set like a thematic symphony of Palladian possibilities, each one an essay in the manner of Roger Morris's Marble Hill at Twickenham. Two of the pedimental façades of the surviving pair were destroyed by Pinch but their quality can be judged by what remains. With their arched and rusticated ground floors, or 'basements' as Wood always calls them, they relate visually to the even more emphatic rustication of the north side and to the arched sections of the south side, but only their dentil cornice links them to the east side. To position the doors rhythmically in a long terrace is simple; it is far more taxing to include three main entrances in one supposedly single villa and Wood's design, particularly for the south-western villa, shows how ingeniously he responded to the problem.

33 The error has arisen as a result of the infilling by Pinch. Originally the villa at the south end was divided into three houses as the villa at the north end remains today. No. 16 was lost as a separate unit when the infilling destroyed its north-facing entrance, but its rooms and its staircase still survive within No. 15. The 1736 parish rate book shows the west side divided into eight properties but only nos. 16, 17 and 18 are occupied. The last two, equally rated, are the semis in the lost central villa owned by Sir John Buckworth and Esquire Greville. By 1740 all eight properties were occupied: two by Mr Carrington, one each by Madam Long, Buckworth, Greville and Mrs George , and two by Mr Westbury.

Queen Square – the central
obelisk with overgrown trees of
misguided later planting

This western range was the last section of the Square to be completed.
Only three houses were occupied in 1736 and it was not until 1740 that all
eight were paying their parish rates, the two houses of the recessed central
villa being rated higher than any other house in the Square except the
central house in the north side.

One strongly unifying factor to these four disparate sides was the
central garden. Its first layout is particularized very exactly by Wood and
restoration to its original condition should be a first priority of any informed Friends of Bath.[34] Wood always saw ideal Nature in its inherent
geometrical forms and he laid out Queen Square like a Union Jack with a
round basin of water at the centre and a needle-pointed obelisk rising out
of the water. The diagonal walks were turfed, the walks dividing the quarters were gravelled and lined with low espaliers of elm and lime. Finally
the whole was enclosed but texturally related to the houses opposite them
by a stone balustrade. There was certainly no intention to have full-grown
trees breaking the skyline and the essential symmetry of the place.

34 For the original design of the garden see *Essay*, 345.

79

Apollo flaying Marcius – plasterwork in the staircase hall of 15 Queen Square

80

Queen Square, East Side – the doorcase to one of Earl Tylney's properties

If these unfortunate intruders from later landscaping were cut down, the north side would command the Square again with its proper authority. It is a deliberately rich composition, so crowded in its fenestration as almost to hint at that baroque busyness which was so popular in Bath a decade before. The attic windows are set very high, immediately below the encrusted cornice, a touch which Wood had picked up, consciously perhaps, from Campbell. The forward breaks of the five-bay centre and the three-bay wings are very shallow; Wood rarely indulged in deep articulation of parts. Where the elevation is most demanding is in the usual profusion of delicate conventional moulding which has been lavished on every possible architrave and cornice. He seems to have taken the illustration of the ideal Corinthian ornaments from the First Book of Palladio, or more probably from Antoine Desgodetz's *Les Edifices antiques de Rome* (Paris, 1682; reissued 1695), and included every possible enrichment to the correct sequence of mouldings for the order. These need to be studied at length to be fully appreciated but make a subliminal impact on every casual glance. The final effect is one of two-dimensional stability with an intense superficial impasto of engraved stone. It is unquestionably an informed elevation, carried out with no expense spared and in the grandest style. Whether it reveals much imagination or spatial feeling is questionable, but it is more inventive than Campbell's proposal for Grosvenor Square, infinitely superior to Price's hotchpotch of styles at Headley and, finally, it was actually built. Achievement is all. A design may survive for scholars to debate its possible Italian progenitors but a completed building project in a fashionable resort inspires general comment and imitation. Until a more direct connection with Earl Tylney can be proven, it must be assumed that Wood achieved this breakthrough in urban design without the help of a noble patron but simply by rallying the limited financial capital and expertise of a small provincial city. His plan of the city may

81

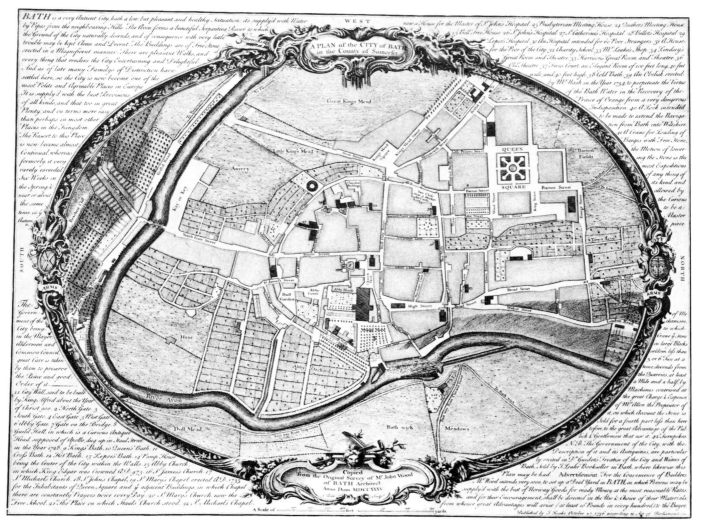

The following text appears within the plan illustration:

WEST

A PLAN of the CITY of BATH
in the County of Somerset

QUEEN SQUARE

SOUTH

NORTH

Copied
from the Original Survey of Mr John Wood
of BATH Architect
Anno Dom MDCCXXXV

Wood's 1735 Plan of Bath records the completion of Queen Square

have been published in 1736 expressly to celebrate his achievement. Queen Square with its garden and chapel features more prominently even than Bath Abbey.

In addition to providing a base line for the construction of Queen Square, the south side range of houses, with its continuation on a markedly different scale in Chapel Row,[35] firmly established Wood's system of different 'Rates' of houses to zone the various areas of Bath's expanding street system. The idea of grading houses into distinct rates according to their number of storeys and fixing certain rates as appropriate to certain streets stemmed from the Act for the Rebuilding of the City of London, 1667. When he moved from London to Bath, Wood elaborated the original four rates into six. The verbal distinctions between them are not as precise as he makes them appear, but for interest his definition of the

35 The houses in Chapel Row are markedly lower in height than the adjoining houses on the south side of the Square and they ended in a 'tenement' so they were obviously intended to fulfil a lower social function. Exactly where they stand in Wood's complex system of rates is not so clear. The south side houses are 5th Rates: a basement, plus a principal and a half, plus a garret. The Chapel Row houses consist of a basement, plus a principal and a half, all on a smaller scale, consequently they must be intended as 3rd Rates.

The southern villa of the west side of Queen Square originally contained three separate houses

house categories was as follows:

1st Rate – a principal storey and a half.
2nd Rate– two full (principal) storeys.
3rd Rate– basement plus a principal and a half.
4th Rate – two storeys (principals) plus an attic.
5th Rate – either a 3rd rate plus garrets, or a basement plus principal
plus a three-quarter storey.
6th Rate – basement plus a double storey plus an attic.

What happened in the actual practice of his building was that, after a few timid gestures of erecting lower rate houses in John Street, Old King Street and Chapel Row, Wood concentrated almost exclusively on the two top rates, thereby distinguishing his areas of development in both height and social class from the contemporary housing which John Strahan and 'the Capricious'[36], as Wood termed them, were building on John Hobbs' land immediately to the south-west of Queen Square.

It is still possible to appreciate this dramatic fall in rate and social consequence by walking from the south side of the Square down Little Prince's Street into Beaufort Square. This is to move directly from Wood's 5th Rates to Strahan's only surviving sequence of 2nd Rates. In design and finish Strahan's houses with their bold Doric frieze and alternating pediments to the ground floor windows are, if anything, superior to Wood's

36 *Essay*, 341.

(left) The chaste Doric detail of John Strahan's low rated houses in Beaufort Square
(right) A 'piratical' house in Kingsmead Square

design of the south side. But because they have only two storeys with a garret added they have never attained the social consequence of Queen Square even though they are nearer to the city centre. The south side today has been restored after bomb damage and still harbours one of Bath's most expensive hotels; Beaufort Square, for all its fine elevations, remains socially nondescript.

Wood cast a wary but sympathetic eye over the buildings of his rival, as he could well afford to do. The rate books of the parish prove that Strahan was imitating Wood in the creation of squares and regular streets, and not vice-versa. When all the exterior walls of Queen Square were complete in 1736 and most of the houses occupied, Beaufort Square did not even exist on the rating schedule, Beaufort Buildings had three houses and Kingsmead Square, which Strahan laid out but whose sub-leaseholders went their own individual way, had only five occupied houses. Avon Street, another major Strahan project, did not exist. In 1737, however, Beaufort Square had twelve houses, Kingsmead Square seven and Avon Street nine. This clearly brackets the years when Strahan was most active on John Hobbs's territory. His houses were of a lower rate, his square could be dismissed by Wood as 'a little open Area'[37] and the whole quarter of the town where he was engaged has remained commercial. The battle was won and lost through height, scale and boldness of concept.

If the words of John Wood quoted in this account of Queen Square have seemed brash, insensitive and lacking in self-criticism there is another episode connected to Wood's actual home life in the Square. This

37 Ibid.

84

is related by him in the concluding chapters of his *Essay* with a strange spiritual exhibitionism which throws a far more direct light upon the kind of man he was.

In 1730 he took as lodgers a rather dubious gentlewoman whom he calls Sylvia and her waiting maid Nash. Sylvia had been closely associated with the disreputable Lindsey sisters who ran the second Assembly House and she had, as a result, acquired a loose reputation. But, 'in the Course of three Years ... by the strictest Observations' – the phrases seem to reveal some emotional involvement – Wood could never 'perceive *Sylvia* to be tainted with any other Vice than that of suffering herself to be Decoy'd to the Gaming Table, and, at her own Hazard, Playing for the Amusement and Advantage of others', so he took her in. A friendship ripened, 'and for about six Months before her Death she lost no Opportunity of viewing the Moon with my telescopes; nor of Talking with me about the Beauties of that Luminary, and what Pleasure Souls departed from this Earth must have, should Almighty God destine them to that Planet'.[38]

All this time her gaming debts were mounting and by September 1731 she owed Wood the considerable sum of £52.3s.4d in rent but still remained a trusted family friend, which again says something about the relationship. Early in the month Wood went, with his wife, on one of his frequent visits to London, leaving his three young children in Sylvia's charge but with 'one of the Master Workmen of the new Buildings, to Lie in the House for the better Security of it'.[39]

Wood was delayed in London and, on the night of 8 September, when he had been expected home, Sylvia committed suicide after deliberate and careful preparation. The account of her last hours is one of Wood's finest pieces of writing. He was always capable of rolling off a standard period sentence to sententious effect but he related her stoic suffering with a dry precision half way between Edgar Allan Poe and a sensational Sunday newspaper.

First she dandled two of his children on her knee then bid Nash good night, 'the first time she had ever done so'. Retired to her room, she pinned scarves together; Wood even records the material and her 'White Garments of every kind, like one that was going to Church to be made a Joyful Bride'. Her first attempt at hanging herself failed but after pacing the room for a time she tried again and succeeded, 'the Silken Girdle ... kept her just suspended till the natural Struggles for Life tortured her to Death and, in Dying, made her bite her own Tongue through in several Places. When Life left poor *Sylvia's* Body, it stretch'd to such a Degree that her Ankle-bones touch'd the Floor of the Room'.[40]

Not until 2.30 on the next afternoon was her body discovered by one of Wood's men, possibly fellow-lodger Thomas Omer, climbing up a ladder outside the locked bedroom. He recovered the key from her clenched hand with a pair of tongs and a 'Free Stone Mason' finally entered the room.[41] After a hasty inquest and verdict of lunacy she was buried in the Abbey late the next day.

38 Ibid., 448.
39 Ibid., 449.
40 Ibid., 450-1. The *Gloucester Journal* of 14 September 1731 recorded the tragedy naming Sylvia as 'Mrs Braddock'.
41 Ibid., 452.

One piece of information resulting from the account is that Wood kept a substantial force of workmen about him at this time. He had not yet completed his own house, No. 9, as he refers to 'a House I then Lived in, in Queen Square'.[42] But the real interest in the macabre story is Wood's own account of how he reacted late on the 10th, when he was told the news of her death, at 'Frocksfield' [Froxfield] on his journey home to Bath:

> the Sun was then Setting; but nevertheless by the Help of Post Horses from *Marlborough*, I reached Home by the Time that her Funeral was over: The Surprize was so great that every Bush I Galloped by looked like an Infernal Spirit; every large Stone and Clod of Dirt that lay in the Road appeared like a Hobgoblin; and Stone Walls resembled nothing but Swarms of dreadful Spectres. The Rustling of the Trees, and the Sound of the Horses Feet filled my Ears with nothing but the Groans and Howlings of People in the utmost Distress; and if the Poet that Described the Journey of *Ulysses* to the lower Regions of the Dead had, in Imagination, seen the Objects, and heard the Sounds which, in Riding near thirty Miles after the Close of the Day, were perpetually Presenting themselves to my Mind and Ears, his Account of a World of Darkness, inhabited by the Phantoms of the Dead, might have received such Improvements as would have filled every Reader with Horror and Surprize.[43]

It is an extraordinary piece of writing, prematurely Gothick in spirit, involved yet analytical, delivered as if in a certain atonished surprise that he could have felt so strongly. Then, abruptly, he cuts the narrative to tell a foolish ghost story about a black hell hound (that turned out to be only a banging shutter) haunting a house in St John's Court. The self-revelation is over without comment or conclusion. But in Sylvia's death chamber a volume of Ariosto's *Orlando Furioso* was found open at pages 74 to 75, 'the story of *Olympia*, who by the Perfidy and Ingratitude of her bosom Friend was Ruined, and left to the Mercy of the World'.[44]

Sylvia's debts to him, Wood writes 'intitled me to the Sole Possession of all her Papers and other Effects, which I Seized on *Monday* the 13th of *September* 1731'.[45] Later her effects were sold 'and the Price of every Trifle was so advanced that the Creditors were all paid, and an Overplus remained for the nearest relation ... Though it ought to have gone to me', Wood added with stark lack of feeling, 'as a Consideration towards the Damages I sustained on the Score of *Sylvia's* untimely Death'.[46]

It is possible that a combination of Romantic emotion and calculating financial concern is essential to the make-up of a great classical architect. Whatever the truth of it all the most revealing part is its open exposition. Wood's nature was not hidden or introspective but laid out as bland and open as the city he designed.

42 Ibid., 448. Wood lived first at No. 11.
43 Ibid., 452-3.
44 Ibid., 450-1.
45 Ibid., 447.
46 Ibid., 452.

Chapter Six

The Lost Cathedral

1734 was one of the pivotal years in Wood's life; 1728 and 1740 were the others and 1754 would have made a fourth if death had not taken him just as he was initiating a new building drive. In the February and March of 1734 he twice had the gratification of escorting the Prince of Orange around Queen Square where the north side and St Mary's Chapel were already gauntly impressive in their scaffolding. For the last five years the Square and its works had absorbed him to the detriment of lesser undertakings. Now it was the time for a fresh impetus and, with his Circus, his Forum and his Gymnasium all frustrated by local interests he had to look outside the city.

By the year's end he had completed a villa, Belcomb Brook, near Bradford-on-Avon, possibly the most conventionally satisfying of all his works, and he had begun the heavy palace of Prior Park for Ralph Allen. Both of these in their separate ways were predictable advances for an architect who had already achieved a major Palladian country house but placed it on a town square. With contacts made in the Bath seasons Wood might easily have become a second Colen Campbell devising country seats for the rich and the noble. But in the same year he began another work which he never illustrated or claimed as his own but which reveals more than either Prior Park or Belcomb about his obsessive interests and the direction of his later designs. This was the cathedral which Wood was to build at Llandaff in Glamorgan on an initial budget of £640, far less than the Duke of Chandos paid for his houses at St John's Hospital.

All that survives of the building are two urns in a garden outside the west front and some pilasters and a ceiling rose transferred to the former Bishop's library.[1] Wood's cathedral was pulled down as soon as funds for rebuilding permitted,[2] but even before it was completed in 1752 it had begun to attract unfavourable comment. It is difficult to imagine a building which, though designed in the same Palladian style, would present a more complete contrast to Prior Park. The one rises high on a hill in a confident 1,000 foot arc; the other lay hidden in a sylvan valley, its modest six bays retired behind a narthex of Gothic ruins. But Wood's Llandaff was a visual creation to equal Prior Park, a beautiful and dramatic composition at least as worthy as the laboured restoration which succeeded it.

Llandaff was the poorest diocese in England and Wales. Its bishops doubled as deans and tended to make ends meet by collecting vicar's cures in English counties. Consequently their neglected cathedral church, already unique in possessing no transepts, became doubly unique after the storms of 1721 and 1722 in possessing very little roof to shelter its services.

---

1 In Bishopscourt, which stands above the cathedral immediately to the south-west and is now a school.
2 Restoration to the Gothic style was completed over the period 1840-69. The work was begun by T.H. Wyatt and continued by J. Pritchard and J. P. Seddon.

At the request of Bishop John Harris (1729-38) Wood had visited the ruined cathedral twice in 1730.[3] Considering his circumstances at that time he was probably eager for any little commission and Chandos's connection with the previous Bishop may have initiated the improbable link.[4] Two years passed before the Chapter paid 20 guineas to Mr Wood 'for surveying this church and for journeys made by himself and some artificers from Bath and Bristol'.[5] Wood's estimate for thorough repairs was £6,366; 2,000 guineas for a new roof alone. The Woodward brothers, a well established pair of masons who worked from Chipping Campden, offered to do a cheaper job for £1,836 with a cut price offer of £849.1.0 to repair just the choir and side aisles.[6] The Chapter compromised by briefing Wood to take charge 'and to confine the expense thereof within the sum of £1,700 including the old material'.[7] His surveyor's fee was to be £100, but as a mere £640 had been collected in 1734 when this brief was written, and the repair and reglazing of a single original Gothic window would cost another £100, there were clearly further compromises ahead.

From a letter which he wrote to the bishop from Bath on 13 July 1734 there has to be a suspicion that Wood was up to his old tricks again as a middleman with commissions on the side: 'I thank God', he wrote with appropriate devotion, 'my Cold is now going off so shall soon take a Journey to Landaff ... I have advice by this post of a large ship that is coming from Norway to Bristol, so shall recommend you to the buying of Deals to lay under the Leads etc., by which you'll save 10 per cent at least'.[8]

But the creator of Queen Square is unlikely to have undertaken such a modest commission in a highly unfashionable part of the country simply for gain. From his subsequent writing it seems that Wood the antiquary had from the start been keenly interested in the site and fascinated by the Welsh background. Llandaff was still, in his time, Welsh speaking with Welsh services in the Lady Chapel and in his *Essay* Wood shows a most un-English familiarity with the meaning of common Welsh place names. When he made his cathedral survey he must already have been familiar with Browne Willis's *A Survey of the Cathedral Church at Llandaff*, (1719) which had claimed a smaller early church on the same site as the oldest in Britain, built between AD 108 and 180 for King Lucius. Noticing the contrast between the Norman work at the east end and the Gothic arches of the nave, Wood decided that the former had survived from Lucius' church and were Roman-Christian in style, built in close imitation of pagan Roman temples. Those temples had, in their turn, borrowed their dimensions from Greek and Egyptian temples and the prototype of them all was, he believed, the First Temple at Jerusalem built by Hiram, the first Freemason, for King Solomon, to measurements dense with divine symbolism.

3 In July and September; see Chandos Letterbooks; 11 July 1730: Chandos to Shepherd and 10 October 1730: Chandos to Bishop Harris.
4 Tyberton papers; Chandos to William Brydges: a series of letters (Jan-Dec 1728) refer to the Duke obliging Bishop Clavering.
5 National Library of Wales, Llandaff Chapter Act Book, 1732.
6 National Library of Wales, LL/Minor Classes/19.
7 National Library of Wales, Llandaff Chapter Act Book, 7 July 1734.
8 Quoted by Canon E. T. Davies in 'John Wood's Italianate Temple' in *Journal of the Historical Society of the Church in Wales*, vol. 6 (1956), 70-81; Appendix E, 81.

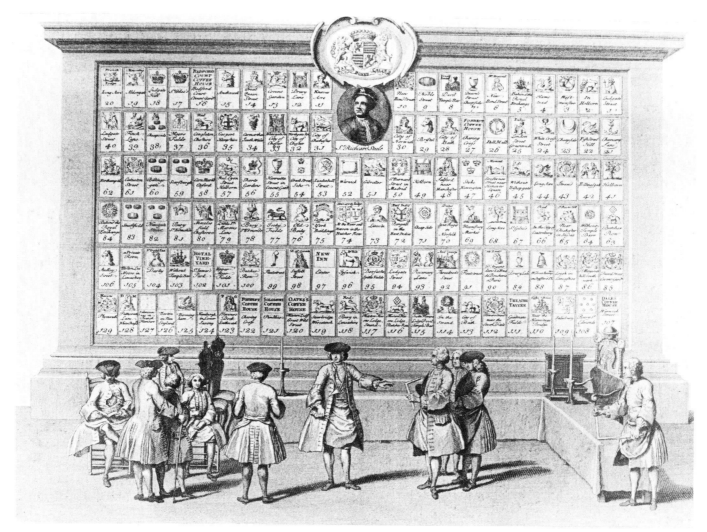

Wood's writings are strongly Masonic in tone and in interests but his membership of the Order has never been proven. Bath was the premier Masonic provincial city of England and had the first grand Lodge outside London, founded 1723/4. Wood's name is not included in the list returns of this Lodge (No. 28, Queen's Head, Bath) made to the Grand Lodge in London in 1725, but there is no significance to this as he was not resident in Bath then and the membership was overwhelmingly aristocratic: Duke of St. Albans (Master), Duke of Bedford, Earl Darnley (Grand Officer of England), Earl of Litchfield, Earl of Craven, Lord Hervey, Lord Cobham, Sir John Buckworth (later Wood's sub-lessee in Queen Square), Sir Robert Waller, Sir Humphry Morroux, Richard Nash. Wood may have joined a minor lodge in London some years before; equally, on settling in Bath, he may have joined the less aristocratic lodge which met at The Bear (No. 113). It is interesting that Wood called his youngest son William Lewis; a 'lewis' is both a dovetail iron tenon for lifting blocks of stone and the name given to a Freemason's son.

As he made his survey Wood found that, if he assumed the first church on the site to have extended no further west than the second bay of

A French engraving of English Freemasons showing, on the rear wall, the lodges of the period. The City of Bath lodge at The Bear (No 113) was probably Wood's own lodge

89

the nave from the choir, he had a close approximation to the ground plan of Hiram's inner Temple with its chamber within a chamber. When this failed to compare exactly he could press an equally plausible comparison with the dimensions of Noah's ark; he was already developing the flexible mind of the over-zealous antiquary. Swayed by his findings and guessing that shortage of money would make the Chapter responsive to any suggested alterations that might provide economies, Wood accepted their commission to supervise the reconstruction.

At some unrecorded stage the Chapter accepted the idea of abandoning four bays of the nave. This left Wood a church with the right proportions: a length of 150 Rhineland or Roman feet and a breadth 75 of the same. The height should have been one-and-a-half times the breadth but that could be fudged by whichever breadth one chose to measure. Hiram's inner court was recreated by surrounding the area of the choir and sanctuary bay wall with arches and a stucco covering.

The rebuilding went slowly; there were pauses for fund raising in 1738, 1740, 1743 and 1749. Meanwhile, quite early in the operations, by 1737 at the very latest from internal evidence, Wood had completed the manuscript of a book in which he virtually argued himself out of his fixation with both the First Temple and with Roman cultural influences. He replaced these, however, with an equally strong obsession with the Second Temple. This had been built on the site of the First by Zerubbabel following the decree of the Emperor Cyrus, 536 BC, and the return of the Jews from the Babylonish Captivity.

In an architectural sense this second obsession was more productive than the first for two reasons. The first was that much less is recorded of this later Temple's proportions in the Bible and therefore it was less restrictive to the imagination of an architect in its inspirational grip. The second was that, because it was built so much later than the First Temple, Wood with his passion for exact dating was able to create links between the Second Temple and the current antiquarian craze in Britain for all things Celtic in general and Druidic in particular.

This Druid mania, whose origins will be traced in a later chapter, was a low-key preview to the forthcoming Gothic Revival, a movement of patriotic historicism. Unlike the Gothick movement, which tended to be seen as a counter force to Classicism, the Druid mania could run in aesthetic tandem with Palladianism. Very little of druidic architecture survived and what there was could be passed off as a particularly primitive proto-Doric.[9]

As a result of much research, writing and dictation to secretaries, Wood was left with two sets of manuscripts. Both survive, one in the Soane Museum and one in Bath Reference Library. They include annotations and whole insert pages in Wood's own hand. From them his first book emerged in 1741, *The Origin of Building or the Plagiarism of the Heathens Detected*. It is a work by fits and turns tedious and fascinating as it traces the origin of all so-called 'classical' forms of building to the Tabernacle, which

9 Wood found that in the piers of Llandaff nave 'the Proportions every where are the most just and wholly answer the Rules of the Doric Order'; Soane MS, fol 132a. An interesting comment on the readiness of classical practitioners to see Doric proportions in unrelated architecture.

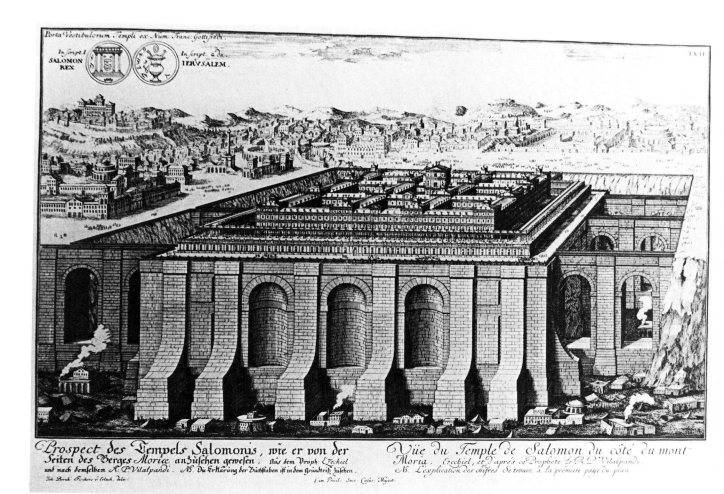

Based on a description by the Spaniard G. B. Villalpanda – Solomon's Temple from Fischer Von Erlach's 1725 *Entwurf*

Moses built to God's precise instructions after the meeting on Mount Sinai, and to the First Temple in Jerusalem. In its published form *The Origin* contrives to restrict itself fairly closely to the theme that the Egyptians, Assyrians, Babylonians, Medes, Persians, Greeks and Romans all stole their architecture from the Jews without acknowledging the theft. The last five chapters of the two manuscript versions with their elaboration of the two sets of links – those between Hiram, the Romans and King Lucius and those between Zerubbabel and the Druids – were deliberately compressed to a few pages in the published book.

A manuscript is easily repressed but what was by now a potential embarrassment to Wood, his reconstruction of the Hiram-Roman inspired First Temple, staggered on.

What Wood did to poor battered Llandaff was to impose symmetry and a highly dramatic classical order upon that part of the church which could be made to correspond to the relatively small inner Temple area which had been enclosed within Hiram's sprawling outer courtyards. When Wood had finished his paring down, there was a two-bay nave, a two-bay choir and a two-bay sanctuary, all with aisles which were flat roofed. He left the Lady Chapel but cut it off from the main body of the church and replaced its east window. The Chapter House was given a neat

Llandaff Cathedral in the 19th century – Wood's classical rebuilding in the ruins of the Gothic nave

octagonal upper storey.[10] An equally neat groined plaster vault with rosettes at the crossing points covered all six bays. The pulpit and bishop's throne faced each other like matching ambos in the form of pedimented tabernacles supported on Ionic columns; beyond them was an arch with coffers of decorated stucco and then the sanctuary, raised up three steps. Finally up another flight of steps was Wood's most splendidly Romano-Jewish device, a reredos and baldachino of Corinthian columns with a pediment, a most un-Protestant fitting. This last, according to the Chapter Clerk Thomas Davies's letter of 23 November 1736, 'my Lord Bishop does not like, because it projects above ten foot, and is like a tabernacle'.[11] This, however, was exactly what Wood intended it to be like: a note of visual authority at just the right place over the Communion table. He had been reading Joseph Bingham's *Antiquities of the Christian Church*[12] and knew that, following Jewish precedent, the altar in early churches 'had a Canopy over it supported by four Pillars standing upon the four Corners of the Altar and in others by twelve'.[13]

It should be stressed that though Wood completely transformed the interior to produce 'a very neat and elegant Church' in an 18th century

10 William Cole (1714-82) copied drawings of the proposed cathedral which the Chapter Clerk, Thomas Davies, had sent to Browne Willis, and Cole's drawings, now in the British Library, are usually cited as being illustrative of Wood's original designs. They are more likely to be Davies's speculations based on, perhaps, the Woodward brothers' sketches. The pigeon-house tower, scorned by T. H. Wyatt, would not have been planned by an architect with an antiquarian bias who meant to keep the ruined west front, the Chapter House has no similarity to the one Wood built, the elevations of the clerestory show none of Wood's rhythm of buttress and fenestration as actually built and the length mentioned on the Cole drawing of 153 feet could not have been achieved with seven bays and a tower.
11 British Museum, Add. MS.5829, fol. 51b.
12 *Origines Ecclesiasticae, or, the Antiquities of the Christian Church*, 2 vols., 1726. Wood frequently refers to this in the margins of the Bath manuscript of *The Origin*.
13 Bath MS., 178.

INTERIOR OF THE PRESBYTERY OF LLANDAFF CATHEDRAL IN 1826
COPIED FROM A SKETCH BY THE REV.ᵈ ALBERT JONES

The choir and sanctuary of
Wood's cathedral at Llandaff

sense, he destroyed very little.[14] The Bishop had wanted to pull down the
first four bays of the ruined nave with the surviving north-west tower, but
that superbly atmospheric approach to the new west door was left, as were
the ogee Gothick windows to the north and south aisles. Only the clerestory was rebuilt with plain round-headed windows.[15] The perpendicular
screen, St Teclan's tomb and the rich Norman arch behind the high altar

14 British Museum, Add. MS. 5829, fol. 51b.
15 All these details are visible in several 19th century engravings of Llandaff.

93

were all scrupulously walled up and plastered over to re-emerge intact in the 19th century restorations, a sign surely of an antiquary's prescience.

When Wood's splended baldachino was torn down in November 1830 an inscription was found on the back wall testifying to the antiquarian reverence with which Wood's men worked and recording an episode so Gothick in its detail as to seem like an invention by Horace Walpole for his *Castle of Otranto*:[16]

> On the south side of this Chansell neare the door is a Tumbe whin a neach now wall'd upit is supposed to be Sant Blawe Tumbe when i opened the Tumbe the Parson buried apar'd to be a Bishop by his Pastorall Staffe and Crotcher. The Stafe when we come to Tuch it it droped to peaces But the Crotcher being Puter but almost perished But wold hold toogether. Betwithin the Stafe there was a large cup by his side but almost perished The most of Puter he was rapt in Leather and the upper part was very sound

John Wood
    Architect of
        Queen Sqr Bath
Thomas Omer
    Joyner and   of Queen Sqr
        Carpenter

There are rare moments when time past lives vividly again, and this is one of them: the confrontation between St Teilawe, his 'upper part' sounder than his pewter chalice and crozier, and the two living men, awed but fascinated in the shadows of the tomb. Without this inscription we would never know what happened to that curious figure Thomas Omer of the 1734 Tyberton letters. He was the one workman for whom Wood ever expressed a personal concern, the man who twice nearly embarked for Georgia, clashed mysteriously with Wood's brother and failed to take Wood's unstated advice: 'Tho the Man's behaviour have not been agreeable to me of late', Wood wrote, 'yet I still think him the best and most Industrious of Workmen as well as a very Civill Sober and Honest Man and thoroughly deserving of any encouragement that can be given him'.[17]

Much anticipated by Alexander Pope, Omer had visited the poet to advise him on his grotto at Twickenham but left abruptly, returning, as the half-literate but evocative inscription proves, to live with Wood in his Queen Square house and share his employer's exploration of antiquities. In the 1740s he was acting as Ralph Allen's negotiator and after Wood's death he is recorded in the *Bath Advertiser* of 17 April 1756 building on his own account in the Vineyards area of Bath. The Chapter Act book records in 1738 'that 5 guineas be given to Mr Thomas Omer joiner for his extraordinary care about the buildings, over and above his wages',[18] an independent confirmation of Wood's earlier evaluation. It must have been Omer who neatly fitted into the pediment of the baldachino a 15th cen-

16 Quoted by D. R. Buttress in 'Llandaff Cathedral in the 18th and 19th centuries' in *Journal of the Historical Society of the Church in Wales*, vol. 16 (1966), 61-76; 64.
17 Tyberton papers; Wood to William Brydges: 13 July 1734.
18 National Library of Wales, Llandaff Chapter Act Book, 1738.

tury painting of the Virgin Mary ascending a starry firmament with the donor bishop in one corner. Recovered intact at the restoration it is now one of the see's treasures, but none of Thomas Omer's fine carpentry remains unless he was the unnamed workman who finally carved the Tyberton reredos after so many delays.

In a scholarly article *'Solomon 'Engothicked': The Elder John Wood's Restoration of Llandaff Cathedral'*[19], Christine Stevenson traced the links which Wood established in his manuscripts of *The Origin* between his cut-down Llandaff, the original Llandaff which King Lucius built in the 2nd century AD and Hiram's First Temple at Jerusalem. But she admits to being puzzled as to why so little of the Llandaff and early Christian last sections of the manuscripts were printed and why Wood never actually mentions that it was he who had carried out the recent 'restoration'. This may be because she has studied the episode in isolation from Wood's next antiquarian hobbyhorse, the Druids.

By the end of his manuscript versions Wood had written himself into a pro-Roman and unpatriotic position which he no longer wished to occupy. The young John Wood of the 1720s returned to Bath determined to restore the architectural glories which, from his reading of Tacitus, he believed the Roman general Agricola had conferred on the city. That was the standard, and largely correct, scholarly position. But by the 1740s an older John Wood, antiquary and Druid fancier, had convinced himself, by an intense but uncritical course of reading, that fine architecture had reached Bath much earlier through the instruction of the native British monarch Bladud, and that by the end of the 5th century BC the city was already glorious with columned temples, *'Troy Novant'* in fact.

The Origin fell uneasily between his two sets of ideas. In the preparatory manuscripts there are signs of an internal antiquarian conflict. On a single page, 186 of the Bath manuscript, he moves into self contradiction: 'It is therefore more than probable', he began, with a clause of reservation typical of a man who thought as he wrote, 'Stonehenge was Built in the time of the Persian Empire and that the Builders of it had in view to Paragon in some respects the Temple erected at Jerusalem in pursuance of Cyrus's Decree ... for the Temple was surrounded by 4 Rows of Pillars and so is the Monument of the Idol at Stonehenge. The Temple was 60 Cubits in Breadth and the Diameter of our Antiquity is much about the same.' Yet a few lines later he writes of 'The Romans having introduced architecture soon after the time of Claudius into England', 500 years later. The discord was even to be illustrated. Wood had prepared a marked plan of the cathedral to print in the book alongside his plans of Moses' Tabernacle and Hiram's First Temple. But he had also drawn plans of the Druid temples at Stanton Drew, six miles from Bath, and it was these which had left him so disenchanted with his theory of Lucius and Roman colonialism.

The more he surveyed remains like Stonehenge and Stanton Drew,[20] the more impressed he became with native Celtic achievement, but the

19 *Art History*, vol. 6, no. 3 (September 1983), 301-14.
20 His interest was moving from Stonehenge, which Inigo Jones had surveyed in 1612, to Stanton Drew, a more local antiquity. Folio 170 of the Bath MS. in a secretary's hand, deals with Stonehenge, but on the opposite page, the verso of 169, is a long analysis in Wood's own hand, prepared as an insert and wholly devoted to Stanton Drew and its links with Pythagoras' planetary system.

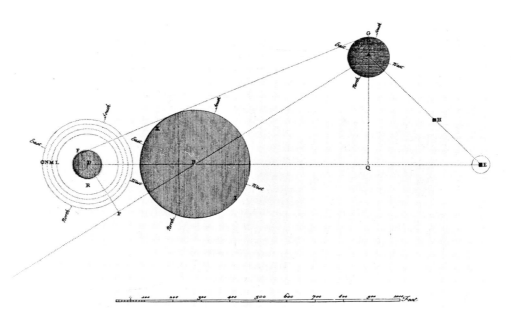

Wood's plan of the circles at Stanton Drew from his *Essay*

harder it became to create any links between these circular henge monuments and Hiram's ruthlessly rectangular Temple enclosures. His solution was to drop the First Temple with its inconveniently detailed groundplan and forge 5th century BC links between the Druids of Stanton Drew, Pythagoras and Zerubbabel's Second Temple which could be considered to have been circular if critical common sense was briefly suspended. Thus a sacred Jewish connection was retained and a Greek scientist was added to give early British architecture a shining origin.

As a result of this conversion Wood scrapped most of the account of Llandaff, including the proposed illustration, reserving his description of Stanton Drew with its ground plan for a later book. All the Druid and Pythagorean parallels found on the back of folios 168, 169 and 170 of the Bath manuscript were actually published in amplified form in his next book, the 1742 and 1743 volumes of his *Essay*, along with two ground plans of the Stanton Drew stone circles. The ground plan of Llandaff was scrapped for ever and Wood 'forgot' his whole involvement in the cathedral rebuilding because he no longer wished to believe that the sacred Jewish forms of architecture had come second- or third-hand to the primitive British through the agency of Roman conquerors and Druid slaughterers.

Both the book and the manuscripts provide fascinating glimpses of Wood's reactions to medieval architecture. They are plain evidence that he had become an antiquary by wide reading and not by practical field experience. It is extraordinary that the east end of Llandaff appears to have been his first experience of Norman architecture. Had he never entered St James in Bristol or All Saints? Was Gloucester Catheral unknown to him or St Bartholomew the Great from his London visits? He seems to have been more familiar with the illustrations in Antoine Desgodetz's monumental volumes, *Les Edifices antiques de Rome*, than with any of these. Consequently his surprised response to the Norman clerestory of Llandaff's choir was: 'the windows that stood over the Great Arches below were three in Number over every Arch. Of which the Windows in the Temple of Peace at Rome in point of form and those in the Great Hall of Diocletian's Bath in respect of Situation are the very Pattern'.[21] They were not in reality very like either of those Roman examples but without previous experience to guide him Wood plunged on to hail them as 'the only footstep now Remaining in Britain that I know of of that noble manner of Building taught the Britains by Agricola and still upheld'.[22]

If Aubrey in the previous century had published his tentative conclusions on the dates and sequence of the stylistic development which he had noted in church architecture, Wood might not have floundered in this way. As it was he mistook the Norman method of ramming a rubble infilling between two courses of worked stone for 'that sort of Work called by Vitruvius Emplecton', while the 'Square Pannels and Roses' of the high altar arch suggested the kind of stucco decoration which Wood was familiar with in the soffits of classical arches.

When he turned from the false familiarity of the Norman work to the refined and intensely pointed Early English arcading of the nave Wood's response shifted abruptly from condescending approval to hostile admiration. The passage was never to be published, which is unfortunate, as it is a most revealing instance of how a man of Wood's generation, sophisticated in the visual subtleties of classical architecture, could analyse a Gothic achievement brilliantly and yet, in the end, kill it by over-intellectualising. It is Ruskin's writing without the affection and without the fire.

As if to defend himself from giving the work its due, he opens by pretending to believe that it was 'erected by Goths and Vandals', which with his detailed knowledge of pre- and post-Roman tribal migrations he would have known was impossible. 'Those People though fond of Introducing Novelty still kept themselves in the principal Arches of their Structures to such forms as were coincident to some of the Works of God', again the note of defensive disparagement before he takes refuge in symbolism rather than enjoying actuality:

> In their Arches they were about to Represent a part of the Great Canopy of Heaven, they therefore chose a portion of the Circumference of a Circle made upon one sixth part of the whole Area for their Purpose, because the Radius of any Circle making the side of an equilateral Triangle, six of such Triangles may be inscribed in the same Circle and will divide the Circumference into six equal parts answering the six days in which the Heaven and Earth were made.

He has now moved his subject into his own area of competence, geometry, and for the remainder of the passage can admire abstractions and figures of his own creation rather than what actually stood there in the nave. Inevitably he wove the analysis into 'an Equilateral Triangle ... a figure the most perfect of all others composed of several lines ... a Symbol of Divinity or Sign of Caelestial Matter as Above'. Then abruptly, the fan-

21 Bath MS., 173.
22 Ibid.

tasy described, he collapsed into a lame repetition of his opening, as if to avoid any expression of merit: 'and the two Segments together makes one third part of the whole Circle to which they belong'.[23]

Though infuriating in what it fails to say, it is a great response, encapsulating the strength and weakness of the period in which is was made. The fascination which it betrays is the surest pointer to the strength of the emerging Gothic Revival, though in his whole career Wood's only executed Gothick designs were the sloping pasteboard battlements of the Llandaff Lady Chapel.

As a testament of personal belief *The Origin* is guarded and instead of an analysis of Beauty in Creation it offers the mysteries of geometry. Like Isaac Newton, whom he often quotes, Wood was under the extreme pressure of having to co-ordinate the new science with his Christian fundamentalism; but because numbers are the essence of proportion in classical building, and proportion is at least a part of beauty, Wood's writings were a sincere exploration of his aesthetics and no more harmful to his intellectual trade than Newton's grotesque exegesis of the Book of Daniel was to scientific thinking.[24]

In the firm front of Christian faith which he presents there is rarely a flash of personal spiritual excess. Probably the most lyrical writing in the book is an account of the pagan Daphnephorian Festival of the Boeotians.[25] But at just one point in his solemn exposition of devout symbolism the mask slips: 'But suppose there was no such Thing as the Deluge, (which in fact wou'd be admitting nothing beyond our Knowledge) How beautiful the metaphor!'[26] It is possible that while raising Llandaff to the correct, divinely revealed proportions he became as unsure of its mathematics as he became doubtful of the capacity and seagoing qualities of Noah's Ark. There has to be some sense of personal failure to explain why the man who published one book to express his pride in the reshaping of a city, and another merely to tell the polite world that he had built Bristol's Exchange, should not mention in even a single line that he had rebuilt a cathedral.

After a while the reader develops a certain wary understanding of John Wood's patterns of belief. He writes as if playing a game to see how far he can go on a line of argument or a provocative theory. When the links in his argument are logically most frail he usually betrays this by a string of rhetorical questions. *The Origin* must have been intended as a salute to the confident fundamentalism of his self-educated adolescence and to the Freemasonry which originally gave him a firm system within which to start thinking. If that was so there are few studies so destructive of conventional devotion as the anthropology and comparative religion into which he was drawn by this book. Before it was well started, the dangerous breadth of his reading and plain common sense were beginning to lead him into the more relaxed and genial atmosphere of his next book where the sun worship of the Druids soon resembled a pre-Christian Christianity, harmless and possible even laudable.

23 Ibid., 180.
24 *Observations upon the Prophecies of Daniel and the Apocalypse of St. John*, 2 parts, 1733.
25 *The Origin*, 23.
26 Ibid., 231.

The City and Tower of Babel cou'd not be the Work of above thirty and forty Men and therefore that City must appear to all considerate People, but as a little sorry Village, the Tower can't be conceived bigger than one of the Crosses common in Country Places. And is it not unlikely but from the Tower of Babel, the High Places in Scripture, and also our Crosses and Maypoles had their Origin? For the High Places were adorn'd with Images, representing the Sun; and the First of May was the Day on which our antient Druids held their great Festival to Beal, or the Sun, therefore to the hour, says Mr Toland, The First of May is by the Aboriginal Irish call'd la Bealteine.[27]

John Toland was an Irish freethinker, a celebrated scandal in his time to all devout churchmen. Fluent in three Celtic languages he had published *A Critical History of the Celtic Religion* in 1702 and *A History of the Druids* posthumously in 1726. More than any other contemporary writers he influenced Wood on things druidic though Wood was also familiar with the works of William Stukeley, if only for statements to contradict and measurements in which to find fault.[28]

There is another feature of *The Origin*, which suggests better than any other, the peculiarly business-oriented and architectural nature of his beliefs. Bound together after page 94 are five illustrations of what is basically the same house. Three are alternative elevations in the three classical orders and two are careful ground plans with details of closets, bookcases and bed alcoves. These come at the end of Book One which relates in a tone of careful reverence how God in person gave Moses the exact dimensions for building his Holy Tabernacle. This was the great portable tent in which the Ark of the Covenant was to rest for several hundred years until Hiram's First Temple had been completed to receive the presence of the Almighty.

Then, without warning, the piety ends and like some brisk estate agent with a hot property to sell Wood opens a sales pitch:

> Let us suppose the twelve Pillars which Moses set up at the Foot of Mount Sinai, covered over in such a Manner as to form a Cottage of that Kind ... and let us suppose those Pillars made after any of the Orders; will not such an Edifice, small as it is, be beautiful, whether the Orders be the Strong, the Mean or the Delicate? On the Contrary, omit Proportion and Regularity in the same Cottage and the Result will be what every Country now Produces, where the People have no Idea of the Fundamental Principles and Precepts of Architecture.[29]

He then offered to design three alternative 'villas' to this God-given

27 Ibid., 26.
28 It is significant that Stukeley's Druid interests led him down the same primrose path of theism and Nature worship; but equally significant of the religious climate of the times is that no less a person than the current Archbishop of Canterbury successfully urged Stukeley to take Holy Orders and that Wood remained convinced of his own Christian orthodoxy.
29 *The Origin*, 93.

A design from *The Origin of Building* for a Corinthian cottage based on the Tabernacle of Moses

pattern of the Holy of Holies with the cool aside: 'but No. 11 is that which is to be executed by the Person for whom these Designs were first made'.[30] No. 11 was the Corinthian illustration, but in the event it was plate No. 9, the Doric and cheaper design, which was actually built in 1738 on the west side of Lansdown for one of Wood's lessees in Queen Square, the surgeon Mr Jerry Peirce. The house, Lilliput Castle, has been subsumed in a later house.[31] It showed, when built, an alarming tendency to go on fire, so it remains, like his Llandaff, only a memory to Wood's readiness to put Biblical theory to the practical test of stone. It provokes a question. Did it ever occur to Wood that in the sequence of three – God, Moses and John Wood – it was he who was perfecting the form and might, therefore, have a claim to be the best architect?

30 Ibid., 94.
31 See Chapter Eight.

100

Chapter Seven

Wood in Defeat
'The comfortless Palace
of Prior Park'

Where the design and building history of Prior Park are concerned extreme caution is necessary. The precise dates of the great house and the exact genesis of its five parts are amazingly obscure considering that it went up in full view of a fashionable city and that Ralph Allen was subject from 1736 onwards to a flow of letters from Alexander Pope. A remarkably accurate 'prophetick' poem, *The Description of Bath*, by the Bath poetess Mary Chandler was published in 1732. This describes the grounds of Allen's house as they were to be developed and is near enough to their actual layout of 1750 to suggest that they had already been planned in 1732 and planting begun. The scale of the house and its brilliant siting can be credited to John Wood with fair, though not absolute, confidence; other attributions become tenuous when they are examined closely. Walter Ison is carefully imprecise on the subject and R. E. M. Peach complained sadly that 'to follow Wood is like groping in the dark without a single ray of light in the shape of a date to guide one'.[1] What Peach seems not to have noticed was that Wood, normally exact to the day in dating his projects, created that 'dark' quite deliberately because he had much to conceal.

Contemporary maps and plans, Thorp's of 1742 and Thorp and Overton's of perhaps 20 years later,[2] lay down some time-markers and Anthony Walker's engraving of the north front, dated 1750, has to be set against Wood's radically different illustrations in the 1749 edition of his *Essay*. Otherwise any general conclusions about the construction of the house have to be reached by weighing Wood's long but evasively phrased description of the building against some notes taken down as the basis for a 'Life' of Richard Jones, clerk of works, by his own account, to Ralph Allen from 1731 to 1764.[3]

The two men, Wood and Jones, were almost exact contemporaries. Jones was born in 1703, Wood a year later, and socially they began not far apart. But Richard Jones was apprenticed to a freestone mason in 1718 in those free and easy days before Wood and Allen between them broke the power of the masons: 'and it was at that time', Jones declared nostalgically, 'a very good trade and had good prices for their work'.[4] So Jones lacked

---

1 R. E. M. Peach, 'Ralph Allen, Prior Park and Bath' in *The Antiquary*, vol. 12 (1885), 218.
2 The survey and plans by Thomas Thorp and John Overton have never been dated more accurately than 1758-63. Thomas Thorp's map of 1742 (An Actual Survey of the City of Bath and of Five Miles around) may be notional as it shows the house and wings complete whereas a drawing of 1743 by L. Rushe (Mellon Foundation; photograph in the Victoria Art Gallery, Bath) shows the house without the east wing.
3 This is known only from a 19th century handwritten copy in the Bath Reference Library.
4 Jones MS.

Drawn from Mr. Allens Road in the Year 1750.   Published Dec. 1st 1752.   Ant. Walker Sculp.

PRIOR PARK the Seat of Ralph Allen Esqr near Bath.   PRIOR PARC la Residence de Raoul Allen Ecuyer pres de Bath

Prior Park – Walker's engraving, drawn in 1750, records that Wood's proposed west wing was never built

Wood's early experience and training in London and Yorkshire, only teaching himself to draw 'to my master's satisfaction'[5] around 1731 when an independent mason's practice near Bath had become less profitable. What he dictated shortly before his death was rambling, obscurely phrased and grammatically unsophisticated. It has also to be approached with the reservation that Jones may well have disliked Wood and been scoring points as he shaped his recollections of the past.

What must have complicated the whole creation of Prior Park was the fact that Allen was no ordinary patron. He was a shrewd, self-made man with a large workforce of masons in his personal employ. Wood and he were already associates in the building and developing business. He will have heard the melancholy history of Wood's technological inadequacy as Chandos Buildings went up. When Allen was building his prestige town house and office in Lilliput Alley he had pointedly used Wood's design but then had the house built by someone else, probably one of his own men. So neither Wood nor Allen began at Prior Park with any illusions about each other.

In his *Essay* Wood gives the impression that the idea of building Allen a seat 'wherein the Orders of Architecture were to shine forth in all their Glory'[6] stemmed from the commercial set-back of spring 1728. Allen was seeking a contract from the Governors of Greenwich Hospital to supply Bath stone for the building operations there and Wood was representing

5 Ibid.
6 *Essay*, 427.

102

him at a public meeting. Ranged against Wood and favouring Portland stone was the formidable trio of Colen Campbell, the Surveyor, and Nicholas Hawksmoor and John James, the joint Clerks of the Works at the Hospital. To secure the contract for such a prestige project was important to Allen but Wood was characteristically over-clever in his advocacy. He confused Campbell with two lumps of stone, one Bath and one Portland, while the Governors still chose Portland because the rival quarry had made a 33% price reduction. It was an unfortunate incident. Wood had made an older man, whose stylistic innovations he admired and closely followed, look foolish in public and he had been worsted himself in a business battle by foes who had suggested that Bath stone would breed maggots like Cheshire cheese. But, according to Wood, 'the Reflections cast upon the Free Stone of the Hills of Bath' brought Allen 'to a Resolution to exhibit it in a Seat which he had determined to build for himself near his Works, to much greater Advantage, and in much greater Variety of Uses than it had ever appeared in any other Structure'.[7] This implies that Allen had decided to build before the Greenwich snub. It also suggests that from the start Wood had it firmly in his head that Prior Park was to be a commercial showcase first and a home for a family afterwards. The profound disfunction of the house as it was to be built probably stems from the conflict which arose between these two aims as Allen, increasingly prosperous and secure, veered from the first to the second.

In their first flush of angry enthusiasm 'several Designs were formed'. Wood does not actually claim that he formed them.[8] Allen was alive and vigorous in 1749 to correct him if he had lied, but Wood does claim that 'an humble Simplicity' took the place of these first Designs and states that 'the Westward Wing of Offices' was begun as the first instalment of that 'humble Simplicity'.[9]

It is here that an interesting character assessment has to be made. Knowing Wood's emulous and combative nature is it likely that he would have returned to Bath and, by his own choice, set about building a rejected design of Colen Campbell's?

There is no easy answer but the question has to be put because that is exactly what John Wood did. The main house of Prior Park has, for its north elevation and original front, an ingeniously adapted version of that first, 1714 design which Campbell had produced for Wanstead House, Essex and which his patron Sir Richard Child had rejected. The plagiarism was quite open and with all three Wanstead designs published in Campbell's *Vitruvius Britannicus* Wood could not have hoped to conceal it. What matters is whether Wood copied Campbell with the idea of out-trumping him,[10] erecting on a hill-top the first version of what was at that

7 Ibid.
8 Ibid.
9 Ibid.
10 Wood writes in the *Essay*, 432: 'Mr *Colen Campbell* having boasted the Justness of the Hexastyle Porticoe Designed by him before *Wanstead* House in *Essex*, it was determined that a juster Hexastyle Porticoe should be executed before this House, and with Columns of a larger Size; and for this End I Designed it with Columns of three Feet one Inch and a half Diameter, which exceeds those at *Wanstead* by an Inch and a half; made the Intercolumniations of that Kind which *Vitruvius* calls *Systylos*; and gave two compleat Intercolumniations to the Flank of our Porticoe, instead of the compleat Interval and small Portion of another at *Wanstead*'.

The north front of Prior Park from the combe

time the most famous Palladian house in Britain, or was he pressed unwillingly to imitation by Ralph Allen who may have had little confidence in his provincial associate and wished to be sure that his money would be well spent on a celebrated but unrealized design?

Wood was not averse to borrowing. Belcomb Brook Villa which he designed in 1734 is a clever adaptation, arguably superior to its original, of Roger Morris's Marble Hill House in Twickenham. But when he was asked to design Prior Park for Allen he must have realized by its scale and its physical prominence that there was a perfect opportunity to demonstrate his own designing talent for the fashionable world to admire. To take the design of another living architect does inevitably suggest a failure of imagination and an opportunity lost. There is a fascinating echo in the episode of Peter Palumbo's frustrated attempt in 1987 to build a Mies van der Rohe design in the City of London several years after that architect had died. Ralph Allen may have shared something of Palumbo's motivation: the wish to realize a rejected vision of an admired master.

Inevitably the preceding chapter on Queen Square raised another possibility. By 1728 Richard Child, now Earl Tylney, had become one of Wood's most important backers in his scheme to build Queen Square, and the great north side of that square was to have the same number of bays

104

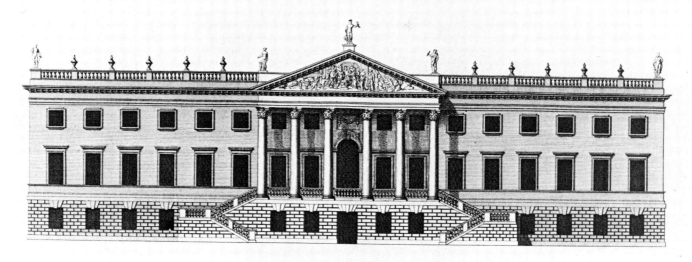

Extends 200

a Scale of 100 Feet.

The first Deſign of the Weſt Front of Wanſted as intended by Sʳ Richard Child Barᵗ
Is moſt humbly Dedicated to my Lady Child

Elevation de la Maiſon de Wanſted comme eſte la Premiere penſé de L'Architecte.

(23) as yet another, the most ambitious of the three Wanstead designs, the unbuilt Wanstead 3. If there is a possibility that Tylney influenced Wood over the one project, there is clearly a chance that he influenced him over the much closer imitation of Wanstead 1 at Prior Park. It would, to complicate the problem, have been equally simple for Tylney to have influenced Allen directly. They were two of a kind, except that Tylney was the second generation of a self-made business family. Allen was also involved in Wood's development of the Barton estate. He had bought five house sites in John Street, just around the corner from Tylney's house in Wood Street, so the two men would have had interests in common and opportunities to meet.

In default of any direct evidence of Wood's precise control over the design of Prior Park the problem has to be assessed by comparing the house that was built with Wood's drawings for it and by considering Wood's account of the building in the light of Richard Jones's recollections.

The real source of confusion in the dating and understanding of Prior Park's evolution is the building which Wood described as 'the Westward Wing of Offices'. It was 'the first part of the Seat that was carried into Execution'[11] in a scheme which Wood describes as having 'humble Simplicity', but which any unbiased contemporary, observing Prior Park's

Colen Campbell's first design for Wanstead

11 *Essay*, 427.

105

giant elevation of 1,000 feet and double hexastyle Corinthian portico, could reasonably have described as one of overwhelming grandeur.

This phrase of 'humble simplicity' is the first warning to a reader that Wood's description of Prior Park cannot be taken at face value. The first edition of Wood's *Essay* made no mention of Prior Park. This was strange because it came out in 1742-43 and by 1741 Allen was in residence in the main house[12] and all the western wing had been completed, so Wood might have been expected at least to mention such a major achievement. If, however, the great house had been a source of friction and disappointment to him he would, for all his combative habit of writing, have been most reluctant to antagonize Allen who was such a force in local politics and the Bath economy. When, in the 1749 edition, he came to describe the house he compromised by describing not what was built, but his original vision of the five detached but related units. He not only described these in ambivalent syntax as if they had actually been built but he even illustrated them in their original forms. As a result, unwary historians, writing after the alteration of the wings by Bishop Baines in 1829,[13] have assumed that Wood's fantasy buildings once had a real existence. In fact Wood had carefully covered himself by adding 'as it was originally designed' to the captions of his illustrations. Pedantic attention to the mood and tense of the verbs in his 'house description' gives an amusingly divergent and more accurate set of alternative meanings. A statement like, 'They were to enter' means 'is not and never was an entrance'. 'Was to have been crowned' means 'was never built', while, 'were all compleated at first' means 'were immediately altered because they were found to be grossly impractical'.[14]

Wood's elevation of the westward offices shows a long, low symmetrical building, Doric and austere. It has a five-bay central block with a tetrastyle portico and rising above this a stubby pigeon tower with a pyramidal roof. There are wings of six bays to each side and it was to face south. Wood wrote in deceptive detail about its stone vaults and timber roof. His only complaint was that:

> in the Execution of the Building the manner of Roofing was entirely altered, Mr *Allen* resolving, at all Hazards, to make use of nothing but Stone for a Covering to this Wing of Offices.[15]

12 *Correspondence of Alexander Pope*, ed. by George Sherburn (Oxford, 1956), vol. 4, 344: Pope to Allen, 14 May 1741; 'Are you got into your New House?' Later that year Pope was staying with Allen in the new house.

13 In 1829 Dr. Peter Augustine Baines, Roman Catholic Bishop for the Western District, bought Prior Park for £22,000 and converted it into a seminary (St Peter's in the east wing) and a boys' school (St Paul's in the west wing). Describing these changes Monsignor James Shepherd in *Reminiscences of Prior Park*, 1894, 70, wrote: 'the classrooms of St Paul's are only a modification of the stables and cow-houses but ... it is impossible to trace in them the humble purposes to which they were formerly put'. Sixty-five years after the Baines alterations Shepherd is already taking Wood's writing at face value without asking why it should be impossible to trace 'the stables and the cow-houses'. A print of 1830 shows the east wing greatly enlarged and the west wing still as Wood had built it. A further print of 1836 shows most of Wood's west wing lost in the new St Paul's college with only his *porte cochère* still intact. (Both prints are illustrated in Gillian Clarke, *Prior Park: A Compleat Landscape* (Bath, 1987), 66-7)

14 *Essay*, 427-33.

15 Ibid., 428.

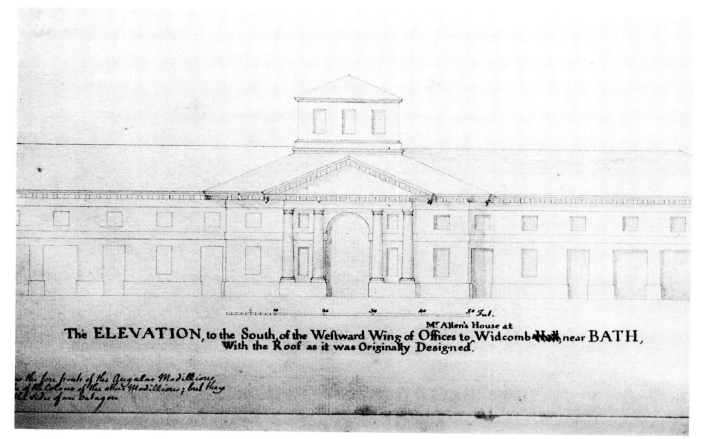

The ELEVATION, to the South, of the Westward Wing of Offices to Widcomb Hall, near BATH, With the Roof as it was Originally Designed.

Wood's proposed design for the west wing of Prior Park

Thus, without telling a plain lie, Wood concealed the fact that not merely was his proposed roof altered but an entirely different building was actually erected. Walker's engraving, drawn in 1750 and published in 1752, and all later 18th century views of the house confirm this.[16] Viewed always from the north, not the south, they show a west building with asymmetrical wings, one of seven and one of six bays. These lie one on each side of a towering pavilion three storeys high with a large Venetian window in its top storey and four pediments around its roof. The composition is clumsy, distracting and incorrect, but anything less like a pigeon cote can hardly be imagined. It has all the air of a separate residence topped with a splendid viewing chamber to command the valley. On the other side of the main block an east wing matches the west wing exactly in every particular. Wood dissociated himself from this east wing and Walter Ison says that 'the work passed into the far less competent hands of Richard Jones, Allen's clerk of works, who altered the east wing in execution and destroyed the symmetrical balance of Wood's design'.[17] In fact Jones preserved the symmetry perfectly by a careful copy of what Wood had already built to the west. Ison has been misled by Wood's text. It is still possible to make out the general lines of Jones's east wing though Bishop Baines raised the roofline by adding a storey when he created his 'College of St Peter' in 1829.

16 The inscription on Walker's engraving states: 'Drawn from Mr Allen's Road in the year 1750, Publish'd Dec. 12th 1752'.
17 Ison, *Georgian Buildings of Bath*, 126.

The question then is what had Wood been obliged to build in the place of his Doric stables, hay house and pigeon cote? The answer is that it was a house for Allen to live in while the central block was slowly mounting upon its massive 800 ton 'Stylobata'. This pavilion house would be intended for servant accommodation when the main house, which was only to have five full-sized bedrooms, was completed.[18] But Allen, essentially a man of simple tastes, found his temporary accommodation so much to his liking that he had a replica of it built for him by Richard Jones in the new east wing. The Revd Richard Graves, who often dined with Allen in the latter's old age, described this as 'a beautiful pavilion and seems to me to have all the conveniences for a private family. It was a favourite apartment with Mr Allen, where he often breakfasted or drank tea with his most intimate friends'.[19]

This section of Prior Park has suffered major alterations but one room with modest stucco decoration has survived among the dormitories and wash-rooms of the present school, and now what may once have been Allen's homely breakfast parlour, the last relic, apart from the chapel, of 18th century decoration, serves as the bedroom for a prefect.

Ralph Allen left his Lilliput Alley town house in 1735. He first gave his address as 'Widcombe near Bath' in a letter to his sister-in-law dated 21 June of that year.[20] Because he did not move into the main house at Prior Park until 1741 it has been assumed that he lived elsewhere in Widcombe parish but this putative house has never been identified and such a double move would have been unnecessary.[21] Alexander Pope stayed with the Allens before and after 1741, always giving his address as 'Widcomb(e)' as if it remained the same. While in residence in 1739 he referred to Bath as 'the Little Town beneath me'[22] and to Allen as living 'on your delectable Mountains',[23] which suggests that the Allens were already living on the high shelf of Prior Park. If they were, then they must have been occupying that lumpish west wing which Wood could not bring himself even to mention. This was because he had been obliged to design it to the specifications of a strong-minded man who knew exactly what he wanted to make himself comfortable for a few years and was indifferent to the niceties of Palladio.

It was not the only reverse which Wood suffered up there on the hill. His whole scheme for the house assumed that it would be approached from the north. Visitors would keep his strictly Doric stable block to their

18 Revd Richard Graves, *The Triflers* (Bath, 1806) 64: 'but by the columns of the hall rising into the second story (contrary to the original design of the architect) the number and spaciousness of the bed chambers is inconveniently diminished, and they are made gloomy and unpleasant'. Bishop Baines appears to have altered the hall returning it to something nearer to Wood's groundplan preserved in Bath Reference Library. What Jones actually did on the ground and first floors of the main house can only be guessed at; Graves is the best witness and Pierce Egan (*Walks Through Bath*, 1819) supports him.
19 Ibid., 64.
20 Quoted in Benjamin Boyce, *The Benevolent Man – A Life of Ralph Allen of Bath* (Harvard University Press, 1967), 61.
21 Clarke, *Prior Park*, gives an illustration of 'The house at Widcombe thought to be the home of the Allens from 1735 to 1737' (38), but Thorp's map of 1742 shows no house that could possibly be in that position relative to the railway.
22 *Correspondence*, vol. 4, 173: letter of 17 April 1739.
23 Ibid., 206: letter of November 1739.

right after climbing up the hill from Bath. Their coach would then halt under a *porte cochère* 59 feet tall. As first designed this was to be free-standing but Allen's fondness for ornamental fowl obliged Wood to link west wing and *porte cochère* by a three-roomed hen house 'built with wrought Free Stone'.[24]

Prior Park – South Front

It was after the *porte cochère* that Wood's system, already confused by Allen's arbitrary alterations, began to break down completely. He had originally designed the great north portico as the front entrance with flights of steps down at each side, after the model of Wanstead 1. When Allen, for reasons undisclosed, decided against steps, the entrance to the house had to be moved round to the south front where, of course, there was no *porte cochère* and where Wood had no Wanstead elevation to guide him. The elevation which Wood devised to dignify what should have been the garden front of the house is one of quite exceptional ugliness.[25] So it is understandable that in his *Essay* Wood steered visitors, whom he still seems to be thinking of as potential buyers of stone ornaments, not house guests, clean away from it. Instead he led them in from his *porte cochère* presumably along the unsheltered quadrant wall. There, he remembered regretfully, he had intended 'a Winding Gallery adorned with a Row of Columns on each Side of it, as well as with a Pedestal supporting a Vase or

24 *Essay*, 429.
25 Not illustrated in the *Essay* but preserved in Bath Reference Library.

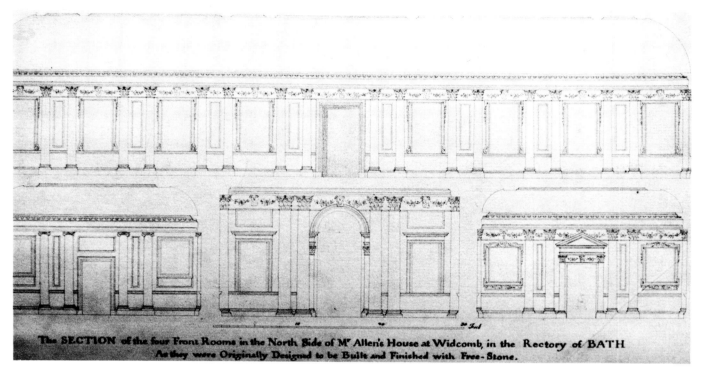

The SECTION of the four Front Rooms in the North Side of M⸱ Allen's House at Widcomb, in the Rectory of BATH
As they were Originally Designed to be Built and Finished with Free-Stone.

The PLAN of the Basement Story of M⸱ Allen's House at Widcomb, in the Cure of Bath,
As it was built A.D. MDCCXXXVII

(top) The interiors of Prior Park as originally planned by Wood
(bottom) Prior Park – basement plan showing the external steps which Wood intended

110

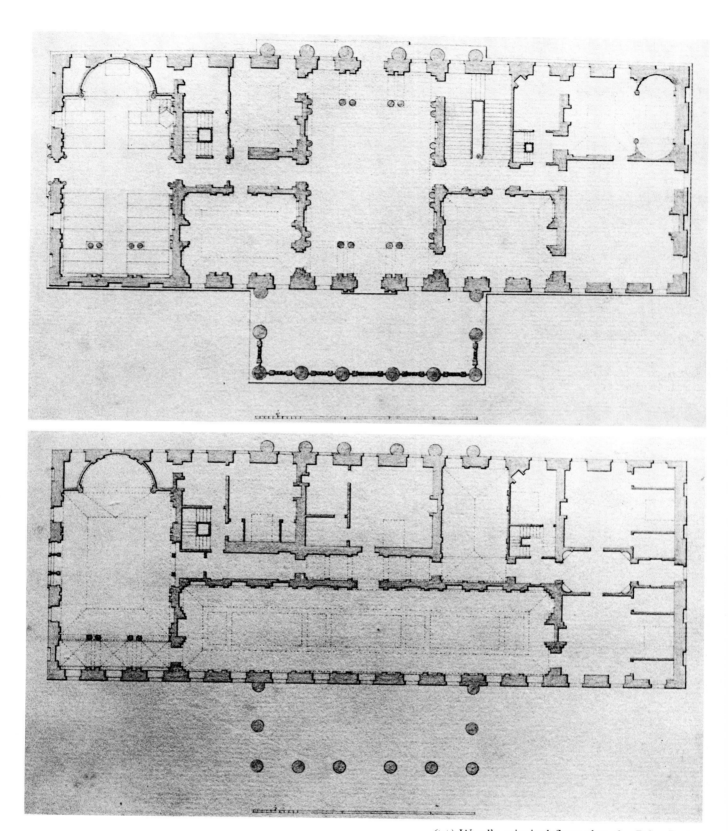

(top) Wood's principal floor plan for Prior Park
(bottom) Wood's upper floor plan for Prior Park

111

some other Ornament in every Intercolumniation, as Specimens of such Kind of Things to recommend the Sale of them'.[26] The passage illustrates how thoroughly Wood had entered into the scheme of devising a house that would double as a commercial showroom.

After the quadrant, because there was no way up to the temple portico, the visitors were to be plunged into a low, dark, featureless tunnel between kitchens and servants' quarters. From this they climbed up narrow stairs to the right and then emerged suddenly into the side of a central hall that had been designed to receive visitors from the north. It could reasonably receive them on the same axis from the south, but was certainly unsuited to an undignified reception out of the bowels of the house from the west. Some neo-Palladian villas are approached from a basement passage but not by stairs between the footmen's bedroom and the butler's pantry.

This route is so eccentric as to rouse serious doubts whether Wood was ever familiar with the house in its completed state. Richard Jones's narrative implies that he was not:

> at the same time began Mr Allen's great house under the direction of Mr Wood up to one storey, the rest was carried on by me till the house was completed. This began after Mr Allen came into to live, and then he ordered me to make drawings for to extend his buildings longer, which was carried on with great success.[27]

This semi-literate narrative would carry little conviction if it were not supported by the general bias of Wood's own account. There is a groundplan of the basement storey in the volume of Wood drawings captioned: 'built 1737'. Wood spends a page and a half describing the very commonplace details of the basement: the architraves, friezes and cornices of chimneys, the kind of rag-stone used for the floors and an apartment 'reserved for Water Closets, if such Conveniences should be wanting within the Body of the House'.[28] Then he abruptly dismisses all the major apartments of the house – hall, parlour, dining-room, chapel and staircase – in just over half a page. Yet earlier he had spent a page and a half on the refinements of a stable block which was never even built.

These are the repressed signs of mountainous disagreements between Wood and Allen. What is likely to have happened is that Allen first insisted on a modified version of Colen Campbell's unused Wanstead design. Wood stomached the humiliation because he saw a way to make it his own and to stretch it out across a superb natural site. His first 'General Plan' was inspired stage scenery. It was Wood's peculiar talent to be able to see the building potential in a certain lie of land. He saw the top of the Widcombe valley as three sides of an imagined dodecagon[29] and blocked it out accordingly, creating Prior Park as an abstract sculptural response to a natural flow of landscape, perfectly in accord with its site. So far Allen humoured him even to the extent of creating an artificial pool at a highly inconvenient point on the steep slope below the house because that was

26 *Essay*, 432.
27 Jones MS.
28 *Essay*, 431.
29 Ibid., 96.

where Wood had fixed the centre point of his imagined geometrical figure.[30] What Allen had already seen were the disaster points in Wood's first draught. From leaving their coach to climbing the proposed stairs visitors would have had a 200 foot walk at the top of a valley designed to funnel up the winds. And where in that grandiose central block was the accommodation for the army of servants with which Allen loved to surround himself? With his essentially urban conditioning Wood had designed an institution rather than a house, or if a house then it would have been the palace for a cold-blooded egomaniac, heedless of convenience or comfort. But in Ralph Allen he had met his match for will-power and purpose.

Wood had first to abandon the noble reserve of his Doric stables and supervise, or perhaps merely sketch out, a comfortable central suite of living accommodation with its grandest rooms on the top floor, something more like an enlarged garden pavilion than a normal house.[31] It was here that Pope was first entertained for three months in the bitter winter of 1739-40. Significantly the poet made no comment on his accommodation. Then Wood was allowed to build his *porte cochère*, which had now to double as a pigeon house because the pigeon cote above the Doric stables had been lost. Whether it was a functional arrangement to have a thousand or so birds fluttering in and out above carriages and guests can be left to the imagination. The three hen houses which he had to construct where he had intended a void can hardly have pleased Wood, and it may have been then that the whole idea of the arched *porte cochère* was abandoned and the interior space filled in, as it is shown in Walker's engraving.

Who designed the quadrant colonnade and open corridor linking the pigeons to the main central house is not known. If it was Wood he does not claim it. But the basement of the main house can be confidently attributed to him because of his praise for its solidity and damp-proof qualities. Also he had learned at Chandos Buildings that the plumbing of water closets was most easily handled if they were set in a row at the lowest part of the house. The final break with Allen will have come when Wood heard that he was not to be allowed his steps to the north portico. That made nonsense of his design and he made a dignified retreat, probably in 1737, holding his peace because he was still anxious to have Allen's support for his hospital schemes down in the city.[32] Richard Jones will have carried on, more or less to Wood's designs. Jones's statement 'The house was about seven years in building'[33] would be correct as the main house must have been begun in 1735, when Allen moved into the completed west wing, and it was finished when Allen and his second wife moved again into their state apartments in 1741.

30 This pool was supported by an artificial dam over which the water flowed down a rocky cascade; this is shown in a Thomas Robins watercolour of *c.*1758 which is illustrated in Clarke, *Prior Park*, 52.

31 The wings to this central pavilion are shown on the Walker engraving (drawn 1750) as being of two storeys; the print of 1830, immediately after the estate was bought by Bishop Baines, is less clear but the pigeon house *porte cochère* still survived at that time though its eastern equivalent had been heightened by two storeys.

32 Allen paid Wood a retainer for five years to answer valuation enquiries. It is not known when this expired but Allen may have devised it as a sweetener.

33 Jones MS.

It would have been then that Allen, dismayed perhaps by the sheer impracticality of what he had conjured up – the heavy, graceless entrance hall, the Stygian connecting corridors along the central spine of the house, the absence of any fine sequence of rooms – hastily ordered a replica in the east wing of the modest comfort which he had just abandoned on the west wing.

What Wood can be credited with is the skilful exterior massing of Campbell's original Wanstead design. It would be unfair to blame him for much else, but as an elevation in a demanding landscape the north front is a triumph. From the Palladian bridge at the foot of the combe only the main house is visible; the ill-proportioned wings were hidden by tactful planting as soon as they were built. By cutting off a bay from each side, raising the roof and deepening the temple portico Wood transformed the relaxed and repetitious Wanstead 1 design, creating a high, hunched mass that commands the vertiginous 400 foot slope with absolute authority.

The only weakness of the elevation is the wide empty space between the bottom of the Corinthian entablature and the top of the windows. Jones was to blame for this because he removed the cornice which Wood had designed over the windows and which would have lessened the gap. On the other side of the house the Corinthian entablature is continued over the south front to crown 'a hexastyle frontispiece' of engaged Ionic columns that appear to be foundering in their surrounding ashlar. It would be comfortable to blame Richard Jones for this disastrous composition but Wood describes the solecism blandly in his *Essay* and the volume of Wood drawings has his design for it, looking every bit as gauche and unfinished as the stony actuality. The pediment seems to be subsiding into the façade because the alien entablature is too high; the doorway is a void, just as Wood inked it in on his drawing, and the fenestration is cut without architraves directly into the masonry. This foretaste of neo-Classical practice leaves a disturbingly large area of plain wall. Round the corner on the east front the windows in their tabernacles hang like picture frames unrelated to the structure by platbands and topped again by the intrusive cake frill of the Corinthian entablature. The doorway here is a fake because it leads straight into the middle of the chapel.

From these confused and unsatisfying façades it is a relief to turn to the chapel itself where Jones seems to have kept faithfully to Wood's designs and produced Wood's one great interior, a place of chilling excellence only lacking the monochrome altar-piece of the Ascension which Van Diest was painting for Allen as early as 1736.[34] It is a chapel high for its length and intensely demanding through the contradictory moods set up by static forms so crowded as to seem to be jostling in upon each other. These result from superimposing Corinthian columns over Ionic, both with their full entablatures, so that two separate rooms appear to have been opened into one. Even though it handles these and has an apsidal ending there is not so much a feeling of movement in the chapel as a preparation for it, as if the Palladian were considering an escape to the baroque but never making it. Wood's lower Ionic stage is relatively dark and con-

34 *Correspondence of Alexander Pope*, vol. 4, 13: Pope to Allen, 30 April 1736; 'you who have been making an Altar Piece'.

114

stricting but then there is a transition to the complex depth and light of the Corinthian order in the gallery at the north, or ritual west, end. If it were in Venice it would be celebrated as a small masterpiece; here it is little visited, overshadowed by the fine chapel of 1844 by J. J. Scoles in the west wing.

Wood's drawings exist for other interiors, the staircase and the 90 foot long gallery.[35] They are conventional, as far as can be judged, rich in Gibbsian manner with a regular punctuation of pilasters and Wood's unvarying garlands with cherubs' heads. If they were ever copied by Jones they did not survive the fire of 1836 which gutted everything except the chapel.[36] When Wood wrote his brief description of the interiors in 1749 he was already gripped by an obsession with the mystical interrelationship of the classical orders. Consequently he described a visitor's tour of the house as an exhilarating educational experience of the Orders in sequence. Only by noting his careful 'they were to' and 'which would have had' does a reader realise that his 'Perambulations for the Curious' is all pure fiction, as also its 'Stables in the Simplicity of the Dorick Dress', its 'Ionick Gallery' and its 'Stone Hall of the Corinthian Order'. Only his 'stupendous Porticoe of the same Order'[37] was really achieved and that under the supervision of another man, the serviceable Richard Jones. Even the impression Wood creates of stonework 'predominant in the In-

The only surviving interior design by Wood at Prior Park – the Chapel

35 Bath Reference Library.
36 Apparently even the Van Diest Ascension survived the fire but it is now lost.
37 *Essay*, 432.

side finishing of the Chamber Story'[38] fades on closer examination. When Richard Pococke went round the house on 29 June 1754 he wrote, 'Most of the rooms are wainscoated with oak and the pannels hung, and one room is wainscoated with what they call gum wood'. The long Gallery, which may still have been stone-lined when Pope mentioned it in a letter to Warburton on 12 November 1741, had become in Pococke's time 'a secret library, the doors, on which the Philosophers &tc are painted, opening to the books of the sciences in which they excell'd'.[39] Clearly the charmless interiors were being completely rethought, but the unimaginative disposition of the entertainment rooms and the unlit corridors which connect so many of them remain intractable to the present day. Wood had a limited experience of interior planning and most of it had been unfortunate.

The final effect of the buildings, as opposed to the grounds, must have been so close to the artificial grandiosity which he had mocked in Timon's villa that Pope wisely refrained from any comment on his patron's 'new house'. Pierce Egan, in his *Walks through Bath*, writing in 1819 before the disastrous fire could be used as an excuse, was more honest:

> But all the majesty of the building is without. Within, everything (if we except the Chapel, which is neat and elegant, and adorned with an altar-piece, by Van Deest) is little, dark and inconvenient; and seldom has so much money been so injudiciously applied, as the enormous sum expended in the comfortless Palace of Prior Park.[40]

For the majesty, Wood may be given most of the credit and for the remainder, Prior Park was principally an expression of Ralph Allen's complex nature. With the annual income of a duke he remained basically the 'low born Allen' of Pope's initial apostrophe. His tastes were not aristocratic in the normal sense but his benevolence was like a power drive. He opened a new quarry simply to give employment to distressed labourers and built a palace with no wish to inhabit it but only a clear desire to surround himself with a large workforce and to make grand gestures.

Those who mention how Allen was 'eulogised' by Henry Fielding as Squire Allworthy in *Tom Jones* seem not to have read the novel. Allworthy in the book is a man of arbitrary temper, a dangerous moralist and the dupe of every smooth-tongued rogue and hypocrite about him. If Fielding was looking for models of such flattering wretches then he had no further to look than Alexander Pope. In his relations with Allen the poet was at his worst, spending years trying to infiltrate the Allen household with little gifts and careful flattery. Then, when he had penetrated their defences, he stayed for months at a time distributing his usual largesse of aesthetic dicta and soaking Allen for presents of money and grotto-building gear.[41]

38 Ibid., 431.
39 *The Travels through England of Dr. Richard Pococke*, Camden Society 1889, vol. 2, 36.
40 Page 215.
41 On 28 August 1737, two years before he finally achieved an invitation, Pope wrote to Allen from Cirencester where he had been 'helping' Lord Bathurst: 'could I be of any service to you in your Wood ... I have a strong inclination to come to you, and if you send me a Messenger hither, or a Line, telling me the First Day you will send or meet me at Tetbury and the hour, I will meet with you there. Adieu. No man is more Truly Yours.'

Wood's lower lodge to Prior Park

During one three month stay, from November 1739 to February 1740, the months when heating bills run high, Pope's letters reveal some of the contrasts in Allen's life-style. After describing how Allen had created artificial employment for hundreds of labourers to relieve the distress of a hard winter, Pope burst out:

> God made this Man rich, to shame the great; and wise to humble the learned ... I have passed this Christmas with the Most Noble Man of England.[42]

In another mood he spoke rather forlornly of the 'Regularity of dining and the Simplicity of the Food, but one Glass [of wine] a day, and four days in six not a drop'. 'I have not experienced so much Quiet as in this place', he revealed to George Lyttelton. 'Tho' I enjoy deep Quiet, I can't say I have much Pleasure or even any Object that obliges me to smile ...'[43]

Only the last chapter of their relations revealed the iron edge of Allen's will. Pressed for yet another favour to Pope's friend Martha Blount, Allen abruptly ended the friendship and retreated into silence. Only when he no longer risked being battened on did he stage a token reconciliation some few days before Pope's death.

42 *Correspondence*, vol. 4, 221-2.
43 Ibid., 206 and 209 respectively.

117

Such was the nature expressed in Prior Park: the gift for grand and visible gestures, the simplicity of personal life, the dullness, the knowledge that money bought all things, friends as well as servants. This was the man who assessed Wood shrewdly, used him, directed him, then sacked him.

Wood's revenge is preserved in the second edition of his *Essay* and, for a man of his temper, it is a subtle one. Ignoring the real house of compromise, he illustrated and described the Prior Park which Ralph Allen could have had if he had submitted his will to Wood's informed taste, and guided readers on an imaginary tour of the house that never was. As a last malicious reference to the origin of the great man's fortune Wood printed the description of the house in the chapter on 'The Trades of Bath', sandwiched ignominiously between an account of an insignificant seal-cutting factory and a discussion on the revival of Bath lace-making.

Even if Wood and Allen had worked in harmonious accord the project of Prior Park was ill-conceived, a piece of the peculiarly English vulgarity of Palladian giganticism. Elevations which Palladio had devised for the administrative centres of small country estates and summer-houses of pleasure were not improved by being blown up to 34 bays. At that scale they are no longer villas and only palaces by their inconvenience. It is no accident that Prior Park, like Wentworth Woodhouse,[44] survives as an institution, not a home.

44 It is the earlier, baroque portion of Wentworth Woodhouse which is still a home; the Palladian half is an educational establishment.

Chapter Eight

A Theme of Three Villas

For all the pleasure he took in the massing of a natural landscape Wood's architectural ambitions were basically urban. No myth has done more to obscure his character than the fiction that in 1729 he bought Eagle House in Batheaston, altered it to his taste and settled there in rural seclusion.[1] A line in Collinson's *History of Somerset*, 1791, stating that a house in the village 'was the residence of the late ingenious architect John Wood' may have begun the legend.[2] The facts are that a late 17th century house on the site was altered in 1724[3] while Wood was still living in London, and in 1729 a front was added to the road by an anonymous mason in a homely but competent West Country baroque.[4] At a later stage a porch was added with blocked columns, a style current around the 1730s but not one which Wood affected for doorways.[5] In 1773, long after Wood's death, his son John was living in the house and actually died there.[6] It was advertised for sale by his executors in 1781.[7] The nearby Shockerwick House has also been attributed to the elder Wood but it is certainly a work of John Palmer.[8]

Wood was city trained and city proficient. In legal documents of his Bath years he always refers to himself as a resident of Walcot parish, where he had his house in the middle of the south side of Queen Square.[9] At one point in his *Essay* he writes movingly, 'to be a Town's Born Child of the Place, descended from a Parent Whose Origin in the City is beyond any Memorial, is still reckoned, by some, as the greatest Honour an Inhabitant can enjoy'.[10]

Wood was, even so, not the man to underplay an architectural achievement, however minor or embowered in unfashionable fields and

1 M. A. Green *The Eighteenth Century Architecture of Bath* (Bath, 1904) canonised the fiction, relying on Collinson's ambiguous reference to an unspecified John Wood who had lived in the house; Collinson was referring, of course, to the younger Wood.
2 Collinson, *Somerset*, 103.
3 This building history, first analysed by M. A. Green, is summarised in B. M. W. Dobbie, *An English Rural Community: Batheaston with St Catherine* (Bath, 1969), 82.
4 Date inscribed in cartouche on roadside pediment.
5 The only instance of the elder Wood's use of blocked columns on any scale is the house he built, No. 41 Gay Street, for a rich Quaker, Richard Marchant; the taste may, therefore, have been due to Marchant rather than Wood.
6 The Younger Wood's son, Richard, was baptized in Batheaston Church on 6 September 1773, implying parochial residence at that time.
7 See Ison, *Georgian Buildings of Bath*, Appendix VI, 237.
8 Shockerwick House has been attributed to Wood by Pevsner (*Buildings of England; North Somerset and Bristol*, 1958, 260). There is, however, a signed drawing by Palmer of the house as executed in the Chapman Collection preserved in Bath Reference Library. The authors are grateful to Mr G. F. Laurence for bringing this drawing to their attention.
9 Wood began to sign himself as a vestryman in the vestry minutes for St Swithin, Walcot on 9 April 1735 and thereafter until his defeat in a vote on a design for a new church in 1739: Somerset County Record Office, St Swithin, Walcot Parish Records, DP/Wal. SW 4/1/1. The same book lists Wood as a ratepayer for Nos. 9 & 11 Queen Square from 1734-54.
10 *Essay*, 76.

hedges. It is puzzling, therefore, that in the 1742-3 edition of his *Essay* he makes no mention of two small country villas and a rural spa building which he had already designed. His omission of Prior Park from the same edition is easier to understand. The connection with the great house had been a bruising one. Richard Jones would just have been beginning work on the east wing, a deliberate copy of Wood's west wing, and in 1742 the smart of dismissal from direction must still have been painful.

In 1749, when the *Essay* came out in its second, revised and augmented edition, not only was Prior Park illustrated and described but Wood had decided to present himself as the creator of an orderly sequence of country houses, each illustrating the particular qualities of one of the three classical orders 'from the Simplicity of a neat plain Dress to the highest Pitch of Elegance'.[11] In reality what he had built had appeared in no kind of order and the three small villas which he had now achieved had little reference to each other. Belcomb Brook Villa (1734) and Titanbarrow Logia, begun in 1748, can be seen as demonstrations respectively of the Ionic and the Corinthian, but Lilliput Castle of 1738 was only marginally Doric. Nevertheless, Wood's account with its illustrative plates tidies them all into a persuasive sequence. They should be seen as the literary mid-point in his obsession with the divinely revealed Orders, first traced historically in *The Origin of Building* (1741) and then more subtly analysed in his *Dissertation upon the Orders of Columns* of 1751. What the account of these originally rather random villa designs also reveals is that between 1742 and 1749 Wood had become more intensely aware of each house site as a natural presence to which his elevations must respond, and of the pre-Roman associations of the Bath countryside. By 1749 the old holy places of the Druids and their Gods as Wood imagined them were becoming very near to being Wood's holy places also. The account of the three small villas is a fascinating demonstration of how a strict Palladian classicist can be drawn by antiquarian enthusiasms into passages of purely Romantic speculation.

On a lower plane these villa descriptions reveal more than Wood intended of the failures and consequent compromises of his building practice. They suggest too why neither Belcomb Brook, Lilliput nor the 'Duodecastyle Edifice' which Wood designed in 1737 for 'Lyncomb Spaw' were allowed to feature in the first edition of the *Essay*. Memories of slight and disaster would have been fresh in 1742; by 1749 recollection had grown selective and mellow.

So confident had Wood grown of the merit of his villa designs that he set the account of them as an introduction to the third part of his *Essay*, that which contains all his major achievements within the city. They follow a comparison between the quarries of classical Ephesus and those of present day Bath. This deftly created an association between Wood's architecture and the temple of Diana at Ephesus, one of the seven wonders of the ancient world. By that time Wood had come to believe that the temple by which 'the antient Britons determined to Honour the Great God *Apollo*'[12] at Bath had been comparable to Diana's temple and he was redesigning, therefore, in the very grandest tradition.

11 Ibid., 234.
12 Ibid.

Belcomb Brook was the first of the three villas chronologically, though it was placed second in the *Essay* description as the representative of the Ionic order, the Golden Mean. Wood described it as 'a small addition to some other Buildings erected for the Offices and Work Houses proper for one concerned in the Cloathing Manufacture',[13] and that was exactly what it was: a mill-owner's house next to, but with its back turned towards, the fulling mills and a scatter of workers' cottages. These last have all now been subsumed within the extensions and stable blocks of a sizeable country mansion, but what Wood built was not more than a small elegant house in which young Mr Francis Yerbury, the descendant of a long-established family of Bradford-on-Avon clothiers, could forget the rattle, bustle and smells of the factory across the yard and look out over his new garden and the River Avon to where 'a Cliff, covered with Wood, rises up and terminates the Southern View with a Beauty that renders the Situation of the House agreeable and pleasant'.[14]

Belcomb was not designed as a house to impress a visitor on first viewing. The entrance is tucked away on the east side. It is essentially a pavilion contrived to grace a view and one from which that view can be enjoyed in living quarters limited to an ante-room, parlour, study, dressing room and two bedrooms. John Webb had done much the same at Lamport. All three of Wood's 'villas' have this common quality of being appointed to allow a man and a woman to enjoy each other's company in a well-appointed privacy. They are not family houses and they assume that servants will be few. In none of the three illustrative plates is a doorway shown. The rich elevations of Belcomb and Titanbarrow are both the garden fronts, while Wood has deliberately turned Lilliput round, without speculation, and shown 'the Elevation, to the Westward', avoiding the entrance front.[15] Possibly he was conditioned by the retiring insularity of the middle class which he served but Wood seems habitually to have considered the façade of a house as a defence against the outside world rather than an invitation to guests. At Queen Square, the King's Circus, St John's Hospital and the south front of Prior Park there is this consistent playing down of the portico, a characteristic oddly out of accord with the open spirit of a city dedicated to entertainment.

But if Belcomb is a reserved house it is also the most lyrical of all Wood's creations, a title easily won perhaps as he usually designed in the architectural equivalent of prose period sentences rather than metric stanzas, yet against the competition of any other architect of his time it remains a most poetic house. Wood described it with negative satisfaction:

> ... no predominant Precept was intended in the Work; the three grand Precepts of Architecture [convenience, strength and beauty] reigning equally in it; and all appearing in that Perfection that is necessary to make a Habitation agreeable to the Posessor, and so far admired by his Friends as to draw their declarations of Applause.[16]

13 Ibid., 237.
14 Ibid., 238.
15 Ibid., plate opposite p. 234.
16 Ibid., 237.

Belcomb Brook Villa from the gardens

When it was built in 1734 Wood was still in that derivative stage exemplified by the central block of Prior Park: Campbell's design with minor improvements. Substantially the garden elevation of Belcomb copies the central three bays of the five-bay front to Marble Hill House, Twickenham, but as built 1724-5 by Roger Morris, not as illustrated in Campbell's 1725 *Vitruvius Britannicus*. Shorn of basement and recessed wings, Wood's composition is less balanced than that of Morris and it is more dramatic. It is also far richer. All three windows of Belcomb's principal floor are Wood's favourite 'tabernacles' rising from balustrades up to triangular pediments though the windows of the half storey have simpler architraves than their Marble Hill equivalents and, being set higher under the cornice, add to the house's appearance of reserve by seeming to tilt their glance upwards. 'The Mouldings in the whole Front, proper to be carved, are all enriched in the best Manner the Workmen were then Masters of', Wood stated grudgingly.[17] In fact the bead-and-reel, single acanthus and egg-and-dart mouldings are applied with a cunning that deepens the elevation, almost subliminally when viewed from a distance. On the Corinthian elevations of the north side of Queen Square, Bristol Corn Exchange and Titanbarrow, Wood applied these enrichments with a consciously heavy hand to give the third order the more voluptuous beauty appropriate to it.

The ashlar of this perfect façade is of a deep golden stone from a local Westwood quarry. Wood preferred the whitest limestone so the choice of material was not his. On the east and west fronts the masonry is only squared and the connecting walls to the rear are of mere rubble so there is a class system to the stonework.

Within the villa there is admirable stucco work in the square parlour, probably by Thomas Stocking,[18] but this is much later and the real interest lies in the octagonal study. Without this room very little would be known about Wood's interior decoration. So many of his drawings feature a conventional wreath of flowers punctuated by a mask, and the device begins to seem unimaginative. But here, looped around the coved ceiling 'in Stucco, performed by a Workman of great Skill in his Profession',[19] the wreaths of full and budded roses delicately soften the firm geometry of the central octagonal panel. This in its turn contains a riot of plump putti who dance on clouds and support more flowers and fruit, an effect which just manages to be both elegant and bucolic. Two niches, two doors, two windows, a fireplace and a built-in writing desk animate every one of the eight walls and the views from the window provide a permanent distraction from the room's purpose. It is the heart of the villa.

Upstairs are 'two Alcove Bed Chambers, with a Dressing Room between them'.[20] The recesses for the beds are given a miniature formality by elliptical arches on Doric columns, an intrusive order which suggests that in 1734 Wood had yet to formulate his theory of the separate quality of the Ionic. There is a civilised intimacy of scale and decoration to the whole

17 Ibid., 238.
18 Gordon Nares in *Country Life*, 22 December 1950, attributes it tentatively to Stocking on the strength of similar plasterwork at Midford Castle which Christopher Hussey gives to Stocking in *Country Life*, 3, 10 March 1944.
19 *Essay*, 238.
20 Ibid.

The plasterwork ceiling of the octagonal room at Belcomb

interior and because virtually nothing else of the kind can confidently be attributed to Wood, Belcomb has some importance. The rich reserve of the exterior and the domestic charm of the interior are more likely to represent his personal taste than anything else that has come down to us and should be balanced against the grand and sometimes inflexible vistas which he aimed to create in his cityscapes.

Quite how complete his control of the work was at Belcomb it is hard to estimate. The choice of the golden stone and his oblique criticism of the mouldings hint at another will than his own, but what seems to have soured his memory of this immensely covetable and successful creation is the 'Octostyle Monopterick Temple' in the garden.

Wood had determined, with his characteristic impetuous instinct for prehistory, that the Belcomb valley was a druidic site, that 'the antient *Britons* dedicated it to their God *Belenus*; and, in all Probability, erected a Pyraea in the Comb'.[21] If there had been a druidic temple then his antiquary's logic inferred that it would have resembled the original round temple at Delphi which Prince Bladud had designed for the Grecians on one of his journeys to the east. The idea of redesigning such a temple on such a site must have excited Wood's instincts as both antiquary and architect so when Francis Yerbury gave the job to a working 'Mason' Wood's reaction was bitter. 'It wants that Proportion which rendered such

21 Ibid.

124

kind of Structures correct', he reported in envenomed print, 'an Error pardonable in the Working Mason to whom that part of the Pavilion was committed, since he cannot be supposed to have ever heard of covered Monopterick Edifices, much less to have known the Rules by which the Antients built them'.[22]

This offending temple formed part of the crowded rococo garden which Francis Yerbury went on to create immediately to the west of his new villa. Given his idiosyncratic feeling for the prehistory of a park, Wood is not likely to have been trusted with the garden layouts. Yerbury crammed a sizeable grotto, a small lake, the temple and a Gothick cottage all within a 200 yard radius of his house windows. This might have accorded with the taste of the 1740s but Wood's approach to landscape anticipated that of a later period and Yerbury, by tree planting and by creating an enclosed garden of artificial events, destroyed the natural view across the Avon which Wood had intended the house to command.

In 1737 the chance to design another round temple slipped through Wood's hands. A local cooper and self-styled 'Doctor' Milsom had discovered a mineral spring in Lyncomb which had the dubious medical property of combining with alcohol to turn a bowl of punch to a blackish purple colour. Snatching at any opportunity to follow Bladud's career, Wood designed a circular spa building to cover the new source. It would have had four doors and twelve Doric columns supporting a frieze, a conical roof and a central chimney, but its only realisation was as an illustration in the 1749 *Essay*.[23] 'Doctor' Milsom sold a share in his mineral spring to Doctor Hillary who was an amateur architect and designed his own 'spaw'. Wood recorded with some satisfaction that the 'lofty Edifice' which Hillary built over the spring at a cost of £1,500 destroyed the source it was meant to protect by the weight of its foundations.[24]

It was in 1737 also that the Duke of Chandos refused to subscribe to a book which Wood had written and which can only have been his *Origin of Building*, finally published in 1741.[25] This means that at this empty time between major projects like Queen Square and the General Hospital, Wood's head must have been full of ideas about the divine proportions for the construction of a Tabernacle revealed by God to Moses on Mount Sinai. His determination to break away from conventional designs like Belcomb is revealed by the seal-engraving factory which he offered to build for Mr John Wicksted. This 'was to have been two and thirty Feet square; of the *Dorick* Order; one Story high; and Covered with a Pyramidal Roof, in the Vertex of which the Funnels of the Chimneys were to rise up'.[26] The similarity to Wood's reconstruction of the sacred Tabernacle is obvious, but it was not built. Wicksted proposed to construct the factory of 'common Wall Stone ... Painted to imitate Brickwork' so Wood withdrew his draughts in a huff.[27] If it had been erected it would have looked very like the 'Lime Kiln Spaw Porticoe' which was actually constructed about

22 Ibid.
23 Ibid., plate opposite p. 82.
24 Ibid., 81.
25 Chandos Letterbooks; Chandos to Wood: 3 November 1737.
26 *Essay*, 423.
27 Ibid.

The PLAN and ELEVATION of
the Lime Kiln Spaw Porticoe, with the
House of the lower Well, near Bath
As it was first Designed.

The Lime Kiln Spaw from the
Essay – another Wood version of
Moses' Tabernacle

J.Wood Arch.   P.Fourdrinier Sculp

this time for Sir Philip Parker Long to counter a rival spa house owned by John Hobbs. Wood illustrated his Porticoe, 'as it was first designed', in the 1749 *Essay*,[28] but whether the completed building was ever quite such a handsome and substantial Doric essay in the Mosaic proportions is uncertian as, like the Lyncomb Spaw, it spoilt the water source it was intended to protect and did not long survive.

28 Ibid., plate opposite p. 80. Wood never gives a date for the 'Lime Kiln Spaw' but by inference from his narrative (*Essay*, 78-9) it was designed after 1729, the date of its discovery, and before 1737 when 'Lyncomb Spaw' was discovered.

126

His fixation with the proportions of Moses' Tabernacle surfaced again on 5 February 1738 at a vestry meeting of Wood's parish, St Swithin's, Walcot. According to Wood, St Swithin's was on the site 'of a Pagan High Place ... a Structure, before it was rebuilt, that answered the exact Size and Form of Moses Tabernacle'.[29] Wood proposed to rebuild again with 'the Size of the Church increased to that of the Tabernacle, so as to have made it a perfect Example of that glorious Edifice'[30] and he put his design before the vestry men. Aware, possibly, of the earlier seal-engraving factory, the vestry rejected his draughts by 25 votes to 10 in favour of another design by the churchwarden Robert Smith.[31] Wood was furious and wrote that it had 'been made a Job of, and the Jobber supported in his Schemes by the Refuse of the Inhabitants of the Parish, in direct Opposition to the Inclinations of the Principal Parishioners'.[32]

This scurrilous passage was censored from the 1749 edition of the *Essay* but it reveals something about Wood's temper and his relations with fellow citizens. In fairness to him it should be said that three of the men who voted against him were illiterate and could only make their mark.

Out of this unpromising wrangle and obstinate obsession the next villa, Lilliput Castle, supposedly the 'Dorick' but more accurately the Mosaic member of the trio, was born. Jerry Peirce, the surgeon for whom Wood built Lilliput high up on the western slope of Lansdown, was a fellow parishioner and one of Wood's early sub-lessees in Queen Square. He was, so Wood suggests, given to throwing boisterous parties and if he was of a convivial genial nature that may explain how he came to let Wood design him a box so odd 'that the Wits of Bath soon gave it the Name of *T. Totum*'.[33] Aesthetically and functionally the building was undoubtedly a failure, which explains why it did not appear in the first edition of the *Essay*. Yet so stubborn was Wood's nature and so capable of self-deception that by 1749 he was featuring it confidently with an illustration though making no mention of its biblical inspiration now that the Druids had overtaken the Jews as his historical heroes and exemplars.

By a chance which has proved unlucky for his reputation, Wood's draughts for both the exterior and the interior of Lilliput, with detailed notes on the construction for his workers, have been preserved.[34] These prove just how cavalier and impractical Wood could be when he came down from the high levels of biblical proportions to the mundane details of supporting a roof and carrying a chimney flue from an outside wall to the centre of a pyramidal roof. To read them is to understand the bitter complaints of the Duke of Chandos and why Ralph Allen allowed Wood to build no higher than the basement of Prior Park.

The strange little building which resulted from lofty theory and hit-and-miss joinery has been lost within 'Battlefields', a later house on the

29 *Essay*, 'Part the Second', 1742, 29.
30 Ibid., 29.
31 Somerset County Record Office, DP/Wal. SW 4/1/1. Robert Smith had been first elected on 9 April 1735. He served for twice the usual period of two years. All this plotting was in vain because neither Wood nor Smith's design was, in the event, ever built. St Swithin's was eventually rebuilt in 1777-80, 1788 and 1790 to designs by John Palmer.
32 *Essay*, 'Part the Second', 1742, 29.
33 *Essay*, 235.
34 In the volume of Wood drawings in Bath Reference Library (ff. 23-4).

Wood's original design for
Lilliput Castle

site,[35] though it is still possible to trace its outlines by looking down from a
high roof onto the complex of additional building. In the end the authentic biblical measurements of the house which Wood later illustrated in *The
Origin of Building* were much reduced. Surgeon Peirce must have decided
that Wood's first design with its five bedrooms and four octagonal closets
was far too grand for the particular social function which he had in mind.
As built with only one fair-sized bedroom and an octagonal dressing room

35 Incorporated by Charles Harcourt Masters in 1802.

128

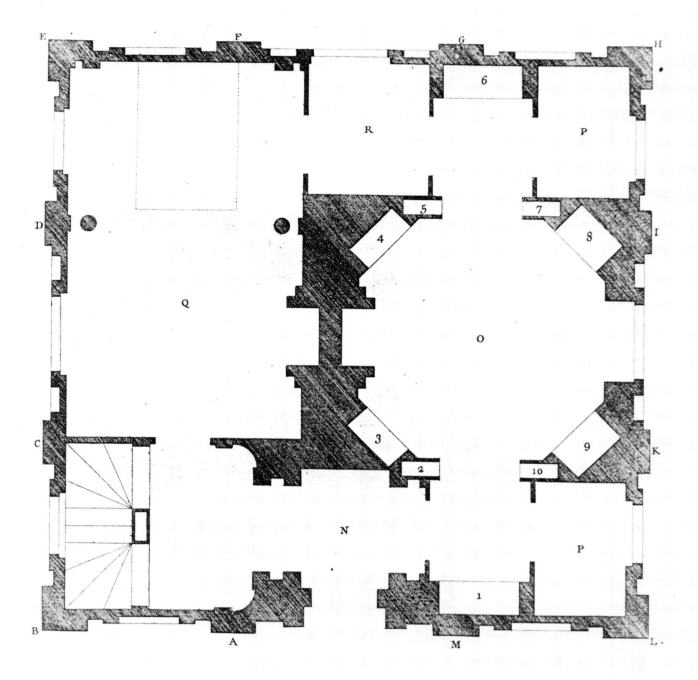

Plan of the first Story.

above a parlour and a closet, it was a 'maison de plaisance', an 18th century version of a 'bachelor's pad' rather than a true villa. Wood's drawings for the fireplace and overmantel in the bedroom are conventional but the roof was coved and it would have made a handsome enough love nest.

To Wood's obvious embarrassment, some years later the pyramidal roof, an essential feature of the reconstructed and adapted Tabernacle,

Groundplan of Moses' Tabernacle cottage from *The Origin* – the prototype for Lilliput

129

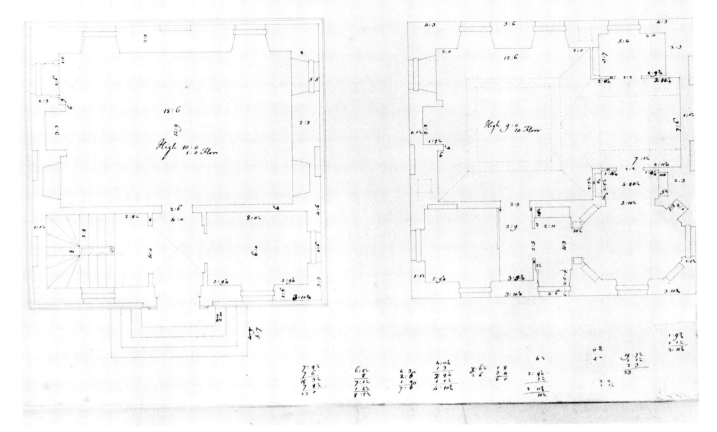

Ground and first floor plans of
Lilliput

proved a fire hazard. 'For from an unreasonable Use of the Kitchen
Chimney it took Fire; and such a Pillar of Flame, Smoak and burning Soot
each time surmounted poor *Lilliput* as was sufficient to have warmed and
kindled any other Structure into one universal Blaze'.[36] Characteristically
Wood brazens the matter out, blames the workmen and the over-hospital-
ity of Peirce, then actually turns the flaw to prove that his Castle had the
true Doric quality of strength.

If the notes which he wrote for his workmen are examined it will become obvious why Lilliput went twice on fire. It was not 'unreasonable Use
of the Kitchen Chimney' that was to blame but a design fault which Wood
had anticipated but left uncorrected. The coving of the bedchamber roof
was to be followed 'to draw the Funnels of the Chimneys in a proper manner from the Outside Walls towards the Middle of the Building'.[37] If any
joists blocked the passage of these funnels 'they may be feathered underneath and if that won't do, omited'.[38] Worse followed. 'It will be proper',
Wood scribbled, 'to cramp the Arch that is to bear the Chimneys to the

36 *Essay*, 235. After the blaze Lilliput was given a flat roof and Wood complained (*Essay*,
   235) that 'the Walls were disgraced with an ill proportioned Balustrade'. But his drawings show that it was originally intended to have a balustrade as well as a pyramidal
   roof. The Doric house in the *Origin of Building* has a deep Doric frieze to its entablature
   but this was not a feature of Lilliput.
37 Annotation to working drawing (f. 24).
38 Ibid.

130

timber work of the Roof, that it might not push too hard against the outward walls'.[39] Hence, of course, the proximity of hot bricks and flying sparks to dry timber, the 'Pillar of Flame' and the subsequent replacement of the pyramid with a flat roof and corner chimneys concealed in the balustrade.

In an engaging instance of a flowing stream of conscious association Wood moved directly from these accidental fires to declare his conviction that the ground where Lilliput stood was the very spot where 'we may suppose those People to have been sacrificed which the Druidical Religion condemned, or allured to the Flames'.[40]

The passage is a perfect compression of the sensibility of the pre-Gothick. Wood opens with some pseudo-etymology, suggesting that a local field name – Upper Rogers – 'seems here to be a manifest Corruption of *Rogus*, a Word importing a great Fire wherein human Bodies were burnt to Ashes'.[41] There follows a persuasive snatch of *Golden Bough*-style anthropology linking the Druids' fiery rites to a surviving practice of Mendip farmers who punished a thief by making him escape from a burning hut. Next Wood expresses the keen pleasure of an early enthusiast for the Picturesque in 'the glorious Landskip' to Bristol and the Severn. Over it all there is a very Gothick savouring of 'the Horrors of Death', the 'Songs of the Bards' and a devotion that will 'embrace Death with pleasure',[42] a foretaste of that feeling for mystery, historicism and doom that was the essence of the earliest Romantics.

Lilliput was a slight and ridiculous building but it is a reminder that Wood, the pure Palladian, was wide open through his antiquarian interests to modifying influences from the most unlikely alternative cultures, Jewish in this instance but with the Druids already in reserve. Lilliput was a small sign of that indiscriminate eclecticism and experiment which was finally to undercut the whole movement of neo-Classicism.

In contrast, Titanbarrow Logia, Wood's last villa, 'begun to be erected in the year 1748',[43] is a conventionally successful composition built for Southwell Pigott down in the Avon valley just outside Bathford where Wood had recently begun yet another of his cube and pyramid structures to enhance a local mineral water spring.[44] Like all Wood's villas, even the giant Prior Park, it consists of no more than a principal storey and a half set on a low basement; unlike the others it follows the accepted villa bay rhythm of 1-3-1. There are no notes to betray the errors of Wood's construction work because he had learnt his lesson and deputed everything. The agreement which he drew up for the costing and the construction is an echo of those which he had made long before for the works at Tyberton or of the practices which had served him on the Harley estate in London. He withdrew from all effort, even that of signing the document.[45]

39 Ibid.
40 *Essay*, 236.
41 Ibid.
42 Ibid.
43 Illustrated and inscribed in the *Essay*, plate opposite p. 240.
44 *Essay*, 69-70 and illustration opposite p. 70 of 'Bathford Spaw', inscribed 'begun to be Executed AD 1746'.
45 The Titanbarrow estimate (copy made by Wood but not signed by him) opens the volume of Wood drawings in Bath Reference Library.

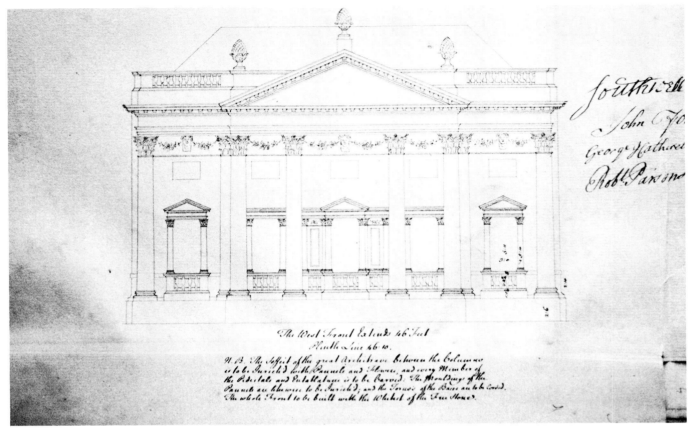

Wood's drawing for Titanbarrow showing his original scheme of fenestration

For £396.12s.2d John Ford undertook the digging, masonry, plumbing, tiling, plastering and painting. George Hatherall dealt with the carpenter's work for £283.18s.6d and for £55.19s.4d Robert Parsons handled the stone and wood carving – the architraves, chimneys and the Corinthian entablatures around the drawing room and staircase. For this was the Corinthian third in Wood's thematic villas of the orders, and the Corinthian order was that symbolized by a lovely young girl. Titanbarrow was 'the edifice that compleats the Gradation of Beauty pursued in the Free Stone Work of *Belcomb-Brook Villa*, and raises that Precept of *Architecture* to its highest Pitch of Elegance'.[46] North, south and east, Titanbarrow was well proportioned but modest in its detail. All the richness of design is concentrated on the north-western elevation: a tetrastyle pediment supported by almost whole columns, the three bays very slightly advanced from single bay wings. None of the errors of Prior Park are made here. There are no tabernacled windows left isolated in blank ashlar. Pilasters frame and link the composition. The entablature is correct and its richness meets a response in the balustrades of the lower windows. As it was originally built the windows of the half storey were blind, cut without architraves immediately below the exuberance of the carved swags and staring masks. This one harsh detail was exactly what was needed to rescue the elevation from predictability and it is unfortunate that they have since been cut through and fenestrated. Time has not been kind to Titanbarrow; all its elevations have suffered some change.

46 *Essay*, 239.

132

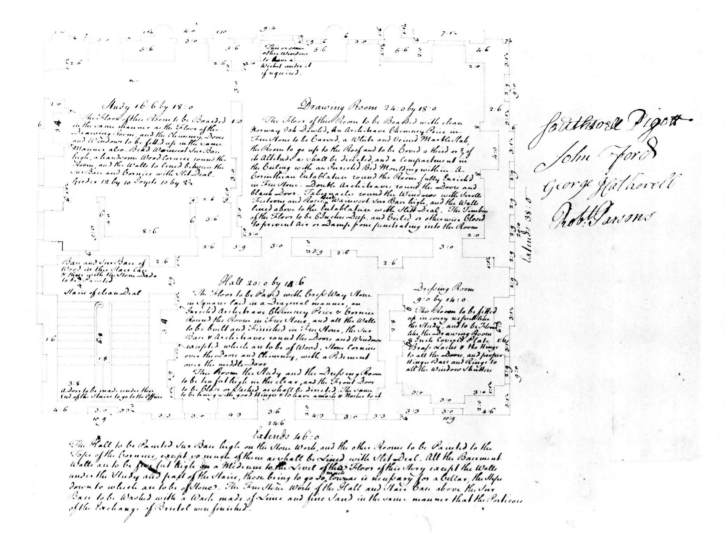

A Wood groundplan for Titanbarrow

This was inevitable as, like its fellows, it was designed to be selfish, a house for privacy where the servants are said to have been lodged in a cottage in the grounds. Three bays of the showfront lit a drawing room with a coved ceiling rising to the full height of the house. A study occupied the other two bays and over it was the master of the two bedrooms with a bed alcove. The loss of the original decoration in this villa is particularly to be regretted as Wood thought so highly of it.[47]

'All the objects', he promised, 'are so remarkable, that they will furnish agreeable Matter for almost endless Conversation'. And if these failed, 'Every Room will command a rich and beautiful Landskip', including the 'Artificial Barrow' after which the house was named.[48] By 1748 Wood was well into his enthusiasm for Druidic antiquities with the Jews coming a poor second.

47 In c.1800 a ceiling was inserted above the drawing room in order to provide more bedrooms; this resulted in the refenestration. Further alterations and additions were carried out in 1937-8 by the ex-Bishop of Bath and Wells, Dr. Wynne: pamphlet by L. M. Dear, *Whitehaven – The Story of Titan Barrow* (Bath, 1972).

The north front of Titanbarrow Logia after modern alterations

As always in his design and planning Wood was aware of the unkempt beauties of Nature which his house commanded; but speaking in the authentic tones of optimistic pre-Romanticism he was confident of being able to match them with the complementary beauty of an ordered Classicism:

> For if Virginal Beauty, in Works of Art, should ever accompany Virginal Beauty, in Works of Nature, here they may be put together with all the Propriety that can be even wished for.[49]

Then, possibly with some relief at the completion of this elegantly phrased and faintly spurious prospectus for the villa suburban, Wood turned to his real interest – the creation of an urban environment on a grand and formal scale.

48 *Essay*, 239-40.
49 Ibid., 239.

134

Chapter Nine

As Carthage to Aeneas – Wood's Imperial Failure

Between Bath's main line railway station and the city centre there still lies an indeterminate stretch of land, part industrial, part commercial, but one of the few level areas in the city. The river, dark, deep and generally ignored, wanders through it past the backside of a Catholic church, playing fields, the crude masonry of lopped-off terrace ends and the junction locks with the Kennet and Avon Canal. On this natural site for the expansion of a town which had hitherto ignored its river communications, Wood planned a Forum, which, out of deference to George II, he called Royal, but which by its scale and imaginative reach was Imperial.

He records and illustrates the prodigy in 'Part the Third' of his *Essay* in its first edition. This section of the book was published separately, probably, for it is undated, in 1743. Apparently the edition was a very limited one because Bath has retained no civic memory of this most extravagant episode in its town planning and it is not mentioned in any of the city's several histories.

The plan was for an enormous rectangle, 1,040 feet long by 624 feet broad, exactly bisected across its length by the canalized Avon and centred upon 'an Octangular Bason of Water' where the river was widened out to create 'the Haven of BATH'. On each side of the river were to be wide Piazzas 'for People to celebrate their Feasts and Festivals, and carry on their Commerce'.[1] For this Forum was no mere pleasure parade like Queen Square or the St James' Triangle. It was to be the hub of Bath, a complete escape from the narrow streets of the old city to classical order and logic. Two bridges were to link the piazzas, the northern one built on the line of the present South Parade where it now ends lamely, high above the river. 'Portico's'[2] were to be built around all four sides of the vast rectangle, interrupted only by these bridges. Raised above the porticoes would be 'Terrasses of fifty feet broad, before four lines of Building, intended to be erected in a Rich and Elegant Manner'.[3]

If Wood, who quotes authors French, Roman and English at every opportunity, had ever shown a knowledge of painting, it would be easier to understand the sources of his inspiration for this astonishing scheme, because it has all the air of a capriccio. Realized, it would have made Bath the picturesque wonder of western Europe: wooded hills in the background and in the foreground, a teeming basin full of ships and barges, with stone steps, columned buildings of golden stone, a turret or two from proprietary chapels and all the animation of Bath's fashionable throng, coming and going with coaches and sedan chairs among the carts

---

1 *Essay*, 'Part the Third', undated but post-1742, 87.
2 By 'portico's' Wood seems to have meant a rusticated wall divided into recesses with arched heads corresponding to the fronts of the house behind and above them.
3 *Essay*, 'Part the Third', 87.

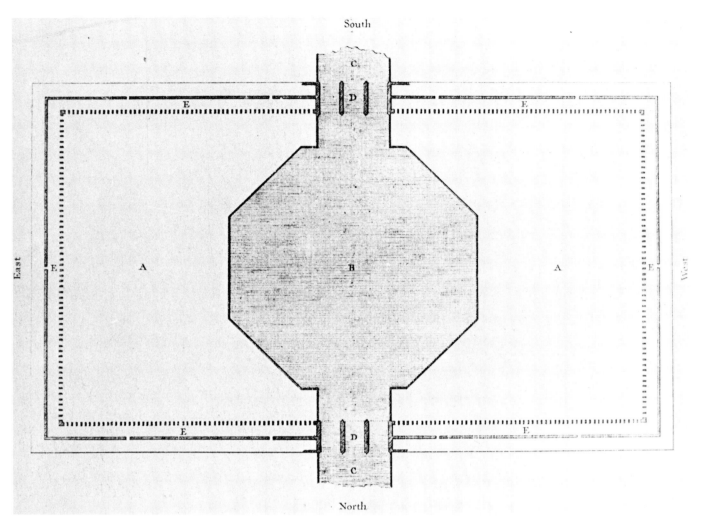

South

East

West

North

From the rare, third, 1743 volume of the *Essay*, a *Royal Forum* to span the Avon

of the country folk. Yet neither Claude nor Poussin is ever mentioned in Wood's writing. If it had been achieved, and there is every sign that Wood took the whole project seriously, the Forum would have out-ranked his hero Inigo Jones's Covent Garden in one bold move, and at the present day, John Wood's statue, of bronze and in a Roman toga, would be looking down on the be-camera'd tourists thronging his broad piazzas.

The best idea of the scale on which it was conceived can be gained from the existing South Parade where the 351 feet of building completed between 1743 and 1749 would have filled most, though not all, of the bottom right-hand corner of the plan. Wood wrote bitterly, in a passage deleted, for obvious reasons, from the *Essay's* second edition, that the whole massive quadrangle, the North and South Parades, Duke Street and Pierrepont Street, would only have made up 'four Fronts of a small Wing' of this overweeningly ambitious project.[4] Even the South Parade as it was built was a poor shadow of what Wood had intended. Its central bays should have been occupied with grand new Assembly Rooms at terrace level and a theatre in the basement below.

All that survives of Wood's ill-fated attempt to equal Lord Bur-

4 *Essay*, 'Part the Second', 1742, 24.

136

The South Parade

lington's Assembly Rooms at York is a printed 'Proposal for Erecting by Subscription an Assembly House in the City of Bath'.[5] It was intended to raise £4,200 by issuing forty shares of £105 each. It would have included a ballroom, a theatre, two billiard-rooms, a drawing room and sizable 'Anti-Chambers' with a flat for a caretaker in the basement. The ballroom, in the form of a double cube of 26′9″, would not, as illustrated, have been an 'Egyptian Hall', but Wood may have had alternative schemes in mind.

This explains why Wood had scornfully dismissed Queen Square 'but as the Barton' compared to 'an Open Area, to be surrounded with Buildings, which I purpose to begin in the Spring of the next Year'. He was writing in 1742. 'It shall represent the Forum or Places among the Antients, where Kings were wont to Convene the People and I will endeavour to give it an Air of Magnificence, equal to any Thing of its Kind'.[6]

That mention of kings convening people is a reminder of how unwise it is to underestimate the apocalyptic, almost mad in normal terms, reach of Wood's mind. Occasional snatches in his casual writing reveal the level at which his imagination was running. There is a page of frantic numerical calculation scribbled onto the manuscript of the *Origin of Building*, and

5 The original is preserved in Bath Reference Library.
6 *Essay*, 'Part the Second', 17.

137

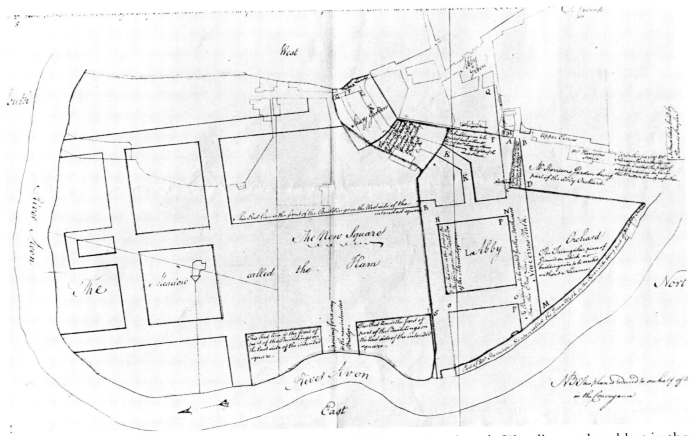

A modified proposal of 1740 for the Royal Forum on the Ham

then, opposite the wild figures, is written in Wood's own hand but in the future tones of William Blake, the gnomic:

> The Angel sent before the Israelites shews the Discontinuance of the Oracle.[7]

Another note written 27 April 1734 and sent to William Brydges along with '6 Dozen of Braughton Water', mentions eagerly 'there is talk (with very good foundation) that the King will have a House built here'.[8]

To such a dreamer there would be nothing improbable in Bath supplanting London as the capital, just as Versailles had supplanted Paris. It would only be a reasonable return to the pre-Roman situation where, so Wood had convinced himself, Bath and Camulodunum were one and the same city, a place glorious with temples to the sun and moon: the undisputed capital of the native Britons, a Troy built again by the wizard Prince Bladud who was himself the Trojans' legitimate heir.

The esoteric faiths to which Wood was prone had a trick of merging easily into his antiquarian research. They would appear finally in the form of a tenacious, almost religious, belief in the symbolic purity of his architectural designs. It must have become apparent from preceding chapters that only a fraction of his schemes was ever achieved, but he conceived so grandly that even that fraction, botched and compromised in its final

7 *Origin of Building*, Bath MS.
8 Manuscript letter in Bath Reference Library.

form, was splendid enough to set London and Edinburgh models to emulate for the remainder of the century, and to embarrass by its nobility the 20th century municipal corporation which has inherited modern Bath.

Towards the end of the fourth part of the *Essay* there is a passage which reveals movingly the inspiration of Wood's planning and his sense of a goal attained. After describing his native valley in terms of affectionate excess, 'A Region that sets Paradise itself before one's Eyes ... the very *Elysium Fields* of the Antients',[9] he closes in upon the city itself as viewed from 'the Summit of *Beaching Cliff*'. 'Bath', he wrote, 'will appear much the same that *Virgil* declares *Carthage* to have appeared to *Aeneas*'; and then the proposed city of his vision blends in with the actual city below him as he remembers the Forum which, in 1749, he may still have been hoping to build. 'Especially', he continued, 'if we suppose the Chapel erected, which is intended for the Use of the new Buildings at the South East Corner of the City'.[10] This is the only surviving hint that he intended another proprietary chapel[11] to stand above the Piazzas beside the proposed Assembly Rooms. Then, instead of listing the real buildings of the city, he quotes thirty lines from Virgil's Aeneid in Pitt's translation. The verse is pedestrian but it deserves to be studied:

> Now o'er the lofty Hill they bend their Way,
> Whence all the rising Town in Prospect lay,
> And Towr's and Temples; for the Mountain's Brow
> Hung bending o'er, and shaded all below.
> Where late the Cottage stood, with glad Surprize
> The Prince beholds the stately Palace rise;
> On the Pav'd Streets and Gates, looks wond'ring down,
> And all the Crowd and Tumult of the Town.
> The *Tyrians* ply their work; with many a Groan
> These roll, or heave some huge unweildy Stone;
> These sink a spacious Mole beneath the Sea,
> Those an huge Theatre's Foundation lay;
> Hew massy Columns from the Mountain's Side,
> Of future Scenes an ornamental Pride.[12]

The identification with the past is absolute. Wood is both Princes, Aeneas and Bladud, controlling the toiling Tyrians and raising a new Troy to equal Dido's Carthage, Aeneas's Rome and Bladud's Caerbran. He was fortunate in the possession of a mind which could take pleasure in the projected as well as the actual and could enjoy the result of compromise almost as much as the ideal form of a first vision.

This last Forum was the third which he had projected on the Abbey Orchard and the Ham. The first was the scheme of 1730 for a Circus and a bridge to open up the much cheaper building land across the river, the Bathwick Estate, which Robert Adam's Pulteney Bridge of 1769-74

9 *Essay*, 440-1.
10 Ibid., 441.
11 More precisely, the only written hint; a chapel appears to be projected in Barry Cunliffe's redrawing of a manuscript plan given in *The City of Bath*, 1986, 128. This, as will be shown, is Wood's plan for a 'New Square' of 1739.
12 *Essay*, 441.

eventually made accessible. The second was a relatively modest, half-way-house of a scheme for a 'New Square' to be built entirely on the city side of the river but with access points to bridge the Avon at a later date.[13] Wood never published this 'New Square' plan or dignified it with a Roman title, but it would have been grand enough to have made Queen Square look like a 'Barton', even though it would have been only half the size of the proposed 1743 *Royal Forum*.

Two copies of the 'New Square' with coloured inks to clarify ownership and notes in Wood's hand, are preserved in the Manvers papers in Nottingham University Library. They are parts (f. 14 and f. 22) of a bound volume of the leases and transactions concerning the Duke of Kingston's estates in Bath in the 1730s and 1740s. On f. 9 and f. 15, both dated 3 July 1739, are the 'Grant to Mr John Wood of the Abbey Orchard under £100 Rent' and the 'Deed of Covenant relating thereto'. The plans appear to have been included as a statement of future aims rather than as a simple clarification of that specific deal. The Abbey Orchard, four acres of which Wood was leasing, covered only 'The Triangular piece of ground on which no buildings are to be erected without a licence' (Wood's note) and the Parades, but the plans cover the whole loop of the river as far as the present railway station. Barry Cunliffe's drawing in *The City of Bath*[14] is based on this, but without any documentary reference and with the wrong date, 1725.

On the far south side of the New Square, which is actually a rectangle, Wood has outlined four more blocks of buildings. Inset into a recess of one of these is what looks to be the proprietary chapel mentioned earlier. Between two blocks on the east side of the New Square Wood has written on f. 14, 'Opening for a way to the intended new buildings', and altered this on f. 22 to 'new bridge'.

It is hard to say exactly what the relationship was between this grand but not impossible project and the third scheme for a *'Royal Forum'* spanning the river. Unlike the *'Royal Forum'*, the 'New Square' would have related easily to the axis of Duke Street and Pierrepont Street and its south side would have matched exactly the dimensions of the present South Parade, which would, confusingly, have formed the north side of the 'New Square'. The likeliest solution is that Wood presented these unpublished plans for a 'New Square' to the Duke of Kingston's agent and lawyers to show that his projects for the city were practical and not disturbingly grandiose. They would explain his continued acquisition of land on the Ham; and indeed, f. 23 records the Duke as licensing Wood's purchase of a 62 year lease on part of the Ham from Richard Marchant as late as 1745. What seems to have initiated this flurry of projections along the river bank was, characteristically, a series of setbacks elsewhere in Bath.

While the Circus was built and the form of the Forum at least illustrated, the actual shape and scale of Wood's *Imperial Gymnasium* can only be deduced. From his first arrival at Bath in 1727 armed with Humphry Thayer's commission 'towards founding a General Hospital', Wood had been obsessed with that scheme but endlessly frustrated in his efforts 'to

13 Nottingham University Library, Manvers MS. 4184.
14 See footnote 11.

140

provide a Piece of Ground for the Building'.[15] He claimed to have devised a new draught for the building every year between 1727 and 1738, when construction was at last begun. At the same time he seems always to have cast emulous, rather spiteful, eyes on John Harvey's small, elegant Pump Room of 1706 and to have poured outraged contempt upon the dilapidated squalor of bathing provision in the King's and adjoining Queen's Baths. Since the former was still in Wood's day basically the Norman construction which Bishop John of Tours had created in the reign of Henry I it is not surprising that there were improvements to be made. What Wood seems to have had in mind was a piece of inspired common sense. He proposed larger and renovated baths, still open to the air but shielded from both wind and prying eyes and with improved slips and pumps for taking the waters externally.[16] Linked closely to these on the site of the Ambrey Field would be a hospital with the healing waters piped in for the sick. The Pump Room could then be enlarged to provide socially for the throng of visitors who came thrice daily to drink the waters. The whole complex, together with toilet facilities, the areas for the gentle exercise so often urged by Bath physicians and the royal tennis courts for the more active would comprise the *Imperial Gymnasium*, the heart of Bath: a leisure centre for valetudinarians and a hospital for the truly sick.

There was a time, early in 1731, when everything might have been realized. But once the kitchen garden in the Ambrey[17] had been lost by a combination of legal delay, over-zealous trustees and unscrupulous local speculators, Wood must have despaired of ever having his ideal hospital site: one near to but slightly below the outpouring of the mineral springs, where the sick could bathe easily and regularly within the premises. The ground which was finally purchased at the very end of 1737 was cramped and unsuitable, set among noisy streets away from and above the hot waters which it was intended to utilize. By 9 February 1738 Wood had prepared a design for the site, Pine had engraved it and it had been sent for the King's approval.

These were months when Bath was indulging in one of its periodic and ineffective frets about the state of its hot springs, and Wood's hopes mounted with the tide of public concern. Not only was there progress on the Hospital but he was required by the Corporation to view the baths and 'not only remove all the Nuisances which then attended both Cisterns, but to make them as convenient for the Bathers, as well as for such as made Use of the Waters by pumping, as the confined Situation of the Place would admit of'.[18] At the same time he was 'encouraged by People of the highest Rank and Fortune ... to extend that Design to a Building which should render the Drinking of the Hot Waters as Convenient as possible'.[19] A lottery was suggested to finance this.

15 *Essay*, 242.

16 Slips were changing rooms. Pumping was an alternative treatment for patients who wished to avoid complete immersion; it should not be confused with the Pump Room where Bath waters were merely drunk.

17 This was the property which Robert Gay had offered as a gift. The offer was withdrawn when the Hospital committee, prompted by Sir Joseph Jekyll, asked for more land on the same site. The Ambrey lay outside the south gate of the city near the Hot Bath.

18 *Essay*, 266.

19 Ibid., 270.

The Royal Mineral Water
Hospital; the attic storey is a
later addition

Both schemes came to nothing. The plan to improve the baths found-
ered on the Corporation's suspicions of the Duke of Kingston's motives
for offering land for an extension.[20] Years later, in 1749, Wood was still
vainly hoping to get his hands on Harvey's Pump Room. He never did.

There remained the Hospital itself. Wood was never one to express
doubts about his own creations. Predictably he described it as 'a Magnifi-

20 The Duke of Kingston offered to give the Corporation a piece of ground on the east
side of the Queen's Bath where Wood proposed to construct two more slips. In return
he asked the Corporation to remove a shed which they had erected against Abbey
House, his Bath residence.

142

cent Pile of Building of the *Ionick* Order'.[21] It is impossible to agree. The design was as practical as the site and the money subscribed (£8,643.10s.9d) would permit. The wards faced the south and a quiet courtyard, the northern front was occupied by administration rooms on the ground floor. But the main north elevation was pedestrian, the windows of the half storey were hunched under the cornice, the break forward of the three central bays was inadequate and the pediment sat low in consequence.[22] It was as if the 11 year struggle had worn the architect out and he merely performed correctly when the occasion came. The lengthy account of the Hospital in the *Essay* demonstrates Wood's interest in the institution and its administrative minutiae – he was himself a Governor – but that circular design of 1731, with perhaps the hot waters welling up in a central courtyard, would have served Bath better as an inspirational focus.[23] Essentially Wood's Hospital represents a failure of committee management and of vision.

This hospital portrait group by William Hoare shows Dr Oliver and Jerry Peirce examining patients

21 *Essay*, 291. This building was begun in 1738 and functioning by 1741.
22 Wood's Hospital was given an attic storey by John Palmer in *c*.1793 and was extended by Manners and Gill in 1850-60.
23 *Essay*, 284. May 1727: 'we then resolved upon making a new Bath in the Center of the Hospital, as the Cistern could be supplied with water from the *Hot* Bath, without losing much of its natural Warmth'.

143

Behind all these half events and frustrations the 'one headed corporation of Bath', Ralph Allen, should not be forgotten. He was President of the Hospital Governors. His money, his stone, supplied without charge, and his directing hand, had lain behind the whole enterprise. It is likely then that his voice had been the decisive one when the scheme for the baths and the Pump Room came to nothing. For more than 20 years it could be said that in Bath Wood proposed but Allen disposed.

This was even more apparent in the events leading up to the launch of the *Royal Forum*. The days were long gone when Bath Corporation would dismiss Wood's building schemes out of hand as 'chimerical'. He had proved himself and proved the value of local land, so now there were political pressures to sway any decision over new developments. Wood's account of these pressures is nervous and equivocal. His own preference seems to have been for 1,000 feet of building on the west of the city at the head of the King's Meadow, not far from Queen Square, with a new Assembly House as the catalyst to the development. But 'Fair Promises', he wrote, 'recommended the opposite side of the City',[24] so obediently he scrapped the Circus scheme of 1730 and on 25 April 1738 relaunched it as the *Royal Forum* spanning both sides of the Avon but with a smaller pilot project, the quadrangle of the Parades, preceding it immediately to the north. That lesser scheme would involve neither bridge building nor river canalizing but would be a prototype to test out Wood's idea for setting a row of houses on a broad terrace raised 18 feet above normal ground level. This was to be fronted with a rusticated wall crowned with a balustrade and obelisks 'to answer every Break in the Front of the Building'.[25]

Up to that point there had been nothing to favour this building project in the south-east of the city any more than the other proposal west of the town in the King's Meadow as both were outside the old borough walls. Now the economics behind the options changed. As a result of a pamphlet fostered by the residents of Queen Square, an Act of Parliament, no less, was passed late in 1738 and this, among other provisions, readjusted the rates for chairmen, relating them strictly to the distance covered rather than arbitrarily to movement outside the city walls. Where visitors and the siting of future lodging houses were concerned this was decisive. Wood claims that it was 'to the very utmost of my Wishes'.[26] There must have been political manipulation at a high level to effect this trivial issue so swiftly and it is hard not to suspect that Ralph Allen was the manipulator. He had failed to invest as a sub-lessee in the best houses of Queen Square. Coming in late he had had to be content with some inferior property sites in John Street and he was not a man to lose such a chance twice. He had learned that Wood could provide good investment opportunities and, after events at Prior Park, knew him as a man who could be handled.

At first things went as smoothly as poor Wood could have hoped. He and his publisher James Leake signed contracts on 22 May and 3 July 1739 with the Duke of Kingston, leasing from him the Abbey Orchard for a peppercorn rent. The Duke was to be paid £100 yearly when the first

24 Ibid., 247.
25 Ibid., 350.
26 Ibid., 248.

144

houses on the North Parade were built. That summer John Wesley was preaching on the Ham, a foretaste of the public assemblies which Wood anticipated for his Forum; meanwhile under the Parade sites the sewers were being dug.

Wood followed the procedures which had worked well on the north side of Queen Square, parcelling out the sites from the Town Wall to the river bank, the whole North or 'Grand' Parade as he preferred to call it. He bound the leaseholders 'by the Article, not only to begin upon, and proceed with all the Houses ... at the same Time; but to build them according to my Design'.[27] This should, in normal circumstances, have been legally foolproof. However, after his experience of Allen's ruthless firmness of purpose at Prior Park, he may well have felt some unease when almost a half, 84 feet out of the 210 feet total, from the prime site central terrace was taken up by Ralph Allen.

The proposed terrace wall might well have lent the new terrace 'a stately look'; the obelisks and balustrades were eventually erected, but as a design the three blocks of houses, separated by Duke Street and Pierrepont Street, were nothing more original than the west, north and east sides of Queen Square as they had been originally proposed but laid out in line. The rich Corinthian elevation of the north side, extended by two bays, was to be repeated exactly, but this time it would be within easy reach

Thomas Malton's watercolour of North Parade with the original obelisks on the balustrade

27 Ibid., 350.

of the two Assembly Houses across the Triangle. Wood intended the grounds of the Triangle to furnish a Spring Walk and the wide terrace before the new houses a Summer Walk. He had plans later for a sheltered Autumn Walk on the South Parade. A formal walk at set times of the day was part of Bath's social ritual.

On 10 March 1740 the first stone was laid to the proposed palace terrace. The foundations and the cellar storey were built. Then the blow fell which was to diminish John Wood's enthusiasm for house building in his native city for more than a decade, until 1753-4 in fact when, with his son to help him and as far away from the south-east quarter as he could get, he made preparations to build the King's Circus, the last and noblest work of his lifetime. And on that site Ralph Allen was not a sub-leaseholder; Wood had learnt his lesson.

For there can be little doubt that it was Ralph Allen who wrecked the Parade project. Wood had always to watch his words and all he dared to write was that 'a Scheme, contrived by one of the Tenants, broke out, to lay aside the Ornaments; to alter the Proportion of the Walk; and to erect the Terrass Wall with Rubble Stone, so as to have no reference to the Building above'.[28] His anger at the aesthetic treachery still brimmed out: 'this Scheme was, in Violation of the Articles, as above, pursued and executed, to the Destruction of a Design, which, on Paper, hath given Pleasure and Satisfaction to Multitudes, among all Ranks of People'.[29]

Only the leaseholders of the central block would have benefited from the considerable economies achieved by scrapping pilasters, pillars, balustrades, window 'tabernacles' and almost all the Corinthian enrichment. There were only three potential villains: John Taylor, watchmaker with a 58 foot 8 inch frontage; George Lookup, gentleman with 66 feet; and Allen with his 84 feet. Taylor and Lookup may have been ready enough to follow Allen's lead but only he would have had the local power-base to defy Wood with impunity. There was to be a sweetener, a pay-off, later to buy Wood's acquiescence, but that would be to another city's advantage, and in Bath the damage had been done.

As built, the 'Grand' Parade is uniform, well-mannered and dull. With its open outlook it is handsome enough; the harm done by its impoverishment is more subtle. Because it was not sufficiently rich, it failed to strike that necessary note of aesthetic consequence which would have raised social expectations and carried the proposed Forum into existence. Building development is a confidence trick; the façade matters. Moving for an easy profit, Allen ensured that fashionable Bath would rise northwards up the hill on steep, difficult building sites, not southwards and near the centres of entertainment. When Ralph Allen's philanthropy is being honoured, this action should be remembered.

The houses of the North Parade were roofed within eight months. Work on the other three streets 'made slow advances'.[30] The subscription which Wood set up on 1 March 1742 for a canal to Chippenham may have been an attempt to breathe commercial life into this riverside quarter, but it failed as did his other subscription for an Assembly House. Work began

28 Ibid.
29 Ibid.
30 Ibid., 248.

146

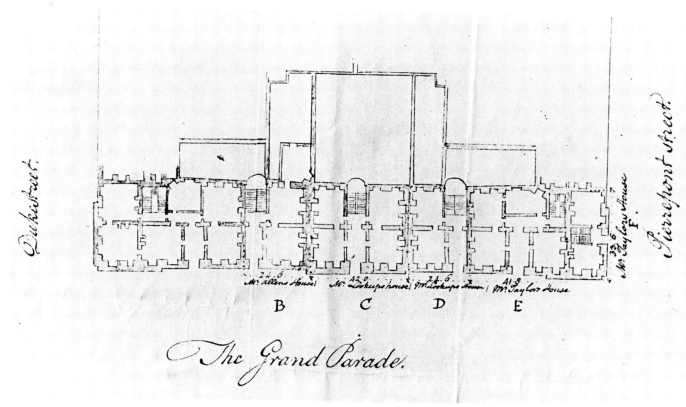

B   C   D   E

The Grand Parade.

on the South Parade on 27 January 1743 but plots were still being as-signed there and in Duke Street as late as 1748 and 1749. Only Pierrepont Street moved quickly, all its plots being sold by 1742.[31] The South Parade was dignified by a balustrade along its roof but it looked out over neither portico nor piazza, while the rear elevations of the tightly laid-out square of houses were inevitably tenement-like by the cheeseparing of Wood's in-itial plan. From the number of masons, carpenters, joiners and plasterers who took leases, old associates of Wood like Samuel Emes included, it is obvious that most of the building was done by the usual cooperation of craftsmen.

It was a discreditable episode of small town politics from which no one emerges with credit. But with that gift for looking on the bright side of every property, which would have made him a successful estate agent if he had been born later, Wood was able to suggest by 1749 that if Prince Bladud's temple of Apollo had still existed (when of course it never existed at all except in his imagination) then its 'Tremendous Look, from the *Grand Parade*, must have inspired Mankind with a Religious Awe, as often as they should consider that the Great God of Heaven and Earth was Adored by them'.[32] More truthfully he reported that 'according to the present Contract' the *Royal Forum* had shrunk to an area of 620 feet by 310 feet 'and this is for Ever to lie Open and Void'.[33]

A groundplan of the houses on North Parade with Wood's standard internal layout

31 The only noteworthy architecture in this area is the portico of Doric columns which Wood designed to carry the elevation on the west side of Pierrepont Street over the en-trance to Orchard Street which he was also developing on a modest scale.

32 *Essay*, 351.

33 Ibid.

Gallaway's Buildings of the 1750s illustrate the general
acceptance of Wood's basic elevations by other Bath builders

Chapter Ten

Civic Pomps in Other Places

The direct result of Wood's rebuff over the design of the Grand Parade was traumatic for the architect and a set-back to the pace and spirit of Bath's development. Disasters strike men variously. When an earlier project collapsed in 1727 Wood had fought back vigorously with alternative sites and new backers. In 1740 he allowed himself to be deflected and, as a consequence, for a whole decade the city marked time. The decent, orderly 'penny plain' façade of the Parade quadrangle and upper Gay Street grew slowly, establishing a standard pattern for the townscape. Lesser architects eventually copied them with Gallaway's Buildings, post-1750, and Bladud Buildings, post-1755.[1] But there was no 'twopence coloured' setpiece to dramatize the city's image and re-establish its sense of style until the King's Circus in 1754, mere months before Wood died. So the 13 year interval very nearly broke a growth sequence which still depended entirely upon Wood's vision and Wood's initiatives.

Secure in his rental income from previous enterprises, he appears to have accepted a second career as antiquary and architectural historian, writing five books in ten years. For exercise in real building design he turned his back on the Byzantine manipulations of Bath politics to work in Bristol and Liverpool. This was Bath's loss but it meant that Palladian façades as the prestige architecture for civic institutions in the provinces reached two great mercantile centres not from London, as might be expected, but from Bath. Wood never received a more impressive testimonial, though Ralph Allen was, almost inevitably, active behind the scene.

Bristol Corporation had been considering an impressive replacement for their old Tolzey or Exchange since 1717, and after 1737 several architects produced designs, at least six from William Halfpenny alone.[2] He was fobbed off with five guineas for his trouble but the designs have survived to make a valuable point about the interaction of functionalism and taste at that period.

Halfpenny lacked training in Palladian façadism. As a result he tried to design functionally, producing schemes for inner courts, some triangular, open at the apex to draw dealers and their customers invitingly from the street into the main trading area. The idea was admirable but the elevations which he produced were gauche, and by 1740 the merchant class of Bristol was becoming conscious of a new style of building in the country.

1 The apothecary William Gallaway began building, after 1750, eight houses on land which he had held since 1738. Wood seems to have approved their design and Gallaway's Buildings was 'new built' in 1753. Bladud Buildings, a plain handsome terrace with front and rear elevations of equal importance (rare in Bath) was begun in 1755 and designed possibly by Thomas Jelly very much to the Wood pattern.

2 Halfpenny's designs are preserved in Bristol Record Office: 1024 (1-16), 04713. Three of these designs are illustrated in Walter Ison, *The Georgian Buildings of Bristol*, 2nd ed. (1978), plate 15. Halfpenny's first draught for the Exchange which differs from those above mentioned was published in his *Perspective Made Easy* (1731), plate 26; Ison also illustrates this alternative proposal.

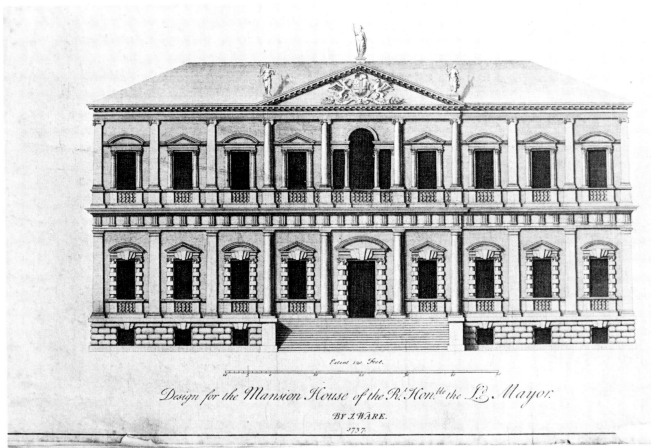

Design for the Mansion House of the R.ᵗ Hon.ᵇˡᵉ the L.ᵈ Mayor.

BY J. WARE.
1737.

Isaac Ware's 1735 design for the London Mansion House

The Council had an engraved plan of the rich and effortlessly correct Palladian design which Isaac Ware had produced in 1735 for a Mansion House for the City of London.[3] This had been rejected in favour of the design by the elder George Dance which was being built, complete with an 'Egyptian Hall', the ultimate cachet of Palladian high fashion, between 1739 and 1742. If London could reject a design of Isaac Ware's quality, Bristol could hardly settle for William Halfpenny's well-meaning but naive provincialism.

It was a councillor, William Jefferies, who had proposed to the Bristol Council in June 1735 that 'it would tend to the Honour and Grandness of this City if some convenient Mansion House were purchased',[4] so he may have been responsible for the presence of the Ware design in the city records and was obviously a man well informed on current architectural taste. That would explain why it was Mr Jefferies, along with a Mr Smith, whom the Council's Committee for the Exchange and Markets required on 19 December 1740 'to go to Bath to treat with Mr Allen or any other persons that will undertake the whole building of the Exchange'.[5]

3 Bristol Record Office, Plan Book B, f. 76. The engraving is dated 1737, a late date, and it may have been specially directed at Bristol by the disappointed architect when he heard of the council's quest for a Mansion House.
4 Quoted in John Latimer, *The Annals of Bristol in the 18th Century*, 1893, 191.
5 B.R.O., Minutes of the Committee for Building the Exchange and Markets, 19 December 1740.

150

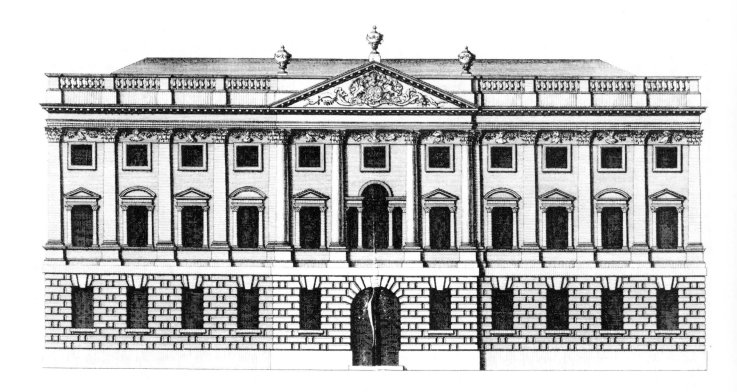

The ELEVATION of the EXCHANGE of BRISTOL, as it fronts North to Corn Street.

This committee had been sitting with no apparent sense of urgency since 1717, but in the autumn of 1740 someone or something had stirred its members into life. They had begun, rather clumsily, to try to contact George Dance through a third person and Dance was invited to visit the city at some time in 1741, but then the prospect of direction from Bath appeared suddenly to become much more attractive and Jefferies and Smith set off.

Considering the enduring rivalry between Bristol and Bath, and the far greater magnetism of the capital, it was not a predictable move; but within weeks all was settled. Dance's visit to Bristol was abruptly called off, John Wood was invited for an interview on 6 February 1741, 'given proper instructions' and asked 'to form designs'.[6] With suspicious efficiency Wood had his designs and his proposal before the committee by 13 February 1741.[7] This suggests that he had prepared them beforehand, probably soon after Jefferies and Smith had visited Ralph Allen in Bath during December. The designs and the proposal were accepted and, in the teeth of competition from Bristol and London, the job was his.

The reasons for Wood's success emerge from the committee's minutes and correspondence: a fascinating and revealing record of Wood's

Wood's design for the North Front of the Bristol Exchange

6 In *A Description of the Exchange of Bristol*, 1745, Wood claims (p. 9) that he attended on 4 February, but the minutes of the committee, usually a careful record, date the interview as 6 February 1741.

7 Ibid., 9.

151

The North Front of Bristol Exchange as built

character and working methods.[8] They must, however, be reviewed in the light of a volume presented to the library of the Royal Academy in 1789 by the Bath artist Prince Hoare. This is a detailed collection of drawings and documents related to the construction of the Bristol Exchange. From its general positive bias towards Wood and the presence of two letters addressed by the carver Thomas Paty to John Wood the younger, it was probably put together by the latter as an act of filial piety to the memory of the father he respected and admired. Certainly his father was in need of some defence from several contemporary Bristolians.

Trouble began for Wood as soon as the committee began to award contracts to the various craftsmen who had tendered for the work. Separate proposals had been printed and published for the three most important contracts: those for the rough masons, free masons and carpenters, which had to be decided quickly, and others for the lesser trades of plasterers, tilers, plumbers, painters and glaziers, which could wait until the

8 We are indebted to E. G. Priest's scholarly thesis 'Building the Exchange and Markets of Bristol' (Dept. of Architecture, University of Bristol, 2 vols., 1980) for our introduction to these. The only limitation of the study is that the author was not directed to the volume: *Bristol Exchange – Wood* in the Royal Academy Library (8516/51A).

building was well advanced.[9] The committee was in burning haste and the free masons' proposals had to be returned by 26 March 1741. The rough masons' contract had already been awarded on 5 March 1741, only five days before the mayor laid the foundation stone. This contract went, with predictable local patriotism, to George Walker, Nathaniel Daniel and William Foot junior, who were Bristol men. But on 3 April 1741 the committee accepted the tender for the free masonry of a Bath man, William Biggs and gave him the lucrative contract for the finer stonework.

Meanwhile Ralph Allen had agreed to deliver Bath stone at the 'Key' (quayside) at the highly competitive price of 11 shillings a ton. This meant that a Bath architect, a Bath stone merchant and a Bath mason had put a package deal together and presented the Bristol interests with competition which they could not hope to rival.[10] The respective tenders tell the tale plainly:

Biggs, a Bath man, had tendered £1,967.18s.9d.
Pitcher, another Bath man, £2,087.4s.6d.
Thomas Paty, a Bristolian, £2,312.16s.8d.
James Paty, a Bristolian, £2,655.16s.8d.
Ireson, from Wincanton, £2,788.17s.8d.[11]

Faced with these figures the committee had no option but to take Bigg's Bath workforce of free masons along with Allen's stone and Wood's design and direction. But the rough masons, working on the same site, were from Bristol and friction was inevitable.

This was not the end of the committee's errors. Wood was to be paid a five per cent commission, but he never gave the committee an estimate even though they began to ask for one on the day, 13 February, when he handed in his designs and proposal.[12] As if aware already that they were

9 The contracts were awarded as follows:
       Rough Masons: George Walker, Nathaniel Daniel, William Foot: 5 March 1741.
       Free Mason: William Biggs; 3 April 1741.
       Carpenters: Daniel Millard the younger, Samuel Jones, Samuel Glascodine;
       21 April 1741.
       Smith: Joshua Donne; 21 April 1741.
       Pennants and Paving: Daniel, Foot as above; 7 January 1742.
       Plasterers: Thomas North, John Griffin; 10 September 1742.
       Tilers and Plasterers: North, Griffin as above; 10 September 1742.
       Plumber: Thomas Hill; 10 September 1742.
       Painter: Daniel Morgan; 15 April 1743.
       Glazier: William Tilling; 15 April 1743.
10 Later, the clerk of works, Edward Foy, referred, in a letter to the committee (B.R.O.,
    01152, 55) of 14 May 1742, to 'The scheme projected for monopolizing the stone at
    Bath recommending surveyors and such workmen as will suit the intention ... I under-
    stand that his lordship our Bishop is drawn into the snare as likewise Mr Cozens'. The
    Bishop of Bristol may have used Ralph Allen in work on his palace which was destroyed
    in the Reform Riots. The Redland Chapel built for John Cossins by an unnamed ar-
    chitect (1740-3) is constructed of Bath stone on a Portland stone plinth, so it may be
    another result of this 'package'. For the building of Redland Chapel and the confusion
    over attribution see Ison, *Georgian Buildings of Bristol*, 54-61, and H. M. Colvin, *Biog-
    raphical Dictionary of British Architects 1600-1840* (1976), 378-9.
11 Figures derived from the back of the account book for the Exchange.
12 The committee minutes for 13 February 1741 record that Wood was asked to produce
    'calculation of the expense of putting his designs in execution with all speed'. No reply
    is recorded.

heading for trouble, the committee appointed as clerk of works, a Captain Edward Foy,[13] another Bristol man, whose qualification seems from the start to have been that he mistrusted and even despised Wood. The committee records are full of his vindictive letters as he worked behind Wood's back, taking the part of craftsmen on the site whenever they had a usable grievance.

Wood ignored Foy completely, addressing his letters in courteous and even relaxed style to the City Chamberlain. It would be easy to dismiss Foy as a malcontent and trouble-stirrer were it not for the resonant echoes which his letters evoke of that other compulsive letter writer 14 years before, Mrs Phillips, the landlady at St John's Hospital, who wrote so many bitter letters to the Duke of Chandos complaining of Wood's incompetence and his delays.[14] It does seem to have been part of Wood's nature to take pleasure in conflict with lesser mortals, but as he moved from the Bath frying pan into the Bristol fire at least Ralph Allen had made generous amends to him for his treachery over the Grand Parade and, at the same time, a profitable deal for Allen's quarries.

Edward Foy lost no time in declaring war. He was appointed clerk of works in March and on 3 April he was writing to the committee, before he had even seen Wood's designs, to describe his 'proposalls ... as mean and low, nay lower than ever I saw any', and begging the committee 'before it is to [sic] late ask advice of some man that is Judge of designs and work such as Lord Penbrook or Burlinton Mr James or Mr Gibbs now all in being and I am sure would be glad to give their opinion on it'.[15]

Fortunately for Wood and the honour of Bath it was the rough masons of Bristol who first revealed professional incompetence when an arch in the basement which they were constructing collapsed on 8 May 1741 because they were not working 'according to the proposals entered into by them'.[16] But by 27 November 1741 Foy was writing:

> I can never bow myself to think that exhibiting an impracticable draft of a building and prattling in terms of art and grand performance is the signature of an architect but the erecting of an aedifice in geometrical proportion and symetry whose compartition shall answer the intention, not of the artificer but of those who pays for the same. [17]

Clearly in the gallery of Wood's enemies Edward Foy was a choice specimen of wordy pomposity. In January 1742 he was reporting to the committee that 'the Freemasons told me Mr Wood never did nor would give any drafts'.[18] The committee then asked for 'proper drafts for the workmen to work by'.[19] In the Royal Academy volume there is a careful, large-scale drawing of the head of an arch in Wood's hand with his exact

13 Foy was an ex-army officer with no recorded previous experience of such work. He may have been related to a previous Mayor of Bristol.
14 See Chapter Two.
15 B.R.O. Bundle J 41(j).
16 Ibid., Committee Minutes.
17 Ibid., 01152, 30.
18 Ibid., 01152, 3.
19 Ibid., 01152, 4.

directions for building a basement and arcade to the south. This is dated 17 March 1742,[20] so Foy had won that round. Soon he was complaining: 'now it is too evident that the stone vendor, the surveyor and his free mason have all a right understanding with one another ... however seemingly they differ, the better to conceal the knot for their several profits'.[21]

While Foy was suggesting that he was in physical danger when he climbed about the Exchange site, Wood was writing to the Chamberlain in an oblique counterblast on 19 February 1742: 'the journeymen that are good hands had rather starve here [Bath] than go to Bristol again.[22] A few days before, on 12 February, Foy had attacked 'these prattling pretenders to architecture that have insinuated themselves up and down these kingdoms which is a growing evil'.[23] According to one of his tap-room spies, William Biggs had boasted 'to the workmen on Monday night last', as they were drinking together 'we will have the captain off too 'ere long'.[24]

Perhaps it was unwise of Biggs to drink in a Bristol pub but clearly he had got wind of a conspiracy. Foy had been appointed clerk of works in March 1741 on a salary, which never rose, of 15 shillings a week. On 20 July 1742 Wood was allowed by the committee to appoint his own clerk of works, a Bristolian and a respected figure, David Lewis, at a salary of a guinea a week, which has all the air of a snub to Foy. The hapless committee was now paying two clerks of work for a single building operation: one apparently to keep the peace and the other to disturb it.

By that July the committee must have begun to realize that they had a battle on their hands and that if Wood was a foe and a Bath man he was nevertheless a foe to whom some form of concession must be made. David Lewis must represent a peace gesture of some kind. The clash which may have brought the matter to a head and revealed to the committee the force of the opposition which they were facing is revealed in the Royal Academy volume where two separate documents have been set next to each other, f. 33 and f. 34, as if representing the younger Wood's despairing comment on the duplicitous truculence of his strong-willed father.

Both documents are dated 13 July 1742 by which time it would have been supposed that the exact design of the Exchange had long ago been settled, since the foundations had been dug a year and four months earlier. Apparently, however, a dispute was still raging with the elder Wood on one side and the entire city of Bristol, his patron and paymaster, on the other as to whether there should be a single storey of building crowned with a balustrade around three sides of the open court in the centre of the Exchange or two storeys for the display of a second order.

In his book *A Description of the Exchange of Bristol* which Wood published in 1745 to record his achievement as favourably as possible, he mentions that 'While the foundation was about it was debated in the Committee, Whether the Place of EXCHANGE should be built in the Manner of a large EGYPTIAN HALL, as I had DESIGN'D it? Or in the Manner of a small PERISTYLE, to comply with the OPINION of the Citizens in General, then startled with the Novelty of a Covered Place to meet in upon

20 R.A. Library, *Bristol Exchange – Wood*, f. 36.
21 B.R.O. 01152, 18.
22 Ibid., 01152, 14.
23 Ibid., 01152, 4.
24 Ibid.

Mercantile Affairs?'[25] Then, however, he deliberately states that he lost the debate at this early stage and obediently made new draughts conformable to the committee's decision to have an open court with a single order of columns and low surrounding buildings on every side except the north to Corn Street. This, he makes clear, was settled before the proposals for the rough masonry had to be returned on 5 March 1741, as was reasonable since an Egyptian Hall with its concomitant two storeys would have altered the costing.

The first document in the Academy scrapbook (f. 33) appears to square with this, though 13 July 1742 seems a very late date for its production. It is 'A section of the Inside of the Exchange from North to South delivered to the Committee this 13th of July 1742' and signed 'Jo. Wood'. The peristyle is shown as it was built, open and with a single order of columns. But the next document (f. 34) is a trenchant and handsomely printed broadsheet, bearing exactly the same date. This called boldly for two storeys around the court to permit the display of a second order. That would have allowed most of the basilican dignity of the lost Egyptian Hall while avoiding the engineering problems of a wide span roof. It was a deliberate attempt to put pressure on the committee men he was supposed to be serving by appealing over their heads, though to whom exactly he was appealing is not clear. It is direct and ingenious in its wording:

> If the inside of the EXCHANGE at Bristol should be finished with a Ballustrade upon the present Order of Columns, that Part of the Building will have all the Advantage possible of Light; but at the same Time it will be *Low, Mean* and entirely *without a Precedent* in any of the Squares or open Places of Antiquity.
>
> But if the inside of the EXCHANGE should be finished with a Second Order that Part of the Building will, I confess, be somewhat GLOOMY as to the Light; but then it will be *Elegant, Magnificent* and entirely *conformable to the Squares erected by the Greeks and Romans*, except in respect of Intercolumniations, and perhaps, to the Size of the Piazza, or open Area.

Two considerable reservations, one would have thought. There follows some of Wood's characteristic manipulation of scholarship to suit himself:

> I don't remember to have read that the Antients ever contrived to let the Sun into their open Places; but on the Contrary, the Grecians surrounded their Squares with double Portico's, to avoid the Rain, the Snow, and every Injury which Men might receive from the Air, or the Sun.

The broadsheet ends:

> Upon the Whole therefore, I submit it to the Consideration of the COMMITTEE for building the EXCHANGE in BRISTOL, *Whether the Inside of that Structure should be finished with a Ballustrade, or with a Second Order.*

25 Pages 11-12.

It must have been an irritating moment for the committee, but they stuck to their guns, kept the courtyard to a single storey colonnade and conceded only a second and milder clerk of works to soothe their disloyal architect. The root of the trouble was that Wood had a frustrated obsession with Egyptian Halls and their potential for a display of a second order. His was an intensely competitive nature. He knew that Lord Burlington had designed one: 'such a House I have, for some time had a view to building almost upon the same footing with the Assembly House at York'[26] and the Assembly Rooms which Wood proposed to build facing his *Royal Forum* in the middle of the South Parade might have had such a hall.[27] By 1742 the prospect of ever achieving either the Assembly Rooms or the *Royal Forum* was becoming faint, though the project was still alive in 1748. Wood must, therefore, have hoped to build, at the expense of Bristol Corporation, an unroofed basilica-style structure which would allow him to experiment with the display of a second order on a second storey. Hence his last-minute attempt to steamroller the committee into a change of heart.

On folio 36 of the Royal Academy volume is pasted Wood's design for this 'second order'. In fact it is nothing less than a more ambitious version of Palladio's illustration of an Egyptian Hall but without the roof.[28] Where Palladio, and Lord Burlington, had a relatively plain clerestory or

A Wood design for a Second Order for the Bristol Exchange

26 *Essay*, 'Part the Second', 1742, 51.
27 See Chapter Nine.
28 For Palladio's Egyptian Hall see *The Four Books of Architecture*, Dover Edition (1965), Second Book, Chapter X, plate 28.

second order of Corinthian pilasters with rectangular windows between, Wood proposed his favourite device of Venetian windows between each pair of pilasters.[29] These would have produced a much richer effect but they would have left the second order, set over the widely-spaced Corinthian pillars of the colonnade, looking top-heavy. By this time Wood was firmly committed to building 'with very wide Intercolumniations'[30] though his first design, whose groundplan he was to illustrate nostalgically in his book of the Exchange, had a closer intercolumniation nearer to Palladio's ideal. In his published writings Wood rarely refers to Palladio, as if he wished to distance himself from the enthusiasm of the fashionable Burlingtonians, but in the Royal Academy documents (f. 4) there is a scrap of paper in Wood's handwriting where he quotes Palladio on Roman and Greek squares. Two pages later, on f.6, there are rough sketches and dimensions of the Royal Exchange at London indicating how competitive he was in his planning. Later there is a groundplan of the aisled and roofed Exchange at Manchester as another suggestion as to how his mind was working.[31] Whether Wood had the technical skill to roof a very wide space is doubtful, and even unroofed, a court with a 'second order' would have been as he admitted, gloomy.

No sign of all these tensions between architect and committee is manifested in Wood's correspondence with the City Chamberlain. Wood simply ignores Edward Foy apart from the one reference to his journeymen preferring starvation to Bristol. What does emerge from these otherwise brief letters is the deplorable state of Wood's health. Always a valetudinarian, he now gives the impression of being at death's door, though never too ill to make a sly point in favour of a cherished scheme. On 14 August 1741, he wrote: 'I intended to be at Bristol today; but as the Clouds seem to gather for Rain must put off my Journey till tomorrow, against which time I must advise Mr Bigg to get the Work in the Hall [he means the courtyard but still significantly refers to as if covered] set out. I woul'd submit it to the Consideration of the Committee whether it will not be too warm in Summer, & too Cold in Winter under Porticos without Rooms over them'.[32] So he was already preparing for another round of the fight. Sometimes, with excuses like: 'If the Weather had continued as it was yesterday I shou'd have attended the Committee this Evening' he reads like some sniggering Jonsonian rogue, a Volpone side-spying his frustrated dupes from the quilts of his bed.[33] At a later date he, who never gave the committee an estimate despite years of pleading, is himself dunning Willoughby, the Chamberlain, for £250 on account, a substantial sum in those days, so that he can lend it to 'Mrs Hopley ... a single young Woman ... this money I have lent her by Mr Triggs desire ... I am in Bed & I find myself something better than I have been, the moment its safe for me to stir out I will make you a Visit'.[34] The loan would, of course, bring Wood interest.

29 For Burlington's Assembly Rooms at York see R. Wittkower, *Palladio and English Palladianism*, 1974, chapter 9: 'Lord Burlington's Work at York'.
30 *Description of the Exchange*, 12.
31 *Bristol Exchange – Wood*, f. 52: 'Plan of Exchange at Manchester Dec. 16th 1743' – by its date far too late to have influenced the course of the building.
32 B.R.O. 01152, 15.
33 Ibid., 01152, 42.
34 Ibid., 01152, 45.

Finally, on 30 March 1743, he writes:

> These few days of Severe Weather have almost demolished me
> [did the sorely tried Willoughby raise a secret cheer at that point?] I
> can neither Eat nor Sleep, & last night I had a Kind of Cramp in
> my Leggs I never felt before: My Asthma however is come to its
> Crisis, which makes me hope to be able to Ride tomorrow.[35]

After letters like these it is hard to avoid the suspicion that Wood was consciously playing a game. The city of Bristol has joined the file of Wood's enranged clients: Chandos, William Brydges, the Bishop of Llandaff, Francis Yerbury who denied Wood his Monopterick temple, Jerry Peirce whose house twice went on fire, Ralph Allen who abruptly disengaged himself; it cannot all have been bad luck. And yet the man, left to his own devices, projected a revived city into being, and here in Bristol was giving the citizens their first correct and classical building. What rain clouds and tempests seem never to have diminished was his appetite for having his own way at his own time.

As if to complete the image of eccentric detachment, this is the first correspondence in which Wood used, on 28 March 1741, his self-awarded coat of arms as a gentleman of the 'ancient *Britons*' to seal his letters. Gone is the classical head which sealed his wax before 1730, and gone the rebus of a tree which he began to employ in October 1730.[36] Now his device, which he also flourished on a larger scale as a book plate, is a shield of rich druidic symbolism. The Druids, according to Wood's etymology, were the 'Oak Men' of Akemancaester, the oak men's town. Acordingly the shield has oak trees, complete with acorns, on a mound quartered with the crescent moons of Onca, his Goddess of the Night, set about a chevron or surveyor's set square.[37] The shield has a rococo trim and is crested by the impressive figure of a naked man, bearded and holding in his left hand a spiked club, in his right an oak bough with acorns. The motto is the lordly DIRUIT, AEDIFICAT but that was not included on his seal which was as well, for the poor Chamberlain had received nothing in the string of letters but evasions and excuses, anything but directions.

In fairness, however, it needs to be said that, if Wood was reluctant to attend the committee meetings, the pages of the Royal Academy volume do emphatically refute Foy's attacks on Wood's actual competence as a designer and director. Wood may not often have supervised construction personally but, when it was necessary he sent exact, often beautifully detailed, working drawings and instructions. For instance, f. 37 and f. 38 are careful drawings of the rafters and roof slope over the porticos of the Exchange, with an elegant and precisely drawn urn to be set on the balustrade. Beside these Wood has scribbled: 'will require twenty good Carpenters to frame & put it up in one time, therefore I do order and direct that twenty Carpenters be instantly employed on the said Roof & that they loose no time. I do also direct that other Carpenters be employ'd upon the Partitions & other work of the Exchange'. Whatever objections may be

35 Ibid., 01152, 66.
36 Both were used on his letters in the Tyberton correspondence; see Chapter Four.
37 For Wood's interest in Onca see the *Essay*, Chapter II in part two: 'Of the GODS, PLACES of WORSHIP, RELIGION and LEARNING of the antient *Britons*'.

DIRUIT, ÆDIFICAT

John Wood

The unofficial coat of arms which Wood designed for himself to use as a bookplate;
the devices relate to the Woodes of Harestone and the Withers of Manydown

raised against the expenditure on the Exchange (it was to cost, including the value of the land, £56,352[38]) there could be no complaint either about Wood's tone of direction or the pace of the work. It was complete and ready for a ceremonial opening on 21 September 1743; a mere two and a half years for a major undertaking on a crowded inner city site. Wood did not have direct control over the subcontractors but he, together with his ill-yoked clerks of work, seems to have led the team efficiently.

In his *Description of the Exchange* Wood records the celebrations of the opening – the processions, the release of minor debtors, the free beer, bells, guns and bonfires – with a certain ironic detachment. 'What PAGEANTRY', he asks sarcastically, 'could illustrate a SOLEMN PROCESSION of the MAGISTRATES and whole COLLECTIVE TRADING BODY of a CITY, that pays the Government a Custom for their Goods of above One Hundred and Fifty Thousand Pounds a Year?'[39] His tone might have been more mellow if there had been any mention of his own name in the self-congratulatory speeches that were made. The Steward of the Sheriff's court, Mr Stevens, did speak of 'this noble pile' and 'the greatness of the design'[40] but John Wood's name was not mentioned. Perhaps they thought that his percentage fee, £833, was reward enough. Over the period it works out as ten times the earnings of a building craftsman.

As usual, authority had not reckoned on Wood's own defiant talent for self-advertisement. Given a prime position in the Royal Academy documents, and another sign that the collection was originally made by Wood's family, is yet another printed broadsheet which has survived here and nowhere else.

It is a vainglorious but wholly delightful composition, a poem entitled *Address'd to Sir Abraham Elton Bt. Mayor and the Corporation*. By this, John Wood the elder must be enrolled among the army of 18th century manipulators of the heroic couplet, for he had often shown himself an admirer of Pope and even loaned the poet his favourite journeyman, Thomas Omer, for a brief consultation on grottoes. In the following lines he contrived to say everything which the civic dignitaries should have said but did not:

> See, see, at length the finish'd Structure rise
> A Structure that with Gresham's Labours vies!
> A stately Pile by publick Spirit plann'd
> Politely finish'd – regularly Grand
> With striking Beauties how it charms our Eyes!
> A Roman Structure gracing British Skies!
> Each Beauty blended in a fine Design
> Such art Palladio – and such Jones – was thine!
> And such is Wood's – who rear-d this spacious Dome
> A finished Wonder for each Age to come ...[41]

38 Gordon Priest, Exchange thesis, 233. Incidentally even Thomas Omer was rewarded. He was paid seven guineas on 28 November 1741 'for drawing a draft and attending'. Wood usually managed to look after Omer in most of his projects.
39 *Description of the Exchange*, 36. It is, of course, possible that Wood intended this seriously.
40 Quoted in Priest, Exchange thesis, vol. 1, 137.
41 *Bristol Exchange – Wood*, f. 1.

It concludes with loyal, if irrelevant, compliments to George II and 'Duke William' (Butcher Cumberland) for their military prowess, promising both, vainly, a statue on the north front of the Exchange. One is irresistibly reminded of the song which Mr Toad proposed to sing to celebrate the recapture of Toad Hall from the Weasels in *Wind in the Willows*, but in fact the verse only claims what is true and what few contemporaries were generous enough to allow. One sheet of the Royal Academy book actually has a ghostly dome and cupola pencilled in by Wood over a finished drawing of the north front,[42] and the sequence of Palladio, Inigo Jones and Wood is exactly what the architect is likely to have stressed, ignoring completely the rival group of Burlington, Campbell and Kent.

If Wood felt the need at this time to sound a note of defiant triumph, the sense of injury must have come from the conflict with Edward Foy and the embattled masons of Bristol. Long after the Exchange was complete the Bristol rough masons were accusing Wood of spitefully underrating their payments because

> Your Worships may Remember you once desired us to Examine Mr Wood's Draught and make remarks thereon which we did and Divers Necessary Alterations was made. Which we humble presume is the cause of his thus using us. Mr Wood did not serve his own friends so for they were paid to their own satisfaction.[43]

So ill feelings endured and it is noticeable that while the Mayor, Sir Abraham Elton, David Lewis and Thomas Paty subscribed to Wood's commemorative volume, Ralph Allen did not, neither did William Biggs nor certainly did Edward Foy!

There remains the quality of Wood's achieved design. Essentially its main north elevation to Corn Street is a palace front concealing a tavern on the right and a coffee house on the left. Both could have been built more cheaply but that was not the point. Business deals proceed easily with the help of alcohol, warm drinks and good food; haggling in open courtyards is for lesser fry, so in that sense the north front was functional, unlike Halfpenny's naive open-ended entrances. If a tavern and a coffee house can suggest that affairs of weight and consequence are proceeding behind their walls, then it is the function of the architect who designs them to suggest it. Wood appreciated this and gave his Bristol clients full value for their money with a stimulating and thoroughly pretentious elevation.

It is not profitable to discuss whether Wood had seen the drawing in Lord Burlington's collection of a Palladio design for the Iseppo di Porto palace at Vicenza. If Wood had not, then Campbell certainly had, and Wood knew Campbell's work.[44] He would also, from his acquaintance with Jefferies, have seen the Council's engraving of Isaac Ware's Mansion

---

42 Folio 18.
43 Committee minutes, letter of 6 September 1745.
44 The relevance of this drawing is discussed by Mike Jenner in *Bristol: an architectural history*, eds. A. Gomme, M. Jenner & Bryan Little (Bristol, 1979), 143-8. There is some similarity between the handling of the north elevation and that unexecuted design which Campbell drew for the east side of Grosvenor Square. Neither that nor Burlington's Iseppo di Porto façade had a pediment so the likeness need not be pressed too hard.

House, which has a Venetian window closely set between the central columns of a tetrastyle portico. He was to design a very similar feature for the Exchange.

Bristol Exchange – detail of the carving executed by Thomas Paty

But the elevation which must be considered most relevant is the north side of Wood's own Queen Square. Higher than the north side and shorter, 11 bays as opposed to 23, the Exchange crams in all of the north side's Corinthian detail and much more besides in a blowsy bucolic free-for-all that still cleverly manages to be 'correct' in the Palladian sense. Its rusticated ground floor is heavy but its pediment, cornice, capitals and frieze of heads and garlands are even heavier. And all between them the windows are packed in between the pilasters and three-quarter columns with enrichment to every appropriate moulding. There are three separate enrichments to the architraves of the first-floor windows alone and the sinuous waterleaf is everywhere prominent. The effect is disturbing and remote from the usual Palladian calm. Yet because the forward break of the three central bays and the tetrastyle centrepiece is so slight, the impression is two-dimensional, restless but never moving. The overall spirit is that of a cheerful West Country baroque. Turks' heads, elephants, camels, rum barrels, bales and pineapples riot symbolically in the ornamental zone between the capitals, but there is no baroque projection of parts and the front is thoroughly Palladian in its lack of containment at the corners. The design simply ends without extra punctuation. It is Palladian

163

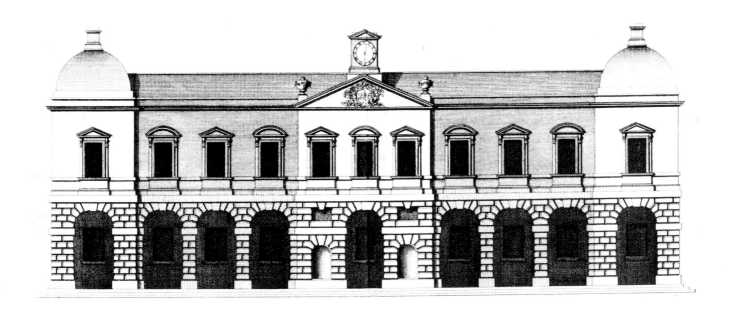

The ELEVATION of the EXCHANGE of BRISTOL, as it fronts South to the General Market.

Wood's design for the South Front of the Bristol Exchange to face the markets

too in its two-dimensional failure to turn a corner. A different elevation just begins, as if for another building. The north side of Queen Square, though far more relaxed, is also more baroque in its containment within taller three-bay end pavilions, though there again the corners are switched rather than turned.

If it can be summed up, the main front of the Exchange is characterized by a cheerful but unsophisticated richness. It represents Palladianism applied to a town palazzo, making its impact obliquely in a narrow street, and as such its works admirably. What Wood learnt from this and from the interior court was the value of symbolic carving in high relief. The foolish gaping masks and gourd garlands that ring the court are a cliché, but the groups in the three tympana representing Asia, Africa and America are quite unclassical and closer to a lively folk art.[45] Penguins hold fish, crocodiles gape, gryphons gambol near camels: all the detail communicates meaning and interest, in anticipation of the even richer work at Liverpool and of the extraordinary Doric frieze which was to enliven the King's Circus.

The south elevation of the Exchange might belong to another building. It is leggy on its stilted arcading, but calm and satisfying like the stables to a great house. The court behind it has been roofed in and has lost thereby some of the richest receding vistas of balustrade above balustrade above columns that Wood ever designed. De-roofed once more and animated with stalls it could still be one of the treasures of Bristol.

The success of the Bristol Exchange is proven by Liverpool's desire to equal it and Wood's own confidence is shown by the firmer rhythms of his

45 Thomas Paty was responsible for the design of these; several of his drawings are preserved in the Royal Academy volume.

164

northern essay. Much is made of the part played by a Liverpudlian lady, Sarah Clayton, in recommending Wood for the Liverpool commission.[46] The truth is that the two cities were conscious rivals for the Atlantic trade and the Lancashire merchants would be excelled in nothing by their rivals of Bristol. They needed the prestige of a Wood design so badly that they were prepared to accept his son as the presiding architect on the site and to make both father and son freemen of the borough before a stone had been laid. Wood's pleasure in the honour can be imagined and he repaid the port of Liverpool with a design of robust character.

This Exchange, now the Town Hall, has been unfortunate in both its history and its surroundings. On Sunday 24 July 1795, only eight years after extensive alterations by the local architect John Foster and by James Wyatt to Wood's original fabric, the entire interior was gutted and all the relevant records were lost. As it was originally built, the Exchange was not free-standing as now, so only the south and the east elevations are to Wood's design. When parasitical buildings were pulled down in 1787 a west elevation was built to match the original one on the east side. To the north, Wood's building adjoins the lavishly-scaled and appointed Mansion House designed by James Wyatt. In 1802 the south or entrance front was given a hexastyle Corinthian portico. A steeply-pitched dome on a high drum was constructed to take the place of the 'massy dome covered with lead'[47] and the light turret of Wood's design which had collapsed in the fire of 1795. Only the elevation to the east survives in more or less the condition which Wood intended, and even here the three central arches of the ground floor should be open to give access to the interior court which was intended to be the heart of the Exchange.

When it came to the design of interior courtyards Wood was not fortunate. That in the centre of the Bristol Exchange was built open, and single storeyed on three sides, much against his wishes. At Liverpool, with a much smaller interior court, he had his chance of an Egyptian Hall again but this seems not to have been considered. Instead he was allowed to build his 'second order'. The courtyard or piazza was surrounded by a covered walk supported on coupled Doric columns. These were without bases, an interesting point as it suggests that perhaps John Wood the younger was edging his father's design towards neo-Classicism. This ground floor was intended for mercantile transactions. Above the walk was a second order of Corinthian columns, almost free-standing, and between these were arched windows with Corinthian pilasters and balustraded bases. If he was not allowed an Egyptian Hall at least Wood was able to develop his drawing on folio 36 of the Royal Academy volume and display a second order. The next step would be the King's Circus where all

46 For discussion of Sarah Clayton's letter see Chapter Four, note 1 of this study. She was inaccurate in saying that Wood 'planned Mr Ward's house at Capesthorne' where he may have advised on the setting up of some rooms much as he did at Tyberton, but her enthusiastic recommendation of Wood: 'except Lord Burlington, there was no person in England that had a juster and better taste in architecture' will have confirmed Liverpool's Corporation in their move to employ him. Capesthorne Hall was rebuilt by Francis Smith in 1732-3; see A. H. & S. M. Gomme, 'Who Designed Capesthorne Hall?' in *Trans. Historic Soc. of Lancs. & Cheshire*, cxxi (1969).
47 From a description of the building by Enfield (*c.* 1769) quoted by J. A. Picton, *Memorials of Liverpool*, 2 vols., 1875, 2, 30.

Liverpool Exchange (now Town Hall) – the East Front which remains closest to Wood's original conception

three orders would be displayed, and it is to be hoped that Wood's health permitted him a second journey to Liverpool to see the courtyard when it was built.

Enfield wrote in 1769 that 'the area is so small as to have somewhat the appearance of a well, and to give a gloomy cast to the walks that surround it'. He also described as 'a redundancy of childish ornament' the carving above the arched window.[48] That was evidently in the style of the

48 Ibid., 29.

166

carving which still enlivens the zone between the capitals of the east and south fronts: naive and vigorous work, symbolic of the city's trade links. Enfield was speaking in the thin fastidious tones of a classical purist.

Detail of the frieze on the Liverpool Exchange

It is remarkable how aptly Wood was able to respond to the harsher climate of the north-west. Even in its present state, altered and overshadowed by much taller buildings, the Exchange-Town Hall has a sturdy masculinity of design, an air of confrontation, where Bristol Exchange has only one of luxury and display.

Where the east and south elevations meet, Wood has modified his earlier Palladian façadism with an almost baroque element of containment. On the east front, the three-quarter Corinthian columns of the hexastyle central portico are organised in the system of 2-1-1-2 and the punctuation of the coupled columns is emphasised by pilasters linked to them on the recessed wings. The pilasters are coupled at the corners of the elevation. Thus, if they do not positively turn a corner to the next elevation, then they certainly acknowledge that a corner is there to be turned; the elevation is not sliced off as at Bristol. Without supporting wings, the building stands tense and self-contained. The baroque note of the coupled columns is heightened by the predominant round-arched rhythms of the loggia and the first floor windows, but the correct Corinthian entablature leaves the remainder of the elevation oddly unfulfilled, lacking the low dome which Wood designed over the entrance.

167

In the garland above the attic windows the animation of Bristol has been repeated and excelled. There is a surge of sea symbolism on John Foster's front towards the Mersey with cherubs on sea-horses, anchors addorsed and Neptune himself. Elsewhere the Indians in feathered head-dresses, the llamas and American beasts are carved with sharp fidelity, by French prisoners according to local legend. The taste of the younger John Wood, who took a house in Liverpool to supervise the construction, is evident in the absence of enrichment on the standard profiles. Though the order is Corinthian, the Exchange is so masculine in feeling that these are not missed. The building was completed in 1754.

These then are the two substantial works of the decade which, on their evidence, saw Wood in his active prime, responding to the challenges which his native city so often refused to offer him. When the two exchanges are set against the dim elevations of his General Hospital in Bath it can be seen what the country as a whole lost by his provincial confinement and what might have been achieved if he had not been kept, from 1740 to 1753, like a Somerset Achilles sulking in his tent.[49]

49 Between 1740 and 1753, apart from the continuing work on the four streets of the Parades quadrangle and the two Exchanges, Wood was active in the following:
    1742 Set up a subscription for the Chippenham canal scheme which failed.
    1742 Completed a design at the request of the Corporation for King Edward VI's School in Bath. This was not built, Thomas Jelly's design being preferred and built in 1752.
    1746 Designed a Spaw building for Bathford which may have been built.
    1748 Designed and supervised the building of Titanbarrow Logia.
    1748 Projected at Nash's urging a scheme for an Assembly House and basement theatre on the South Parade; not built.

Chapter Eleven

Father and Son
The Records of Partnership

It was the increasing frailty of his health which must have led Wood to accept defeat on the Parades tamely and to cut back his commitment to work in the city. One result of this was that he began to develop with his eldest son John the kind of creative partnership in architectural design which he had always needed, but from which his temperament had previously precluded him. Without this productive period of training and exchange, 1740-54, neither the King's Circus nor the Royal Crescent, Wood's crowning achievements, could ever have been built.

After the frustrations of early summer 1740, Wood took up his fieldwork of research into prehistoric stone circles with a new seriousness. An old supporter of his London days, the Earl of Oxford, was in Bath and Wood spent two days, 6 August and 7 August, interesting him and Lord Duplin in his recent visit to Stonehenge. The Earl commissioned a fuller report and at Michaelmas, Wood paid a second visit, via Avebury, to Stonehenge where he made a careful survey of the monument. In the second of two long letters or reports which he sent the Earl, on 11 December and 15 December,[1] later published in an extended form in 1747 as *Choir Gaure vulgarly called Stonehenge, Described, Restored and Explained*, he mentioned with obvious pride the help he had received from 'my eldest Son ... in this his first practical Lesson of Surveying'.[2] The precarious state of his health appeared in his mention of making another visit 'in the Spring when the Days grow long and warm; as little Excursions and Exercise of this Nature are necessary for my Health, under my Asthmatical Disorder'.[3] A 'little smoky Hut in the Body of the Ruins' belonging to a Gaffer Hunt had caused Wood considerable distress when he used it as a temporary refuge and office, 'as I want Breath to rise from my Chair when I am once settled in it'.[4]

The Corporation minutes of Bristol reveal that bad health often kept Wood away from meetings of the committee overseeing the construction, 1741-3, of the new Exchange;[5] and the complaints of the workmen, including one that Wood was proposing to rest the jamb of a chimney in the coffee house on a girder, emphasise the architect's need for a painstaking and practical assistant to shield him from Lilliput Castle-style errors of design. In 1740 the younger John Wood was barely 13. It is apparent, from the fact that he deputised for his father in Liverpool from 1749 to 1753, and successfully continued the King's Circus which had hardly begun

1 British Museum, Add. MS. 7354, 7355.
2 *Choir Gaure* (Oxford, 1747), 49. This was the year when the younger Wood matriculated at University College, Oxford: he never took a degree.
3 Ibid., 33.
4 Ibid., 32.
5 See Chapter Ten.

when his father died in May 1754, that the two worked well together. The building of the Royal Crescent (1767-75), a work projected by the elder Wood as from the grave, was to be a striking proof of the son's fidelity to even the most ambitious and testing of his father's schemes.

The most valuable and revealing evidence of their interaction of respective aesthetics is preserved in the 84 'Wood' drawings which have been collected together in one fascinating, if disjointed, volume in the Bath Reference Library. Most of these drawings have writing on them: directions for workers, captions to rooms or detailed figures in ink and pencil giving directions, but none of them are signed. Fortunately ample specimens of the writing of both men exist to identify their very distinctive hands. In addition the drawings themselves, with the exception of a number of designs related to Prior Park which seem to have been handled by an outsider preparing them for publication in the 1749 *Essay*, are all executed in the sharply contrasted draughtmanship of either the father or the son.

Wood the elder drew with delicate fine lines undifferentiated from each other whether he was delineating outside walls or the slightest subsections of an order. His son used a system of contrasting thick and thin lines which varied from drawing to drawing but was always consistent within any one plan or elevation. For instance, on f. 9, a basement plan for Buckland House, Berkshire, the vertical lines on the right-hand side are thick for the external wall, thin for the internal. Two sides of any rectangular figure are consistently thickened on their top horizontal and left-hand vertical, producing a subtle perspective effect as of light falling. He also, unlike his father, often shaded in shadows cast by projecting elements of a building.

Such shadows are also a characteristic effect achieved by hatching in the engravings made by P. Fourdrinier to illustrate the 1749 edition of Wood's *Essay*. The set of Prior Park drawings which combine the fine lines of the father with the shading of the son, drawings such as the main front to the north, or the westward offices to the south, are all drawn on a much smaller size of paper. These may be specialized drawings on which both men were co-operating to prepare them for Fourdrinier to use as models. Not all these scaled-down drawings were published; the uncouth south front was wisely withheld. As a mark of the elder Wood's enduring memory of the slights inflicted on him by Ralph Allen, on f. 48, the dodecahedral site plan of Allen's house has the words 'Capital Seat' crossed out and 'House and offices' inserted above. Elevations of the house are captioned 'As it was first designed' to distance Wood from the work, but the basement, which he actually built, is captioned 'As it was built AD MDCCXXXVII'.

Criticism has been expressed in an earlier chapter of the east end of Prior Park as it was finally built. Folio 55 proves that this disconnected design was actually Wood's responsibility and not that of Richard Jones, that he prepared it as an illustration for the *Essay* but never used it. One sign, however, of his own dissatisfaction with the Corinthian entablature that sits so uneasily on this elevation is f. 29, an alternative design for the same front which he even had shaded as if for publication. The ground and first floors of this elevation are as built, but in addition it features a plain but

170

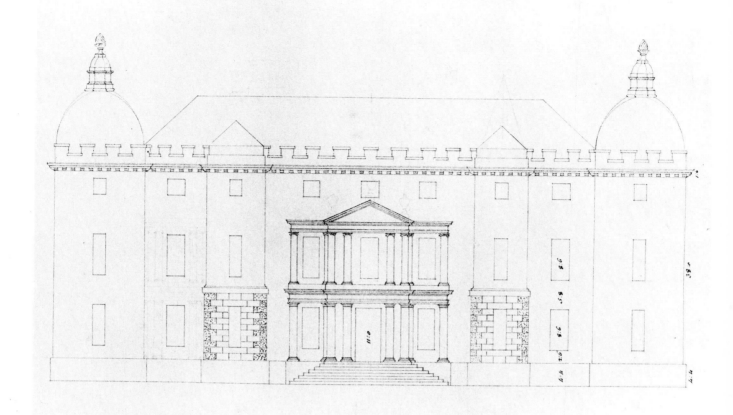

A villa in the castle style from
the volume of Wood drawings in
Bath Reference Library

top-heavy attic floor, with urns to punctuate the breaks on the roof line.

These are all footnotes to past events, along with the drawings for Lilliput Castle and Titanbarrow which have been discussed previously. The real significance of the volume lies in the drawings where father and son have commented on each other's designs either by alternative schemes or by pencilled additions. These suggest that the relatively blank years from 1740 onwards were not idle by intention, but times when the two Woods were often putting forward serious plans for several major country house projects.[6]

Perhaps the most remarkable of them is that covered by the sequence ff. 67-74: eight drawings which proved that on paper the two Woods had anticipated by a comfortable margin Robert Adam's castle-style designs of 1763 and after. They include alternative groundplans and alternative elevations for three of the four fronts of an existing irregular towered house, one probably of Elizabethan or Jacobean origin. A directional note on f. 69 states that the east front was 375 feet 'From the River' so the drawings

6 Folio 60 is for a house to be built in Phoenix Park, Dublin (later Viceregal Lodge), for the Ranger Mr Clements, an official in the Irish Treasury, so the Woods were casting their net widely. Folios 33 and 34 are alternative schemes for a church, the first by the father, the second, much more sober and neo-Classical, by the son. These were probably designed for the proprietary chapel on the *Royal Forum* which Wood was still hoping to build in 1749 (see *Essay*, 441).

171

may relate to the old house at Kelston, four miles down-stream from Bath, dilapidated at that time and one which the prospective owner, Sir Caesar Hawkins, is known to have been thinking of rebuilding in the 1750s.[7] Wood believed that it had been originally designed by Vignola himself for Sir John Harington so he is likely to have wanted to improve upon rather than replace what he thought was a design by an Italian and a Renaissance master. That would explain why he made this rare excursion into castellated Gothick on a scale to rival Inveraray Castle.[8]

The entrance front to the north exercised the elder Wood's imagination most acutely and there are two alternative schemes for this in the drawings. Both boldly emphasize the existing four towers with pineapple finials to the domes on the outer projecting pair and pyramidal tops to the two inner turrets. In each scheme the classical element is given another theatrical emphasis with a columned, double-decker three-bay portico at the central doorway. One scheme throws in additional columns to enliven the other recessions of the front. There is no attempt to apologize for or underplay the clash of styles, a castellated parapet with a dentil cornice below it neatly restates the stimulating union, and the whole effect would have been wildly picturesque yet symmetrical if it could only have been realized. The elder Wood's south front is milder as it has fewer projecting units to cope with. Its towers still have their flourish of pineapple finials and the 11 bays are handled with a fenestration pattern 1 round, 3 square, 3 round, 3 square, 1 round. This is the front for which the younger Wood offers a far more severe and restrained design. His towers have domes with only chimney pedestals on their tops and none of his windows are allowed the frivolity of round-arched heads. The generation gap between the two designs is almost as dramatic as the house itself. Though tutored by a strong-willed father the son obviously has absorbed a neo-Classical morality of austere self-discipline.

This engaging series of drawings is preceded by another one, equally revealing though lesser in shape. In these – ff. 61, 62, 63, 65 and 66 – the Woods may even have been playing a family game to see who could out-point the other in creating the most bizarre design for a medium-sized country house. It is not easy to imagine any of these designs being offered to a serious client but it could be that they were created when the views from the 'Mount of Earth' above the Vineyards in Bath almost 'seduced' Wood 'into a very great Expence, by erecting a House, in a military Taste, upon it'.[9] Any of these designs, if they had ever been followed, would certainly have been considered a rank betrayal of the classical spirit of the new city, but we have Wood's printed word as testimony that he would personally have enjoyed living in such a Gothic rather than classical house – a paradoxical revelation.

The statement appears in the 1742 edition of the *Essay* when the younger Wood was still only 15 and the latter's design f. 61 is quite crude

7 Hawkins had been trying to purchase the seat of the Haringtons since 1751; the property was finally conveyed to him in 1759 and demolition of the manor, witnessed by Pococke, began in 1764. A new mansion was then built on a different site, further east on a bluff overlooking the Avon. This has been attributed (by Pevsner) to the younger Wood without documentary evidence.

8 Built by Roger Morris for the 3rd Duke of Argyll, 1745-60.

9 *Essay*, 257.

172

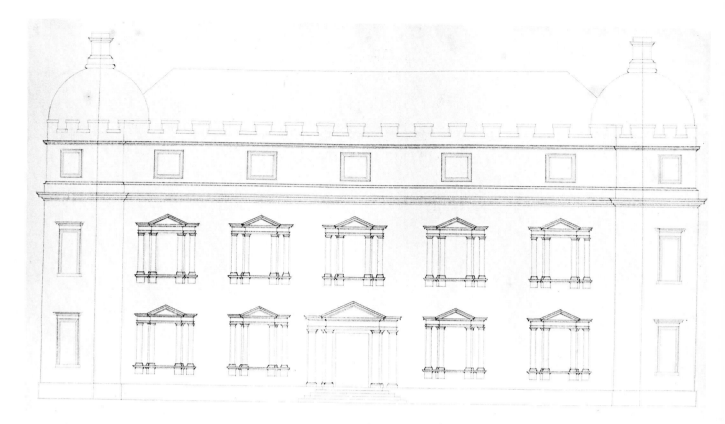

A castle style villa with tripartite windows from Wood's drawings

enough in conception for 'Schoolboy Gothick' – a five-bay barn with a castellated parapet – even less inspired than the Gothick castle of Tregenna which he was to build in 1773-4 for Samuel Stephens outside St Ives, Cornwall. As if spurred on to emulate this disaster, the next drawing, f. 62 by the elder Wood, is even more impossible. He has added corner turrets to f. 61, making it seven bays, retained the castellated parapet, given it a tripartite classical central porch and then, in an orgy of the incorrect, repeated the porch nine times across the nightmare elevation in the form of tripartite windows. Folio 63 is more sober, but the strangest of all this collection, and indeed of the 84 drawings in the whole volume, is f. 66 with its groundplan of f. 65 proving that the concept was being visualized seriously. Folios 61, 63 and 66 could all be elevations for the same experimental house but f. 66 can only be described as Artisan Mannerist. It would not be completely out of place as an effort of late Victorian historicism and it is not possible to fit it rationally into any known episode of 18th century revivalism. Its windows are mullioned and transomed and shown again as such on f. 65, the groundplan. The only explanation must be that Wood was drawing a survey of a real but lost 17th century house.

One of the great virtues of the 84 drawings is their ability to surprise by revealing talents and interests which would never otherwise have been credited to the elder architect. Perversely he seems to have reacted to the automatic austerity of his son's designs by exploring more richly and daringly than he had before. The last drawings in the volume, for three, or possibly only two, very grand, five-bay villas with tetrastyle porticos, show that in these last years he was moving deliberately from his fixation with a

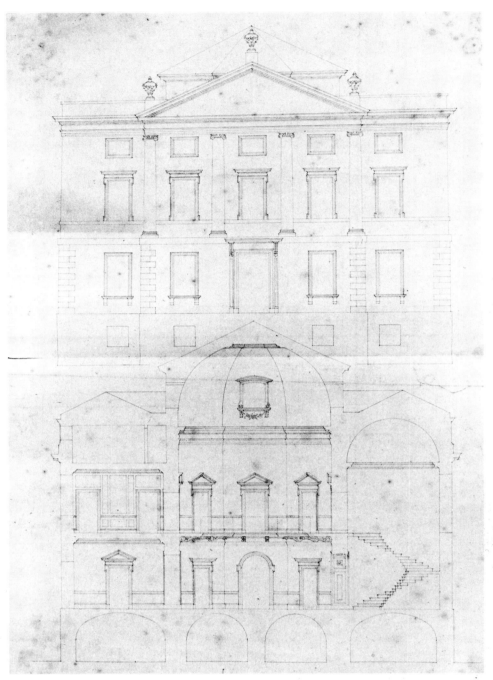

A Taylorian villa drawn by Wood

pyramidally topped box towards the suavity of Robert Taylor's designs of the 1750s. Folios 76 and 77 represent the first stage: a reserved fastidious Corinthian block with a low, perfectly acceptable, pyramidal roof. Then after the bridge designs, ff. 79 and 80, which suggest how imperial his *Royal Forum* would have been if Allen had only supported him, we turn to the sequence of ground and floor plans with elevations: ff. 81-84. There are probably two variant elevations here to the same house, f. 83 Ionic and f. 84 Corinthian, but it is just possible that f. 83 was intended as the main front and f. 84 as an elevation to the garden at the rear.

174

A first reaction on seeing these last drawings is that they must be by the younger Wood because they mark such a forward leap in style. The plan of the principal floor has a much more sophisticated sequence of rooms than any which the elder Wood ever built. The vestibule leads into a wide octagonal space reaching up the whole height of the house within the crowning eight-sided pyramid. A sectional view shows what vistas its galleries would have commanded. Then, continuing axially beyond this, a stair cantilevered boldly out of the wall spirals up to the top floor. An airy lightness pervades the whole interior yet the drawing hand and all the writing on the room plans are definitely those of the elder Wood, and the wonderfully rich Corinthian elevation, f. 84, has an absent-minded quality about it which suggests the characteristic inconsequentiality of his design: the front door, if it is a front door, leads out into thin air with no means of access.

These designs end the volume appropriately, because in them the younger Wood has clearly influenced his father to follow the fashionable innovations of the early 1750s, risking their structural difficulties because of his own youthful self-confidence at being able to handle them. The elder Wood has not, however, succumbed to the arid geometrical refinements of his son but preserved his own favourite surface enrichments and correct display of the orders with their ornaments. It is a true union of talents across the generations and, as with the four-towered classical castle displayed on ff. 67-74, the regret must be that a patron was never found to finance their realization in stone.

After these palaces of only paper possibility there remain two real houses to be credited to the elder Wood which are not normally included in his canon. The first is not from the volume and has left neither design nor documentation, only the firmest possible stylistic attribution and some support from local hearsay. It is that façade (some panelled rooms have travelled with it) which since 1936 has looked out over steep, green parkland from the end of Sion Hill Place, Bath. The travel agency millionaire Thomas Cook had it rebuilt there to extend his previous end-of-terrace house. Prior to that date it had stood as numbers 24 and 25 in Chippenham High Street, built, possibly for Thomas Figgins a rich clothier, at some time between 1749 and 1777, the dates of his occupancy. However, a curiously precise local legend states that its Chippenham presence was the result of yet another rebuilding and that it was first erected at Bowden Hill, Wiltshire, just off the old road from London to Bath, in about 1738.[10] That date would place it as a prototype for the Bristol Exchange, which was completed in 1743, and this infinitely assured façade is nothing more than the street front of the Exchange in a more relaxed dress. The ill-related attic storey has gone and the elevation is reduced to seven bays.

10 The wealthy MP for Calne, Benjamin Haskin Styles, began to build a house on a new site in the grounds of his existing house at Bowden Hill in 1738 when it was seen under construction by John Loveday. But Styles died a year later, in 1739, leaving this a mere shell. The supposition is that there were two major façades. The grander of the pair was bought by Figgins to arrive eventually, via Chippenham, at Sion Hill. The other, plainer in style but strongly reminiscent of Wood's style, was probably re-erected as late as the 1770s at Southbroom House in Devizes where it survives among later accretions in Devizes School. Apart from the stylistic evidence there is proof (*Essay*, 426) that Wood and Ralph Allen were both familiar with Bowden Hill.

1 Sion Hill Place in Bath – a much travelled facade probably designed originally by Wood for Bowden Hill in Wiltshire

Without their pedestals the three-quarter columns and pilasters in Wood's favoured Corinthian stand more easily on the string course above the polite gravity of its rustication. Garlands and masks form a frieze under the cornice, one more elegantly conventional and less international in theme than the frieze of its prototype.

Because it has broken away from Wood's hitherto invariable country villa rhythm of basement, principal and half storey it is easier to believe that it was always intended for a High Street. But the last villas in the volume were also variants with basement, two principal storeys and a half storey or an attic, so these could have been the experimental drift of his design under his son's influence. The journey of these stones to Bath completed a peculiar symmetry of design, for if this is Wood's last house in the city boundary then it is a natural expansion of his first: that splendid but cramped portico on Ralph Allen's town house with the same device of a Venetian window distributed between four columns.

The second house is more controversial and would be better described as a genuine shared attribution. It is Buckland, one of the earliest in the volume, a building previously attributed to the younger Wood and certainly built after his father's death.

This high, poised, ornate and thoroughly Palladian design never fell convincingly into the younger Wood's spare and increasingly neo-Classi-

176

Buckland House – the central block represents, within 19th
century additions, a design by the elder Wood executed by his son

cal oeuvre. In the volume, its drawings, ff. 7-22, are exactly detailed and all are in the younger Wood's drawing hand of thick and thin lines. But not only is the lettering his father's, both in ink and pencil, but on one of the side elevations (f. 17), designed in austere contrast to the charming entrance front, his father has sketched in, in notably frail pencil lines, a Venetian window and pilaster strips. They look quite inappropriate on the plain domed side entrance where the son has been trying out some advanced volumetric exercises; but in that bare desert of blank wall and windows without architraves his father's protest comes over with some measure of pathos.

It is on the front elevation (f. 8) that the older man has had his way. A design from Palladio's *Second Book of Architecture*, Le Ghizzole, has been anglicized with the usual inset of Venetian window within tetrastyle portico, and all the pleasant clichés of masks and garlands. At the end of the long, low connecting wings stand small pavilions with more than a family likeness to the formal Doric design which Ralph Allen rejected for the westward wing of offices at Prior Park, and over the central block is an unemphatic but definitely pyramidal roof as a last salute to the Tabernacle of Moses. Much was changed, particularly in the side pavilions and first floor groundplan, when Buckland was eventually raised,[11] and the younger John Wood must be given every credit for being able, with his more reserved and sensitive nature, to cope with the whims of a rural patron, but it remains essentially a house of the older Palladian generation.

So the volume of drawings is a preparation for that strange, almost haunted, process by which two of the elder Wood's most individual and, in the case of the Circus, most conservative designs, were filtered out posthumously over the years through the simplifying aesthetic of his son. When all credit has been given to the younger Wood for his constancy and his efficiency, what made both Circus and Crescent remarkable was the vision and the complex inspiration which came directly from his father. The blind elevations and anticlimactic siting of the younger Wood's Assembly House is a plain instance of what happened when that dead artist projected no more.

11 The original younger Wood design is given in *Vitruvius Britannicus* volume 4 (1767), plates 90-3; for the early 20th century remodelling by Romaine Walker see *Country Life*, 15-22 May 1915. The house was built in 1755-7 for Sir Robert Throckmorton who was living at No. 15 Queen Square in 1754 just before the elder Wood died.

Chapter Twelve

'Some enterprizing Druid'
Prehistory and Palladian

As the climax of a great builder's lifework, and with his death seeming to be timed like some pagan sacrifice to hallow its foundations, the King's Circus is not an easy construction to appraise. There has always been a tendency to regard it more as a prodigy than a success. This is understandable. A Roman amphitheatre, which is what it always suggests, was, after all, a place for Christians to be eaten in, not to live in. Nor can many visitors have walked up Gay Street, looked around and exclaimed: 'Ah! I see you have re-erected here the circular temple to Apollo of the prehistoric Druids and divided it into 30, sixth-rate middle class houses'. Though that was exactly what the Woods had really done.

So in that sense the Circus is a very private creation. No one interprets it as its creators did. But would that have surprised them; was its symbolism intended only for Freemasons with an antiquarian bent? The question is not as perverse as it seems because the symbolism of the Doric frieze, just above eye level, which captures the attention of everyone who walks its pavements, is wholly and permanently incomprehensible: a Wood family joke which no one is likely to share or ever accurately interpret.

Of the three projects which Wood threatened to impose on the city after his return in 1727 the Circus is easily the least functional. Towns need an open forum or market place yet Bath still manages without one; spas need a healing centre though Bath has yet to get its act together; but does any town need a residential circle which doubles as a place to play games in? And what games? Only the Spaniards and prancing black bulls could have given the King's Circus a dual function. John Wood himself despised games and rejoiced that pig racing and football were banished from the old Bowling Green when it was enclosed in Ralph Allen's garden.[1] Can he ever have honestly intended his *Grand Circus* to be, as he stated, 'for the Exhibition of Sports'?[2] Cobbled all over and with a raised and covered reservoir in its centre the Circus as it was built might have been designed to discourage any kind of frivolous activity.

In its present state, with its superb but wholly inappropriate centrepiece, the Circus continues to bewilder. Having got into it, on what does one focus? What has happened to the view? Subsequently, how does one get out? The tourist buses rotate about the great grove of plane trees that obscure and confuse the intensely limited vistas of the place, then they head for the easier satisfactions of the Crescent where, if there is again little on which to focus, there is at least a beginning, an end and a view.

The sudden unfolding of the Royal Crescent raises the question of intention. If the term 'ha-ha' had not already been pre-empted to describe a sunken fence, the Crescent could have been described as the grandest

1 *Essay*, 244.
2 Ibid., 232.

The King's Circus – an engraving after George Speren of 1757 showing the south-western segment standing alone

'ha-ha!' in Britain from its power to evoke astonished exclamations from a newcomer entering it from Brock Street. Any architectural writer with a fair talent for words can make the accidental appear like a contrived and delightful surprise, but was the Woods' street planning frustrated or deliberate? Were the setpieces intended to achieve visual connections and satisfying vistas? Was an English version of Clementine Rome thwarted by ignorant city councillors and should the Circus have been, like the Place des Victoires in Paris, a circle criss-crossed by roads and a central incident in the passage from one busy section of town to another?

What the Woods actually built is only half their importance. The other half is the way in which later architects were obliged to follow them in Bath by the physical direction of their streets and their style, so it is necessary to take a critical look at the way Circus and Crescent have worked and continue to work in the cityscape.

For a start the external impact of the Circus is, despite its almost 1,000 foot circumference and 42 foot height, virtually nil. Wood thrilled to imagine how the 'Carn'[3] or circular temple of the sun set up on Lansdown hill by Bladud 'must have inspired Mankind with a religious Awe'.[4] But any latter day Aeneas who looks down on Bath from Beechen Cliff will be hard put to it to pick out even the site of the Circus, though the

3 Ibid., 126.
4 Ibid., 351.

180

Crescent opens its arms distinctly from a distance. Because Wood went to 'a great Expense of Stonework' and shifting of 'superfluous Earth'[5] to cut a level shelf out of the steep hillside, the Circus bursts unexpectedly upon anyone on the main approach up Gay Street, remaining hidden until the last few yards of the climb. Thus he deliberately threw away the resonance of linked parts which the Circus could have had with Queen Square if it had been built on the slope and visible from the bottom of Gay Street. Connection was not, therefore, his aim.

As a result the visitor steps into a superbly ordered claustrophobia. Wood resisted the temptation, strong to an English Palladian with a fondness for pediments, to give any of the three equal segments a central feature. And because only three roads enter the Circus at the points of an imagined equilateral triangle there is no escape vista out of the enclosing walls as there would have been with four roads. In the account of laying its foundation stone, the *Gentleman's Magazine* for 7 February 1754 stated that the three streets would be 'each terminated with a fine building'. The reality is that Gay Street drops steeply out of sight, Brock Street offers a distant glimpse of trees and keeps the Crescent for a second and even more stunning surprise view, while Bennett Street, which should have led uphill to Assembly Rooms poised elegantly on the slope, only stumbles around an unpunctuated corner. Bennett Street marks the stage when the

The Circus as originally paved – a watercolour by S. H. Grimm of *c*.1773

5 Stated in a letter now in the Braikenridge Collection, Bristol Central Library; quoted by Ison, *The Georgian Buildings of Bath*, 230.

181

younger Wood lost the vision of the elder and is the one real failure of the Circus.

This apart, the spatial containment is astonishing. The Circus has 30 houses, not 33 as most accounts claim, disposed in three equal segments about a circle with a 318 foot diameter. Each segment is composed, without relief or variety, of three storeys, even in height though not in fenestration, and fronted with paired, plain-shafted, three-quarter columns in rich versions of the three classical orders as they were understood in the early 18th century: Doric, of a kind, to the ground floor, Ionic, to the first floor and Corinthian to the second, each with their entablatures. Topping all is a parapet with later round portholes for the attic chambers and giant acorns on each forward break. Columns above columns and windows above windows yet its doors without architrave or emphasis, the houses create an effect that is essentially of the elder Wood, of privacy and reserve: a watchful order to keep the world away behind the deep, wide moat of basement areas, an anonymous ostentation for those first sub-lessees who included appropriately in their number the Rt. Honourable William Pitt, most victorious of 18th century Prime Ministers.

Happy the building operation which has no history. The younger Wood was not a man given to confrontation. He had trouble for several years, rather surprisingly, in buying an adequate source of water, but when that was resolved the three arcs of buildings went up without protest from the sub-lessees, who included the usual mix of carpenter-speculators, architect-builders and gentry. At the Circus the columned façades were clearly an inducement to the leaseholders to buy and not, as at the North Parade, an extra to be cut to save money. The leases were granted for the south-west segment (that on the left at the top of Gay Street) between 1755-67, for the south-east 1762-66 and for the north (the last to be begun) 1764-66.[6] Meanwhile the younger Wood had been developing Brock Street with its uninspired elevations and was ready in 1766 to lease the ground for the Royal Crescent from Sir Benet Garrard at a rent of £30 for the first two years, rising thereafter to £220. This compares with the £163 a year rent which his father had agreed to pay Thomas and Margaret Garrard for the nine-acre site of the Circus in 1753 and the £100 rent agreed in 1739 for the Parades site with the Duke of Kingston. Bath land values were rising sharply.

What is hard to appreciate, now that Bath's northern slopes have four other south-facing crescents (though only one circus), is the way in which the Woods redirected the whole of the city's development. They drove it upwards and northwards by building Gay Street like a pointing arrow to link with the Circus and the Crescent. Thereafter the flat and easy building sites on the north side of the valley floor fell to industrial development or housing of a lower social order. But there had been nothing inevitable in the process. If the Parades had been finer and the *Royal Forum* had been achieved, the entire growth of the city would have been different.

It will have become apparent in earlier chapters that the historical inspiration behind Wood's schemes was complex, by fits and starts both conformist and laterally inspired. In 1727, when Wood returned to Bath, the

6 Ison, *The Georgian Buildings*, Appendix V, 230-1.

term 'circus' must have had a double connotation for him: part ellipsoid Roman Colosseum, part Druidic stone circle. But by 1754 his mind had been conditioned by 24 years of wide reading and enthusiastic theorizing. As a result the elevations and the dimensions of the Circus present a palimpsest of Wood's interests and beliefs gathered over a number of years.

He was not only influenced by obvious precursors like Vitruvius, Inigo Jones, Scamozzi, Perrault and Gibbs. He was deliberately deploying the classical orders to honour the men who he believed had created them: the Prophet Moses and the Jewish architects of the First and Second Temples of Jerusalem. The circular shape in which he cast them was not a reference to Rome but to the dimensions and form of the prehistoric stone circles at Stanton Drew and Stonehenge, a commemoration of a glorious native Druid culture which he believed to have flourished in pre-Roman Bath.

Wood was a positive and devout Freemason. Once he had retreated from London to Bath, his local patriotism and his highly competitive nature seem to have trapped him in a pattern of provincial intellectualism which drew him further and further apart from standard thinking on classical architecture and world history. No one who has enjoyed the trenchant and often hilarious pages of Wood's *Essay* will need any warning on the processes of Wood's logic or the level of his impartiality. The first was arbitrary, the second was zero.

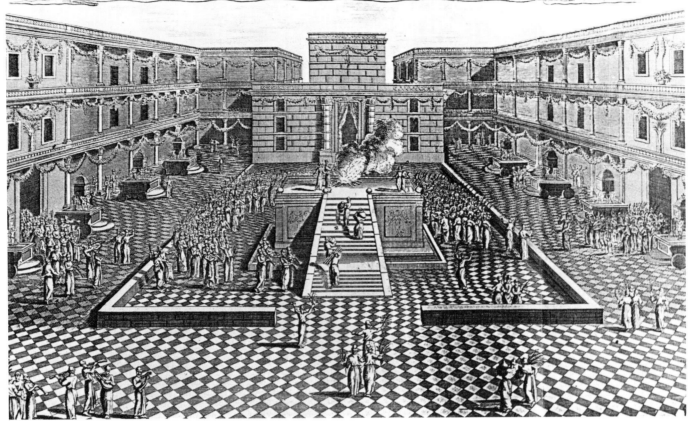

The interior of Solomon's Temple from the 1754 edition of Josephus' *Works*; markedly similar to Wood's Circus design

That self-confidence which drove him to reshape Bath in a short lifetime made him an outrageously bad historian. He was spiteful, ungenerous and adapted all information to suit previously fixed notions.

It was an established part of Freemasonic tradition that the God-given but endlessly debatable three Orders of Solomon's Temple were brought to Greece and the West by Pythagoras. The story as Wood inherited it appears in *The Constitutions of the Free-masons* written by James Anderson and published in 1723 when Wood was young, impressionable and in London, working as a joiner and builder.

> Pythagorus travell'd into Egypt the Year that Thales dy'd, and living there among the Priests twenty two Years, became expert in Geometry, and in all the Egyptian Learning, until he was captivated by Cambyses King of Persia, and sent to Babylon, where he was much conversant with the Chaldean MAGI and the learned Babylonish JEWS, from whom he borrow'd great Knowledge, that rendered him very famous in Greece and Italy; where afterwards he flourish'd and dy'd when Mordecai was the prime Minister of State to Ahasuerus King of Persia, and ten years after Zerubbabel's TEMPLE was finish'd. AM 3498, 506 Ante Ch.[7]

This was the story, remote in apparent relevance to north-east Somerset,

7 Anderson, *Constitutions*, 21.

184

which fascinated Wood and which he was to weave into the very fabric of Bath's early history. To achieve this and to equate the dimensions of Zerubbabel's Second Temple with those of his circular Circus would appear superficially impossible, yet Wood contrived it without a literary blush or logical hiccup. One day he will be acknowledged, not only as Bath's greatest architect, but as her first writer of historical fiction.

From the start he was able to draw on a body of antiquarian studies which had arisen in response to the Elizabethan mood of English patriotism and the subsequent Jacobean expansion of this into British patriotism. To give accord and union to a disparate island of Saxon and Celt the most ingenious legendary history had been spun. With such a wealth of tales recounting 'British' glories and the exploits of ancient 'British', pre-Roman kings, Wood had no need to invent, only to appropriate and manipulate.

Camden's first *Britannia* of 1586 collected classical source material together with much Celtic tradition and settled the Druids in the general educated awareness. Its 1600 edition contains an excellent Dutch engraving of Stonehenge, and when Michael Drayton published his first volume of *Poly Olbion, Great Britaine* in 1613, the Druids were established historical properties, the true heirs of biblical Jewry and classical Greece. 'For the Druids, being in profession very proportionat in many things to Cabalistique and Pythagorean doctrine, may well be supposed much ancienter than any that had note of learning among the Romans ... In other matters, privat and publique (so is Caesar's assertion) they used Greeke letters'.[8] Most relevant to Wood's later researches is:

> The ancient Britans yet a sceptred King obey'd
> Three hundred yeeres before Rome's great foundation laid
> And had a thousand yeeres an Empire strongly stood
> Ere Caesar to her shores here stem'd the circling flood.[9]

These kings were supposedly descended from Brutus, a Trojan prince wandering the world, like Aeneas his great grandfather, after the wreck of Troy. He founded *Troy Novant*, which was supposed to be London until Wood reshaped the chronicles and made it Bath, and it was Brutus' grandson six times removed, King Bladud, who according to Drayton's research discovered the properties of the hot waters of Bath:

> As he from learned Greece, that (by the liberall Arts)
> To Stamford, in this Isle, seem'd Athens to transfer;
> Wise Bladud, of her Kings that great Philosopher
> Who found our boyling Bathes: and in his knowledge hie,
> Disdaining human paths, heere practiced to flie.[10]

The waters of the hot springs were thought to be governed by Apollo the Sun God who was worshipped by the Druids under the names of Belin, Belenus or Bel.

8 Drayton, *Poly Olbion*, 167.
9 Ibid., 112.
10 Ibid.

Stonehenge from Fischer Von
Erlach's *Entwurf* of 1725

At the command of James I, Inigo Jones began a study of Stonehenge
in 1620 which resulted in a book *The Most Notable Antiquity of Great Britain,
Vulgarly Called Stone-heng, On Salisbury Plain, Restored*, ghosted by John
Webb his son-in-law and first published in 1655. This reads more like the
writing of a bad scholar than a good architect. It decided that the Britons
were not capable of stone buildings, that Stonehenge was 'artificially made
of pure Sand', and, therefore, a Roman work.[11] Reissued along with two
even more worthless studies of Stonehenge in 1725[12] it then included very
fine engravings of the monument and a plan showing the stones enclosed
with a circular ditch with three entrances. This is the plan that has been
put forward as the source of Wood's design for the Circus.[13] It could have
influenced his design for the garden in front of the Grand Parade,[14] but
by 1740 both William Stukeley and John Wood himself had surveyed
Stonehenge and found that the circular ditch with the three entrance gaps
was a fiction.[15]

The triangle within a circle is a symbol of the Trinity in Eternity, a
Masonic sign which Wood used prominently in the reredos he designed
c. 1729 for Tyberton Church in Herefordshire,[16] so the symbol could

11 Jones/Webb, *Stone-heng*, 2nd ed. (1725), 22.
12 The two other studies: Walter Charleton, *Chorea Gigantum or the most famous Antiquity of
    Great Britain vulgarly called Stone-Heng*, and John Webb, *A Vindication of Stone-Heng Re-
    stored*; a further study came out in 1730: Rev. S. Wallis, *A Dissertation in Vindication of the
    Antiquity of Stonehenge*.
13 By Stuart Piggott in *The Druids*, 2nd ed. (1975), 144-5.
14 Illustrated in the *Essay* opposite page 320. These entrances on the Inigo Jones plan
    were based on the points of an equilateral triangle as were the paths on Wood's pro-
    posed garden in front of the North Parade. The three roads entering his Circus scheme
    of 1730 were not equilaterally sited which suggests that at that date Wood had either
    not seen the Jones plan or, more probably, was not yet deeply involved in prehistory.
15 In *Stonehenge a Temple Restor'd to the British Druids* (1740), Stukeley asserts 'we discern
    that Webb's equilateral triangles forming the cell are fancies: his three entrances across
    the ditch are so too' (page 3).
16 For Tyberton reredos see Chapter Four.

have had double appeal. Wood had already written of the circumference of a circle as representing 'the Great Canopy of Heaven' and an equilateral triangle as 'a figure the most perfect of all others composed of several lines ... a Symbol of Divinity or Sign of Caelestial Matter as Above'.[17]

There was a resurgence of Druid writing around 1700. A brilliant new edition of *Britannia* in 1695 aired some of Aubrey's theories on prehistory and in 1702 the notorious Irish freethinker John Toland, fluent in three Celtic languages, introduced the figure of Abaris the Hyperborean, Priest of the Sun, in his *Critical History of the Celtic Religion and Learning*, containing an account of the Druids, though not a flattering one. The three Stonehenge books were reissued as one in 1725 and Toland's *History of the Druids* was published in the next year. By that time the Druids had become part of the assault made by reason on the established church, their role shifting slightly from British patriots to Christian Theists before their time, enlightened lovers of Nature who just happpened from time to time to burn a few willing victims alive in wicker cages. This was their image when the antiquary William Stukeley took up pre-history in preference to Roman studies, and at much the same time John Wood began to establish to his own satisfaction the complex web of Zerubbabel's Temple, Pythagoras, Zoroaster, Abaris the Hyperborean, Bladud and the stone circles of pre-Roman Britain.

According to Wood's compression of many authorities, Pythagoras and Abaris did indeed visit Babylon and Jerusalem to observe the new Temple, but Abaris was only another name for Bladud the Prince-Priest of Apollo, Sun God of Britain. It was probably he who taught Pythagoras astronomy and he who built the famous round temple at Delphi, Apollo's shrine, before returning to build Bath in *c*.483 BC and another temple to the sun. Bath was *Troy Novant* and attracted many of the wisest Athenians when that city was wrecked in 480 BC during the Persian wars. Bladud reigned happily there until he killed himself in a flying accident on Solsbury Hill.

All this farrago Wood relates in several chapters, quoting many authorities, Jamblicus, Porphyry and Diodorus Siculus in chief, arguing his points and his dates with convincing relish. The next step was to leave the dry world of books and find architectural traces of this Abaris-Bladud who had travelled so widely just when the Temple was newly built. There were three stone circles near Bath at Stanton Drew, and an easy half day's ride away were Avebury and Stonehenge. Inevitably Wood proved that one of the Stanton Drew stone circles was modelled on the Temple in Jerusalem. In the first chapter of the Book of *Ezra*, Wood found this decree of Cyrus of Persia to the Temple-building Jews:

> Let the Foundations thereof be strongly laid, the Height thereof threescore Cubits and the Breadth thereof threescore Cubits, with three Rows of great Stones, and a Row of new Timber.

That was all he needed. He had a measurement, 60 Cubits, the precise English equivalent of which could be debated, now he had only to find Druidic circles with diameters which could be reckoned as 60 Cubits and

17 *The Origin of Building* (Bath MS.), 80.

Stanton Drew from the air

(top) Wood's supposed Moon Temple at Stanton Drew showing the 'porticoes'
(bottom) A stone at Stanton Drew

Bladud from the *Essay*

near them three (or four) rows of great stones.

His very impressive specimen was Circle D, the north-easterly of the three circles at Stanton Drew. There are two plans of the stones in his

190

Essay.[18] These repay study as Wood's interpretation of them as 'a Model of the Planetry World'[19] as taught by Pythagoras is impressive but it is Wood's letter to Harley with its exposition of the dimensions which is important.[20]

> Now my Lord, let anyone read Cyrus's Decree for building the Temple at Jerusalem, view the stones which I suppose to be a Temple to the Moon, and strictly examine the Dimensions of that supposed Temple. He will instantly find Cyrus's Decree was absolutely the Druids guide in that part of the work at Stanton Drew; for each Temple is 60 Cubits broad, and each Temple is surrounded with four Rows of Pillars.

There were 30 pillars in the outermost row and its diameter across was 316 feet augmented, however, to rather more by the thickness of the pillars themselves. The other circles had 28 or 29 pillars each, these numbers most probably being related to the days in a month. At this point it is necessary to stress that the diameter of the Circus which Wood eventually built is 318 feet and there are 30 houses in its actual circle, and 30 houses also in the Crescent which according to Smollett's *Humphry Clinker*, the architect of the Circus also designed. Wood had managed to squeeze a 60 Cubit, 316 feet plus, diameter out of Circle D, his Temple of the Moon, by including some stone lines and an earth bank to the east which were quite outside the actual circle. But the most interesting pointer to what purposes lay behind his antiquarian jaunts was his discovery that the much larger, though much less impressive, Circle B, his Earth circle, was the remains, not of a temple, but of a circle of houses. Here, of course, was an excellent precedent for his long frustrated *Grand Circus* in Bath. The theory which Wood confidently proposed was that Zoroaster had set up a college of priests in Babylon

> in imitation, no doubt, of that in Jerusalem ... In imitation of that it is highly probable some enterprizing Druid in Britain assumed the superintendancy of the rest of these priests, deserted the established method of assembling under Oak Trees for religious purposes and so erected Temples at Stanton Drew, one in honour of the Sun, another in honour of the Moon, whom they, according to Mr Toland, principally worshipped, and between them raised an Habitation for himself and the rest of his College ... the stone at no 37 is different from the rest, probably part of the Arch Druid's House.

The letter concluded with an imaginative description of a druidic procession across the river – 'What can be more grand and magnificent? What more solemn?'

The next step was to find the 60 cubits at Stonehenge while at the same time reducing Stukeley's favourite circle to a lower status than the

18 Plates 1/2 and 3/4.
19 *Essay*, 148.
20 British Museum, Harleian MS. 7354.

circles near Bath. When he reached there on a blustery Michaelmas day Wood made a point of improving on and contradicting most of Stukeley's published measurements; though Wood confirmed that 'the outer Row of Stones were designed to amount to 30 in Number'. He then proved the Stanton circle to be older because it expressed a lunar cycle of eight years whereas Stonehenge, like Avebury, expressed a 19 year lunar cycle as observed by Meton 'in the Summer Solstice of 430 BC' and must, therefore, have been built after 430 BC.[21]

With the superior antiquity of his Somerset circle established Wood went on to discover the predictable 60 Cubits of Stonehenge:

> I have supposed a Verge of 5 feet broad, now worn away, to have incompassed the Temple. On that Supposition the area remains are exactly the breadth of the semidiameter of the Temple by which the whole was 306 feet in Diameter or thrice the Diameter of the Temple; this was increased to 316 feet by the 5 foot Verge and the whole was environed by the outward row of Stones in the treble Portico.[22]

So in the end he found what he intended to find.

If he had lived his biblical span John Wood might have expounded in a revised edition of his *Essay* the symbolic significance of the Circus and the Crescent. In default of his witness the verdict must lie open. It will probably be allowed on the evidence of his books that he believed the three orders of architecture to be Jewish not Greek and given by God to Moses. Hence the great display of them on the elevations of the Circus can be seen as a devout Freemason's hymn of praise to the Divine Architect. No other building in Britain displays the Orders in the same isolation and repetition.

Then there is the more contentious Druidic matter. The Druids, as Wood repeats again and again in the opening to the second book of his *Essay*, were the 'Priests of the hollow *Oak*'.[23] Is it a coincidence that the parapet of the Circus is topped by as many giant acorns as there are double columns? Is it a coincidence that the 30 outer stones of Circle D at Stanton Drew and Stonehenge are matched by the 30 houses of the Circus and Crescent? And were the Circus and the Crescent intended as symbols of the sun and the new moon? Wood claimed that both Sun and Moon temples had stood on the hills north of Bath and that Apollo-Bel and Minerva-Onca were the natural presiding deities of the hot springs. The Circus and the Crescent, therefore, beneath their overwhelmingly classical ornament, could be expressions, by a first generation Palladian, of that romantic straining after the darker historic past which was, within 100 years, to shatter the classical tradition into eclectic fragments. As Tobias Smollett is the only firm source for the elder Wood's authorship of both the Crescent and the Circus, it should be noted that two passages in Smollett's *An Essay on the External Use of Water*, published in 1752, two years before Wood's death, prove that he was an ardent Wood admirer

21 Ibid., f. 5.
22 Harleian MS. 7355, ff. 8-9.
23 *Essay*, 138.

Aerial view of the Circus and Crescent

and fully conversant with the architect's schemes for Bath. Referring to a lost design by Wood for restructuring the Baths, Smollett writes: 'Mr *Wood*, the architect, to whose extraordinary genius they [the Corporation] are indebted for a great part of the trade and beauty of the place; yet they have industriously opposed his best designs, which, had they been executed, would have rendered *Bath*, in point of elegant architecture, the admiration of the whole World' (p. 39). Later in the same essay he wrote sympathetically of waiting 'until the other more magnificent scheme of that ingenious architect shall be carried into execution' (p. 48). He must, therefore, be accepted as a reliable and informed witness when he wrote of Wood having 'planned' the Circus and 'projected a Crescent'.

The least digestible of the coincidences is that of the Cubits. Wood had added and supposed and contrived by earth banks and thicknesses of stone to extend Circle D at Stanton Drew and Stonehenge into the 60 Cubit diameter which Cyrus had ordered for the Second Temple at Jerusalem. Was it only an accident that he would finally have given the same 60 cubit diameter to his Circus in Bath?

Rather than to dismiss all this as a chain of coincidences, it seems easier to believe that it was deliberate design, in which case the buildings mark the apotheosis of two obsessions: one with the splendour of a lost and native civilization, and one with that civilization's early links with the Israel of the Prophets, classical architecture made not only British, but Christian and numinous.

When Druids and diameters are laid aside it is the sheer proliferation of columns in the Circus, 648 of them, which remains the most enduring impression of the great circle. To display them with such magnificent abandon Wood must have been making a point or testing a theory. He had a theory in fact, not by any means his own, that if the three columns of the divinely revealed Order were placed correctly one above the other a theorem of perfect form would be achieved. In his pursuit of this he often sounds like an old alchemist questing after the Philosopher's Stone or the Elixir of Youth. The handicap he set himself was that the columns with their proper bases and entablatures had to be of equal height, as they are, 216 times over, set around the Circus. But mathematically this should be a near visual impossibility. A Doric column should be 8 times its diameter in height, an Ionic 9 times and a Corinthian 10 times; 'in effect we may' Wood wrote 'see in them the most lively Symbols of the Robust Man, of the Grave Matron, and of the Sprightly young Girl'.[24] But the problem is that 'the clear Shaft of the *Dorick* Column decreases at Top the eighth Part of the Diameter at Bottom',[25] and the next two orders above it must do the same. Now to attain the ideal combined display of 'Columns over Columns' they must be so designed that 'they will, when joined together, represent the clear Trunk of a strait and well grown Tree of the same length ... the Tree of the Forest furnishes us with that sort of Diminution for their clear Shafts which were practised by the Antients in their most perfect Works'.[26] Wood here clearly displays his characteristic feeling for natural parallels.

In stony reality, however, if each column is diminishing by an eighth part of its diameter as it rises, and if the diameter at the base of each column is the same as the diameter at the top of the column below it, to produce this 'Tree of the Forest' effect, then the diameter at the top of the final Corinthian column will have become ludicrously spindly: an eighth reduced by an eighth reduced by an eighth to a mere two-thirds of the base.

Nor, in the mathematical minuet of the correct Orders, is that the only problem. In proportion to its height, a Doric column must carry a wider entablature than the other two so if, as in the Circus, it is intended to allow all three tiers of orders exactly the same height, then it will be neces-

24 *Dissertation*, 27.
25 Ibid., 29.
26 Ibid., 29-30.

A Druid from Rowland's *Mona Antiqua* of 1723

sary to cheat over the relative proportions of Doric column and Doric entablature, which is what Wood did. Another impossible correctness is that the intercolumniation is supposed to be a proportion of the column's diameter at base. But when the columns are doubled as in the Circus, each pair of columns must stand exactly over the pair below it; therefore the intercolumniations cannot vary to reflect the diminishing diameters at the base of each order.

What is most surprising in all this tangle of geometrical relationships is the fact that Wood should have chosen to deploy columns and tiers of even height in his vast demonstration setpiece of the Circus. Organically

A section of the east segment of the Circus

considered, the storeys of a house should diminish as they rise. In late 17th century and early 18th century English classicism this was the rule. Wood actually commented in his *Dissertation* on how superior the effect was when the shafts of each order were of one and the same diameter at the bottom and each order kept to its correct relationship of height to diameter: 8, 9 and 10. Then, he wrote, with these columns of unequal height but correct proportions 'as the Orders advance towards Virginal Beauty and Elegance, the Columns increase in their Altitude, and thereby one Order receives a Majesty above the other, even in Miniature upon Paper, which words can scarcely describe'.[27]

27 Ibid., 30.

196

Inigo Jones after Van Voest –
Wood's enduring hero figure

Why then, merely to achieve this 'Tree of the Forest' effect should he have thrown away all this 'Majesty' when he designed the Circus with its columns and tiers of equal height? The answer can only be that 'By the Draughts of the Banqueting House at *White Hall* inserted in *Campbell's Vit. Brit.* as well as in the Book of Designs published by the late Mr *Cant*, or *Kent*, it appears that *Inigo Jones* intended to give the World a Specimen for placing Columns over Columns of one and the same Altitude ... and if he had avoided some Things in his Sample, the Harmony of the Orders must, in the Words of Mr *Campbell*, have produced, in the highest degree, Strength with Politeness, Ornament with Simplicity, and Beauty with Majesty'.[28]

Wood's architectural hero figure and exemplar was Inigo Jones. With his strongly competitive nature Wood was disinclined to close re-

[28] Ibid., 28.

197

lationships with living contemporaries. He had clashed with Campbell and, though he was well aware of Burlington's work, he was never part of his circle. Established away in provincial Bath, Wood seems deliberately to have dissociated himself from London architects handling Palladian models and linked himself with Inigo Jones as a great master who was both patriotically British and conveniently dead. There was, according to Wood, a strong local tradition that the mother of Inigo Jones had been a Bath woman, related to the Trym family and that Jones had, out of sentiment, given the city the design for its Guildhall. Wood took the story seriously and claimed to detect similarities between the elevations of the Guildhall, the temple of Jupiter in Rome and, almost inevitably, the Tabernacle of Moses. Though declaring judiciously that Inigo Jones had improved on Scamozzi in his handling of the Ionic volutes, Wood found even his hero wanting in other details of the design.

This fault-finding was typical of Wood. In the matter of setting columns above columns he intends to improve even on Jones who 'if he had avoided some Things in his Sample' would have achieved harmony; and Wood cannot resist a silly punning jibe at Kent, 'Mr *Cant*', only one year after his death. Yet the *Book of Designs* (*The Designs of Inigo Jones consisting of Plans and Elevations for Public and Private Buildings* (1727), which Kent published, is one of the most beautiful books of architectural designs ever produced in this country, and Wood must have come closer to an appreciation of Inigo Jones by poring over the great canvas-backed pages of this book than he ever did by visiting Whitehall and Greenwich. It was the awesome detail and scale of the illustrations for the projected palace at Whitehall coupled with the existing Banqueting House which must have lured him completely into 'Columns of one and the same Altitude' in the Circus. Vitruvius urged diminution by a fifth at each stage and Palladio himself illustrated no example, but Jones had attempted it and Jones was, for Freemasons, 'our great Master-Mason', so Wood set out to follow and to surpass him.[29]

It is unlikely that any of Wood's contemporaries would have felt the need to relate so closely to a man of the early 17th century. No one else designed anything remotely like the Circus and it is in a sense a Caroline rather than a Georgian building, still implicit with that air of the novelty of the classical orders, over-reverential in just the same way as those towers of the orders which several colleges and the Bodleian in Oxford built before the Civil War. In his own time no professional architect would have felt any pressure to design the Circus with quite Wood's deliberate naivety. It is an adolescent design from a middle aged man.

The metope sequence of the Doric frieze in the Circus underlines this impression of a metaphysical approach more proper to the previous century.[30] A large number of the metopes ae based, often closely, on the illustrations in a large folio called *Emblemes* published in 1635 and put

29 Anderson, *Constitutions*, 39.
30 In Wood's *Origin* there is an illustration of Federico Zuccari's house in Florence and a short account of its symbolic significance relative to the architect's character. This instance of Wood's awareness of Italian Mannerist practice is discussed by Rudolf Wittkower in 'Federico Zuccari and John Wood of Bath' in *Journal of the Warburg and Courtauld Institutes*, vol. v. (1943), 220-222.

198

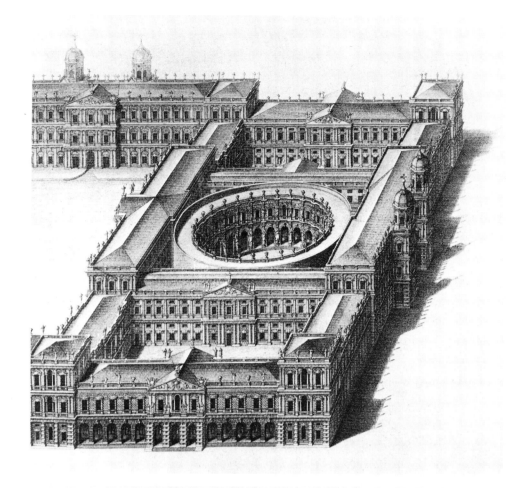

(top) A section of the design for a palace at Whitehall, variously
attributed, but considered by Wood to be a work of Inigo Jones
(bottom) Decorative metopes from the Whitehall Palace designs

199

Portrait of George Wither from his *Emblemes* – the link between his coat of arms and Wood's self-awarded achievements is plain

together by a poet, George Wither. Anyone who takes the book[31] and walks around the Circus with it will quickly prove the truth of the assertion. The link is so unlikely that few serious architectural students will accept it until they have made a personal visit and their own discoveries. There is a further, clinching, proof of Wood's intellectual and emotional involvement with the dead poet and his works. Wood quartered Wither's heraldic device of three crescent moons above a set square or chevron, illustrated on his protrait in the *Emblemes*, with his own rebus of an oak tree when he invented the 'coat of arms' that first appears as a seal on his letters to the Bristol Corporation in the 1740s.

George Wither (1588-1667) was a third-rate Caroline poet. When he was taken prisoner by Royalists in the Civil War, Sir John Denham asked for his life to be spared 'for that whilest GW lived he [Denham] should not

31 A facsimile was published by the Scolar Press in 1968 and reprinted in 1973.

200

be the worst poet in England'.[32] The illustrations in the book are the 'Emblemes' of the title and are earlier Dutch work of the Van de Passe family originally published in 1611.[33] Wither merely added doggerel lines of some, often slight, relevance to the pictures, pointing a sententious moral. Underneath the tortoise, for instance, on page 86:

> For which respects, the Tortoise represents
> That man, who in himselfe, hath full contents;
> And (by the Vertues lodging in his minde)
> Can all things needfull, in all places, finde

and so on for thirty lines of rhyming couplets.

By no means all the 525 metopes are taken from the *Emblemes*, but the majority of them refer in more or less detail to the book. Often a single detail like the harrow on page 160 is taken out of its picture and carefully copied as a single carved metope on houses Nos. 1 and 2. Whoever designed the metopes cut human figures from the *Emblemes*, though hands are common, and avoided depressing symbols like death's heads and hourglasses. Snakes are the most frequent symbol in both the book and the Circus: a snake around a rose, twined round an urn, a bough, a wheatsheaf or jug, seized by a bird or gazing into a mirror. Wither was baffled by these Dutch snakes and varied their significance wildly between wisdom and vice. Winged, burning or pierced hearts are almost equally as common.

For examples of links with the book, the south-east segment of the Circus, that on the right-hand side going up Gay Street, is rewarding. Starting at Bennett Street corner the very first metope, a helmeted head on a pedestal is from page 145; the second, the Sun and heliotrope, is from page 140; the fourth, a Janus, from page 138; the sixth, a face from a cloud blasting a tree, from page 147 or 243; the seventh, a grumpy dolphin, from page 72; the eighth is probably the tortoise, and so on.

The metopes in the three intercolumniations of house No. 21 are of particular interest. The dolphin appears again, this time with a non-Wither barrel; the hand grasping a sceptre is from page 137; a hand shaking a tree is from page 217; the face blasting a tree appears again and there is a saw cutting a tree from page 183. But the metope which underlines the whole improbably joking spirit in which Wood must have embarked upon this iconography is the 36th from Bennett Street corner. This shows four faces blowing into a cloud and they are not taken from a Van de Passe illustration but from the last page of the book where Wither had the ingenious idea of turning the whole into what he calls a 'Lotterie', a game in fact for telling one's fortune.

In the illustration above the four blowing faces, representing the four winds, is a circular dial divided into 56 sections. Pinned to this is an arrow which can be spun and on the opposite page Wither, a Puritan, nervously explains the rules for his dubiously moral device in his usual execrable verse. The eyes had to be shut, the arrows spun once for a page number

32 Quoted in the Introductory note to the Scolar Press facsimile: *A Collection of Emblemes*, 1968.
33 As illustrations to Gabriel Rollenhagen's *Nucleus Emblematum Selectissimorum*.

(top left) A crocodile from
Wither's *Emblemes*
(top right) Crocodile metope
from the Doric
frieze of the Circus
(bottom right) Compasses from
Wither's *Emblemes*
(bottom left) Compass metope
from the Circus

and once again to decide in which of the four subdivisions of the book the player's page lottery had fallen. Then the emblem of that page with Wither's exposition of it was the player's fortune.

Though Wither was apologetic about the element of chance, this expensive book with its circular game was popular and a cheaper version of it, pirated by Nathaniel Crouch, was still being reprinted in the 1720s.

It appears that the iconography of the Doric tier of the Circus is of no deeper significance than a Puritan's parlour game, something to pass the long winter evenings with just a spice of impropriety, of dabbling with hidden things. Perhaps it was a favourite remembered toy of John Wood's own childhood, recalled for its circular shape and very general reference. The mind that was drawn to the symbolism of the classical orders and the moon temples of the Druids seems to have been able to slip easily into the more relaxed mood of a family joke. The pages of the book and the sequence of the metopes are quite unlinked though students will find the south-east segment the richest stalking ground.

In addition to these, Wood has taken many of Inigo Jones's metopes from the Whitehall Palace illustrations: trophies of arms with bows, arrow, spears and axeheads. Others are illustrations of fables and there is predictably, the Freemasons' coat of arms and the arms of the Carpenters. Trophies of Masonic implements are fairly common, including one added in 1962. The Masonic device from page 143 of *Emblemes* with a hand from a cloud inscribing with a pair of compasses appears on both house No. 22 and No. 23. This particular emblem with its attendant verse by Wither may have had a major significance for Wood. The compasses describe a circle and Wither saw this as a symbol of a 'constant round', a 'constant resolution', 'constant liking', 'constant labour' and 'perseverance'. Wood's own career had been marked by constancy and perseverance particularly in his determination to build a grand circular structure, long frustrated but now finally achieved in the King's Circus itself. One sequence at the Brock Street end of the north segment where Andrew Sproule was the lessee, appears to have a theme of revelry and the arts. Other metopes like an

(top right) Heliotrope from
Wither's *Emblemes*
(top left) Heliotrope metope
from the Circus
(bottom left) The Four Winds from
the gaming board
in Wither's *Emblemes*
(bottom right) Metope of the Four
Winds from the Circus

A Thomas Malton watercolour of the Royal Crescent (*c.*1780)

artist's palette (No. 25), a blackboard (No. 15), and a waterwheel (No. 23) may refer to the professions of an original lessee. The two houses, Nos. 7 and 8, which William Pitt leased, have a definite concentration of trophies of arms and symbols of war and triumph.

The absence of any such humorous and human devices on Wood the younger's Brock Street or on the Crescent which, though he did not conceive, he must certainly have drawn out in detail, refutes any notion that it was he who devised the metopes. While he was in Liverpool (1749-54) he joined a sociable club called the Ugly Face Clubbe but that is his only recorded comic gesture. His book *A Series of Plans, for Cottages or Habitations of the Labourer, either in Husbandry or the Mechanic Arts* (1781), reveals him as desperately solemn and, in his enthusiasm for plain spare housing for those in want, the absolute antithesis of his father. It is impossible to imagine the father agitating like the son for more privies for the poor or declaring:

> ... to make myself master of the subject, it was necessary for me to feel as the Cottager himself; for I have always held it as a maxim ... that no architect can form a convenient plan unless he ideally places himself in the situation of the person for whom he designs.[34]

34 Introduction, page 1.

Yet it is easy to understand how such a sensitive and conscientious person was able to carry the most ambitious projects of his father through with unruffled ease. Easy also to see why such a decent and cautious soul, one who took modest pride in having erected 'sixteen dwellings for the impotent poor'[35] of St Ives, should have almost spoilt the great Crescent by touches of moderation and economy.

There is such a profusion of coupled columns on the Circus between its richly ornamented cornice and its animated Doric frieze that the absolute lack of architrave or any kind of enrichment around its ranks of windows and its doors tends to pass almost unnoticed. That fining down of detail was a feature of the younger Wood's drawings and when he came to build the Royal Crescent he no longer had his father's detailed drawings to guide him, only a general notion of the overall conception. As a result, not only does the Crescent mark a complete change in scale, from rank upon rank of small columns in the Circus to one giant Ionic order striding upon a single base, but there is the absolute minimum of enrichment in this English Palmyra, with base and cornice as bare as the windows and doors. The effect is debatable, as is the understated central feature of one round-headed window between doubled columns.

The anonymous but perceptive author of *The Stranger's Assistant and Guide to Bath* wrote:

> The rustic basement of the latter [the north side of Queen Square] on which the pillars stand, gives an air of stability and firmness which is wanting in the Crescent, where it was even more necessary than in the other, as the pillars are much larger, and of the Ionic order, which being originally intended to stand under the Corinthian, were thicker in proportion, and of consequence the want of an apparent support to them is more conspicuous.[36]

The Ionic was the order recommended by Vitruvius[37] as appropriate to the moon goddess and, therefore, well chosen for this Crescent of the new moon, but the choice is unlikely to have been the son's. The startling originality of a row of houses in the crescent shape must again be the inspiration of the father who believed that a temple to the moon goddess had stood higher on the same hillside, who had found crescents in the trilithons of Stonehenge, laid out Prior Park as an angular crescent and described the Beechen Cliff as being 'in the shape of a large Cressant'.[38] What the younger Wood built was a wild Palladian conceit modified by timid neo-Classical treatment; but nothing can wholly distract from a building venture which takes its scale and its shape from the broad hill it rests on and throws a formal palace façade wide open to the soft richness of a broad river valley. The Royal Crescent is the exact architectural point at which Classical and Romantic confront and accord. In a sense, once it had been built, conventional streets of parallel houses were outdated.

35 Wood the younger, *A Series of Plans*, 221. The younger Wood's design for an almshouses at St Ives is given on plate IV of the same book.
36 Page 58.
37 *The Origin of Building* (Bath MS.), 188.
38 *Essay*, 52.

No 1 Royal Crescent with the fenestration restored to the original dimensions

After it, the only possible advance for a city was towards informality, and that would always be a kind of retreat as the garden city denies the nature of what a city is intended to be. That geometry among the trees which the elder Wood had first experienced as he dug his canal in Bramham Park had finally matured there on the slopes of Lansdown.

The Aftermath

There remains the matter of Wood's posthumous reputation with the confusion of attributions, the muddle as to his origins and a certain dwindling of his credit. This began early. In a letter to Stukeley dated 6 August 1763, Bishop Warburton, who married Ralph Allen's heiress and must have often heard his father-in-law speak of Wood, described the architect as 'a great fool, and not less a knave, to my knowledge'.[1] Significantly the letter gave Stukeley his first news of Wood's death, nine years after the event.

But the downgrading has continued to the present day. In *The Georgian Buildings of Bath*, the standard work on the city, Walter Ison could write of the younger John Wood:

> The finest achievements of the son surpass those of the father, both in breadth of conception and subtlety of realization. In fact, the work of the younger Wood represents the highest point of the Palladian achievement in Bath.[2]

Two factors appear to lie behind this process of diminution. The first was Wood's own tactical error in producing an elder son with exactly the same Christian name to follow him in his profession, completing his major projects and using, as at Buckland, his father's designs. The second was Wood's open adoption of a second profession, that of an 'antiquarian', for which he was academically and critically quite unsuited.

Ironically Wood's greatest building schemes would never have been conceived if he had not been a bad antiquary, and his last two ventures would never have been completed if he had not had a dutiful and efficient elder son to 'ghost' his romantic projects into the realization of stone. These factors in Wood's career may have worked to cloud his reputation but they are inseparable from his achievement. Wood was not to know that future enthusiasts for the architecture of his century were, largely, to admire it for qualities of restraint, balance and elegant understatement. These are not the qualities of Wood's antiquarian writing but neither are the Circus nor the Crescent architectural equivalents of the minuet. His writings then, have been, and remain a heavy handicap to his reputation.

Any mention of the divine symbolism of Solomon's Temple at Jerusalem is as suspect to a modern architectural historian as talk of the Protocols of the Elders of Zion would be to a modern political analyst. Both would be considered eccentric and disturbing, the marks of a back-street zealot. But if Wood had not been able to inflate his designs with religiosity, to confuse the *Troy Novant* of Brutus, which was London, and the Camulodunum of the Romans, which was Colchester, with his native Bath, then his imagination would have been crippled. He could not have envisaged a round sun temple of *Bel* or *Onca's* crescent temple of the moon in its 'first Appearance' standing superbly on the northern slopes above a wholly mythical city of the 5th century BC. And without this ability grossly to manipulate historical fact, then it is questionable whether he

1 Surtees Society, Vol. 80 (1885), 277.
2 Ison, 7.

could have projected such schemes of joint classical and romantic composition as the King's Circus and the Royal Crescent.

William Stukeley could talk of Wood stuffing his writing 'with fabulous whimsys of his own crackt imaginations, wild extravagancys concerning Druids, without the least true foundation and knowledge concerning them'.[3] The reality was that both Wood and Stukeley were searchers in a prolonged national quest for an authentic historical image. It had been initiated by the Tudors with their search for Celtic credentials and their revival of King Arthur. Camden's *Britannia* had been part of it as had Sackville and Norton's *Gorboduc* and Shakespeare's *Lear* and *Cymbeline*. When England assumed its Augustan image a growing historical sophistication had come to indicate to all but an eccentric minority that Rome was a more rewarding cultural symbol than any patriotic prehistory. In that sense John Wood was dated and provincial. His standard elevations such as those of Gay Street follow a conventional Palladian, London pattern. But for the poetic set-pieces, for the Circus and the Crescent which are what really make Bath a place of pilgrimage, he looked back to a combination of the Druid delusions of earlier historiographers and to courtyards filched from that impossibly grand and, had it ever been realized, possibly rather vulgar, Palace of Whitehall. Born a decade or so later, Wood might have taken to the Gothick with enthusiasm, but in his generation a natural Romantic made the best of it by enlivening Classicism with an imaginative (if largely fictitious) Prehistory.

From Wood's last months of life there are signals that he was aware of his isolation and was over-reacting in an effort to assert a national standing. When he laid the foundation stone of the Circus, the *Bath Journal* of 18 February 1754, quoting from an earlier *Whitehall Evening Post*, described the event in language that was unctuous, mercenary and assured:

> A general Joy diffuses itself through every Rank of Inhabitants here, on the Prospect of the Advantage that will arise to the Trade of this City from the New Buildings going to be erected on the North Side of the Town, after the Designs, and under the Directions, of that celebrated and eminent Architect and Antiquarian, John Wood, Esq., who this Day laid the first Stone towards the Execution of them, with great Solemnity, amidst the Acclamations and unanimous Applause of Thousands. His Buildings, already erected in this City, have been of so great Benefit to this Place in particular, and to the Country in general, that while they remain standing Monuments to the World of his Taste in Architecture, they will with grateful Hearts be looked on by our latest Posterity, as the Works of that great Benefactor, and the Name of WOOD, the Restorer of Bath, will always be sacred here.

This may read like self-parody but it is impossible not to suspect that Wood penned it himself. His use of the word 'sacred' deserves to be noted.

As if in divine retribution for hubris the *Bath Chronicle* was printing his obituary only three months later. But the sonorous flow of self-con-

3 Surtees Society, Vol. 80 (1885), 276.

gratulation continued as from the tomb and it seems very likely that Wood – always, with his leg-cramps, asthma and chest infections, a convinced valetudinarian – had written this also in anticipation of a combative final dissolution. All, that is, except the first words:

> Last Thursday Morning, about Three o'clock, died after a long and tedious illness, in the fiftieth Year of his Age, John Wood Esq., one of His Majesty's Justices of the Peace for the County of Somerset, celebrated for his Designs, Plans and Skill in Architecture: more particularly in this, and a neighbouring City, the second great Mercantile Trading City of this Kingdom. All which is known to be the Effect of his great Genius: as well as undefatiguable Study and Application, in this very noble and useful Science: Amidst a world of Calumnies, Falsehoods and Discouragements, which he bravely surmounted: He not only raised himself in the Esteem of his Superiors: but in the Compass of a few Years, by an honesty and commendable Industry, obtain'd an handsome Competence for himself and Family – In a word, he had no enemies but those who either envied Him Themselves, or went too far in crediting the defamatory Reproaches and Scandals of Others.

Written in the grand tradition of monumental inscriptions this intensely personal statement contains much truth. If only it had been written by some dispassionate outsider. It must have occasioned, as was intended, much head-shaking in Bath, that 'world of Calumnies, Falsehoods and Discouragements which he bravely surmounted'. There is bitterness, but it is a curiously triumphant bitterness with its bourgeois satisfaction in the family's 'handsome Competence' and its pride in having shaped Bristol as well as Bath.

John Wood died on 23 May 1754. It was a death perfectly timed. The architect's uneasy business relationships within the city and his administrative slackness had left Queen Square flawed and the *Royal Forum* a non-event. Now he left a son perfectly indoctrinated with his concepts yet possessed of a quiet and orderly disposition: a man apt for the negotiation of water rights, the drawing up of binding leases and the legal safeguarding of grand prospects in perpetuity.

The younger Wood must have needed a cool financial head to cope with the terms of his father's will.[4] One sister, Jane Maria, obviously her father's favourite, was left a dowry of £5,000. Naturally her marriage to Henry Coulthurst Esquire soon followed.[5] Another sister, Elizabeth, was left £1,000 to be invested for her and for her subsequent children. She married William Street. John's brother, Thayer Allen, his Christian names a permanent reminder of the father's frustrated hopes for support in early building ventures, was left £1,500 to set him up in a trade or business. He also succeeded to the father's holdings in the city of Bath (as opposed to those in the parish of Walcot) when the mother, Jenny Wood, died in 1766. It is hardly surprising in the light of these provisions that the younger John Wood was to die in debt.

4 Public Record Office, P.C.C. 186 PINFOLD. Summarised by Ison, 235-6.
5 Recorded in the *Bath Journal*, 15 July 1754.

That part of the elder Wood's will dealing with funeral arrangements required that he should be buried 'wrapt up in the cloaths then about him', indicating a nervous distaste at the thought of any hand, even a friendly one, intruding upon his physical privacy. The stipulation that no more than £20 should be spent upon his interment explains the stoic simplicity of his black stone slab in the north aisle of the village church at Swainswick. There was to be no SI MONUMENTUM REQUIRIS CIR-CUMSPICE for John Wood. Possibly his family roots lay in that pastoral quiet. There was no family residential connection with the area until the early 1770s when the younger Wood moved into Eagle House in the next parish, but John Wood's youngest son William Lewis had been buried in Swainswick church four years before his father, 18 December 1750. All Wood's adult connections had been with Walcot parish immediately outside the city walls and he seems to have made the gesture of his last move to Swainswick to shake off the dust of a city that had frustrated and failed to acknowledge him over the years. Finally he lay where his hero Bladud, priest-builder and king, had fallen Icarus-like. In its sense of tempestuous drama and historical absurdity the end was wholly appropriate to the man.

So 'the Restorer of Bath', as he rightly styled himself, remains without a monument in the city he redesigned. It is to be hoped that, before the end of a century during which Bath has cashed in richly on the image which Wood bequeathed it, some body of grateful citizens, led by local Freemasons and a Preservation Trust, will set up a statue to his memory.

It should not be some mean plaque on a house wall or a symbolic twist of contorted bronze but the man himself, larger than life, gesticulating grandly on a plinth. The place to set it would be in the King's Circus where Wood intended George II to ride. He could be dressed in his plain surveyor's clothes, as in the portrait, but a Roman cloak should be draped over one shoulder. On his brow the sculptor might risk a garland of the Druid's oak leaves, one hand would point to the strange circle of stone houses around him and on his face there would be just a hint of a mocking smile.

Wood's final resting place under Solsbury Hill – St Mary the Virgin, Swainswick

Appendix One

Dates relevant to Wood's Life and Career

24 August	1704	Wood baptized in St James' Church, Bath
	1705-6	John Harvey's Pump House built
	1707	George Trim lays out Trim Street
Spring	1708	Harrison's Assembly House built
Winter	1711	Bath-Bristol Navigation Act passed
	1715	8,000 visitors in the Bath season this year
	1716	Humphry Thayer buys the Old Bowling Green and the Abbey Orchard for speculative development
	1720	William Killigrew adds ballroom to Harrison's Assembly House
		Dr. Bettenson begins a court of houses on the Bull Garden (south of Priory)
		Thomas Greenway begins St John's Court
Winter	1721	Wood leases a plot of land on the Cavendish estate in London
12 July	1722	Wood working for Lord Bingley
	1723-32	Wood building on the Cavendish estate
	1724-7	Wood working for Bingley in London and Yorkshire
27 May	1724	Avon navigation subscription opened; Ralph Allen takes share
Summer	1725	Wood prepares designs for Bath while in Yorkshire
31 December	1725	Wood in London to interest Robert Gay in his designs
18 February	1726	Wood signs contract to dig on the Avon Navigation
31 March	1726	Wood approaches the Earl of Essex with his designs
Spring	1726	Wood approaches the Duke of Chandos with his designs
Summer	1726	Wood working in Yorkshire
12 October	1726	Wood's second approach to Chandos
21 November	1726	Wood signs agreement with Gay to build a street on the Barton Fields
	1726	Wood commissioned by Humphry Thayer to design Dame Lindsey's Assembly House
		Wood plans developments for the Bowling Green and Abbey Orchard
	1726	Wood prepares General Hospital scheme for Thayer
		John Hobbs employs John Strahan to lay out streets in west Bath

23 January	1727	Wood signs articles with Chandos to rebuild St John's Hospital
Spring	1727	Wood in London designing Allen's Bath town house
	1727	Wood designing houses and loggia for east side of Orange Grove
16 May	1727	Wood takes lodgings in Bath at Mr Silcock's and prepares Hospital design for the Ambrey
	1727	Ralph Allen buys the Combe Down quarries
12 June	1727	George I dies; Wood's Barton Fields scheme with Gay collapses; Wood's 'Chimerical' scheme for the city rejected by the Corporation
17 July	1727	Wood paid off from work on Avon Navigation
Winter	1727	Wood working at Tyberton
January	1728	St John's Hospital almost complete
25 February	1728	Wood's first son, John, baptized in Bath Abbey
Spring	1728	Wood's dispute with Colen Campbell over stone for Greenwich Hopsital
27 September	1728	Work begins on Lindsey's Assembly House
October	1728	Wood building small house on west side of Barton Street
18 November	1728	Circular Hospital scheme chosen for Ambrey site; Allen joins Hospital Committee
28 November	1728	First leases taken for Queen Square, south-east corner
10 December	1728	Ground broken for Queen Square
27 January	1729	First stone laid at Queen Square
12 February	1729	Wood at Cirencester with Lord Bathurst
	1729	Wood designs Lyncombe and Widcombe Poor House
Winter	1729	Lindsey's Assembly House completed
	1730	Wood erecting sizeable houses in John Street
6 April	1730	Lindsey's Assembly House opened with a public breakfast; scheme for Circus on Abbey Orchard displayed
May	1730	Circus scheme approved, then abandoned.
July	1730	Wood visits Bishop at Llandaff
14 January	1731	Gay offers free gift of land for Circular Hospital
16 January	1731	Hospital Committee asks Gay for more land – no answer
3 February	1731	Wood proposes St Mary's Chapel scheme to Gay
26 February	1731	17 people contract to build on Queen Square, South Side
8 March	1731	Wood leases ground on Queen Square, South Side
	1731	Wood designs an obelisk for Orange Grove
5 February	1732	Altar for Tyberton church completed
25 March	1732	Foundation stone of St Mary's Chapel laid
12 October	1732	Leases taken for Queen Square, North Side
Autumn	1733	Wood designs a second storey for Harvey's Pump Room – rejected

	1734	Wood building Belcomb Brook Villa
Spring	1734	Restoration of Llandaff begins, continues until 1749
25 December	1734	St Mary's Chapel opened for Divine Service
21 June	1735	Allen resident in west wing of Prior Park
	1736	Wood's Plan of the City of Bath published
January	1736	Queen Square completed
	1737	Wood writing first version of *The Origin of Building*
		Basement storey of Prior Park's central block completed – Wood sacked
		Lyncomb Spaw building designed by Wood
15 August	1737	Wood designs seal factory in Widcombe – not built
9 December	1737	Humphry Thayer dies
22 December	1737	Wood prepares new Hospital design – not built
	1738	Lilliput Castle built this year and probably the house at Bowden Hill for Benjamin Styles
11 January	1738	Hospital trustees debate Hospital scheme and new Baths
9 February	1738	Wood completes Hospital design, Pine engraves it
1 April	1738	Corporation quashes Wood's scheme for a new Pump Room
25 April	1738	Treaty for a 'Grand Forum' on Abbey Orchard
6 July	1738	William Pulteney lays foundation stone of Hospital
10 November	1738	Queen Square obelisk begun
Autumn	1738	Act of Parliament on Chair rates favours eastward extension of city
		Strahan's King's Mead development completed
3 July	1739	Contract for *Royal Forum* signed; work begins on sewers
October	1739	Assignments for plots on the Grand (North) Parade granted
10 March	1740	First stone of the first house of Grand Parade laid
Michaelmas	1740	Grand Parade ready for roofing; Wood surveys Stonehenge
	1740	Wood builds house now known as 'Chandos Buildings'
6 February	1741	Wood asked to form designs for the Bristol Exchange
13 February	1741	Exchange designs accepted
10 March	1741	Foundation stone of Exchange laid
Spring	1741	Central block of Prior Park completed by Richard Jones
	1741	*The Origin of Building* published
1 March	1742	Wood sets up subscription for a Chippenham Canal which fails
10 September	1742	Wood completes a design for King Edward's School – not executed
	1742	First Part of the *Essay towards a Description of Bath* published

27 January	1743	First stone of South Parade laid; work continues until 1748
21 September	1743	Bristol Exchange opened
	1743	Second and Third Parts of the *Essay* published
	1745	*A Description of the Exchange of Bristol* published
	1746	Wood designs Bathford Spa building
	1747	*Choir Gaure* published
Spring	1748	Beau Nash urges Wood to design an Assembly House on the *Royal Forum*
	1748	Titanbarrow Logia and Liverpool Exchange begun
	1749	Second edition of the *Essay* published with extensive revisions
	1751	*Dissertation upon the Orders of Columns* published
18 December	1753	Contract signed to buy nine acres on the Barton Fields for the King's Circus
7 February	1754	*Gentleman's Magazine* records Circus foundation stone laying
23 March	1754	Circus site moved to the north
23 May	1754	Wood dies in his fiftieth year

Appendix Two

Contract drawn up by Wood between Bath craftsmen and William Brydges of Tyberton

Memorandum it is agreed this 16th day of Sepr 1728 Between William Brydges Esqr of the one part and Michael Bray John Fussel and Benjamin Fussel of the other part as follows viz.

Imp For Transome Windows half a Crown each Window
For two light Windows eighteen pence each Window
For Door Cases two Shillings a peice
For naked Flooring three shillings a Square
For Partitioning half a Crown a Square
For Roofing four shillings a Square
For Boarding the Floors three shillings a Square

The sd Michael Bray John Fussel and Ben. Fussel doth agree to perform the aforesd Work in a workmanlike manner and the sd William Brydges doth agree to pay them the aforesd Prices in manner following (viz) the Sum of Six Pounds Six Shillings at the Signing of this Agreemt Three Pounds three Shillings more three weeks after the date of this Agreemt and the residue of the money Accruing from the Measuremt of the Roofing and Flooring in the Offices when the sd Roofing and Flooring is finished together with the Residue of the Money for making the Window frames and Door Cases when the sd Window Frames and Door Cases are finished And as the sd Michael Bray John Fussel and Benjamin Fussel goes on in finishing the Partitioning and Boarding of the Floors of the House and Offices the sd William Brydges doth agree to pay them as often as they shall have finished a peice of Work the value of such Peice of Work provided it is not under Four Pounds in value by measure It is lastly Agreed by the Partys hereto that the aforesd Work shall be measured by John Wood of the City of Bath Architect and if any dispute shou'd arrise about the sd Work the same to be determined by the sd John Wood

Witness

Appendix Three

Letter from Wood to William Brydges
illustrative of Wood's expertise
in fitting up an interior with woodwork

Sir

Bath March 19th 1729

I am very concerned to hear by yours of the 7th Ins^t that you have been ill. I have Receivd a Bill from Mrs Payne for £24:10s wch will be payable the 26th Ins^t. I have acquainted Greenway with what you wrote about the Man and he promised me that he wou'd write to him to know the reason of his Idleness.

I have sent you herewith the first draught of the Salon the Chimney of wch you seem to like it being to be Executed in Stone I must own it will have a very good effect but must prefer the Chimney in the new design the Jaumbs and Mantles bounded with the red lines being all the Stone work and the rest is intended to be Wood work and this Chimney will be proper if you Execute either of the draughts for the Room. On the backside of the draught of the Steps for the Stairs is the Moulding of the Chimney Piece which is to project before the Wain-scott 3½ Inches, the Plinth (or Beginners as the Bath Workmen term it) is to be half an Inch wider than the Jaumbs & to project before the Nose of the Architrave a quarter of an Inch so that the Plinth will be 9 Inches wide and will project before the Wainscot 3¾ Inches. In the new Design for the Salon I have drawn a Sconce on one side of the Chimney wch will cost about 50s if you woud go to the expence of such Sconces for all the margins A B C D E F G H I K L M it woud not only make the Architecture of the Room much better but serve instead of Furniture. I mean Common Sconces & Curtins & Peir Glass wch must come to more than £30. the draught is drawn by the same Scale as the first design, the Coves in both draughts are the same and the Entablatures of the same height only in this new design I have left out Modillions & have made the Entablature quite plain, the Pannels and the Margins are in a line with one another, and the Ground of the Ornaments round the Pannels is designed to project forward one Inch, the Grounds are each one foot wide, upon which there is to be an O.G. 2½ Inches wide nailed in thus [diagram] the Wainscot under the Sur-Base must be quite plain, the Architraves round the Doors must be 6½ Inches wide, the Doors 3:3 wide and 8 foot high in 8 Pannels according to the Draught, (wch may served for the Doors of the whole house) I have figured the framing of the Doors, all the Stiles and Rails 4 Inches broad, except the bottom Rail wch is 6½ Inches, and the next Rail upon wch the Lock must be set 6¼ Inches wide; and what ever Moulding the Door is worked with whether O.G. or Quarter Round, or Quarter round & O.G. it must be added to the breadth of the framing. I have made a Draught for the Hall Door supposing it to be four feet wide and nine feet high the Framing without the moulding which is quarter round and O.G. is 5 Inches and a half wide, ex-

216

cept the bottom Rail which is eight Inches and a half wide, and the Rail on which the Lock must be set which is eight Inches wide, the outside of the Door is represented by the Draught the Pannels are raised with a bead upon the rising the inside of the Door must be the same sort of Work wth the Hall.

If the Salon is executed after this new design the Pannels must be one Inch thick at least & Canvas shou'd be Glewed at the back of the Joynts, the Pannels ought to be glewed up (-) with & planed over, and if they were planed over upon the Backside & primed with Oyle & Coulour it would not be money ill layed out, the top Rail & the Joynts of the framing must be as I have marked upon G with Pricked lines & then if the Margin G or the Pannels shoud shrink when the Ornaments comes to be put on the shrinking will be hid, and it woud be proper to have the Wall work framed & put up directly and the Cornice and freeze may be put up but the Architrave Base & Sur Base & the Ornaments round the Pannels ought not to be put up untill the Wood has done Shrinking (which will be in one years time) the Work must be painted twice in Oyle as soon as it is fasten'd up against the Walls, for this Maxim must ever be observed, that as often as the Pores of Wood is exposed to the Air (or wch is equal) if it is moistened with any Oyley substance that will penetrate into the Wood it will Cause it to shrink (that is the Pores when they are open will Close) and if this method is followed the Work will be done in the best manner and tho it is so plain yet it will have a better effect than an Ornamental Design unless Executed in the best manner which cannot be done but at a great expence.

I have draw a Step for the Stairs at large, the String board is to be plain with a Bead at the bottom, I suppose the Steps to have twelve Inches Ground, Six Inches rise and to be Six feet long, it Wou'd be proper to have a very large twist at the bottom at least 2 Steps and a half. The Ballisters shou'd be two Inches and a quarter Square and two foot four Inches high, so that if you agree for the laying the Strings, setting & Working the Steps Working the hand Rail & puting up the Ballisters it may be Worth about four Shillings a Step if done with Deal.

Inclosed is a draught of the Altar, if you have a Person that can execute it in Plaister (I mean the Ceiling) it will be better than in Deal Painted, but nothing can be done to the Ceiling till the Wood Work is done and put up because the Ribs of the Cove must answer the Margins between the Pannels. I will order the Altar to be gone on with and finished as soon as possible, I think you concluded to have a Mahoggony Rail & Ballister before it.

When you have agreed for the Stair Case Mr Symmons must let me know how many Ballisters will be wanting & he must give me the heights of those under that part of the Rail which is ramped & twisted – before I can order them to be turned.

When ever you go on with your Painting I can send you a Man to Work after the rate of 10s for every hundred yards.

I am sorry to hear of the damage you have receiv'd by broaken Glass, it was safe & whole when opened at Bristol so that what is broake was after it went from Bristol.

    I am

      S^{r}

        Your most obed^{t} & most hum: Servt

          Jo: Wood

Select Bibliography

1. Manuscript Sources

Bath Reference Library: Volume of Wood Drawings; 2nd MS of *Origin*; MS Life of Richard Jones

Bramham Park Estate Office: Estate Maps

Bristol Central Library: Correspondence in Braikenridge Collection

Bristol Record Office: Minutes of the Committee for building the Exchange; Wood's correspondence with the Committee

British Museum: Harley Estate Records and additional Harley papers; Cole's drawings of Llandaff

Hereford Record Office: Tyberton Papers

Hoare's Bank: Bingley's Account Books G & H

Huntington Library, California: Chandos Letterbooks

Lincolnshire Archives Office: Monson Papers

National Library of Wales, Aberystwyth: Llandaff Chapter Act Books

Notting University Library: Manvers Papers

Public Record Office: Wood's will

Royal Academy Library: Bristol Exchange – Wood volume

Soane Museum: 1st MS of *Origin*

Somerset Record Office: Walcot Parish Vestry Records

2. Unpublished Theses

Bertram, William, 'The Origins and Building of Queen Square, Bath' (Architectural Association, 1963)

Brownell, Charles Edward, 'John Wood the Elder and John Wood the Younger: Architects of Bath' (Ph.D., Columbia University, 1976)

Buttress, D.R., 'An architectural history of Llandaff Cathedral' (MA, Manchester University, 1965)

Coates, Ann Barbara, 'The two John Woods, 18th-century architects of Bath' (RIBA, Dec. 1946)

Priest, E.G., 'Building the Exchange and Markets of Bristol' (Dept. of Architecture, University of Bristol, 1980)

Stevenson, Christine, 'John Wood the Elder and *The Origin of Building*' (MA, Courtauld Institute, 1981)

3. Primary Printed Sources

Anderson, James, *The Constitutions of the Free-Masons, Containing the History, Charges, Regulations etc., of that Most Ancient . . . Fraternity* (Bernard Quaritch, 1723)

Anon., *The Stranger's Assistant and Guide to Bath* (R. Cruttwell, Bath, 1773)

Bingham, Joseph, *Origines ecclesiasticae, or, the Antiquities of the Christian Church* (Robert Knaplock, 1708)

Campbell, Colen, *Vitruvius Britannicus* (Campbell, 1717-25)

Collinson, John, *The History and Antiquities of the County of Somerset* (R. Cruttwell, Bath, 1791; reprinted by Alan Sutton, 1983)

Derrick, Samuel, *Letters written from Liverpoole, Chester, Corke, the Lake of Killarney* (L. Davis and C. Reymers, 1768)

Desaguliers, John Theophilus, *A Course of Experimental Philosophy* (John Senex and W. Innys, 1734-45)

Desgodetz, Antoine, *Les Edifices antiques de Rome dessinés et mesurés tres exactement* (J.B. Coignard, Paris, 1682; reissued 1695)

Drayton, Michael, *Poly Olbion, Great Britaine* (M. Lownes, 1613)

Egan, Pierce, *Walks through Bath* (Meyler & Son, Bath, 1819)

Fischer von Erlach, J.B., *Entwurf einer historischen Architektur* (Vienna, 1721; facsimile ed. by the Gregg Press, 1964)

Graves, Richard, *The Triflers* (London, 1805; Bath, 1806)

Halfpenny, William, *Perspective Made Easy* (J. Oswald, 1731)

Horsley, John, *Britannia Romana; or, the Roman antiquities of Britain* (J. Osborn and T. Longman, 1732)

Jones, Inigo, *The Most Notable Antiquity of Great Britain, Vulgarly Called Stone-heng, On Salisbury Plain, Restored* (London 1655)

Kent, William (ed.), *The Designs of Inigo Jones consisting of Plans and Elevations for Public and Private Buildings, with some Additional Designs* (London, 1727)

Musgrave, William, *Antiquitates Britanno-Belgicae* (J. March, Exeter, 1719)

Newton, Isaac, *The Chronology of Ancient Kingdoms Amended* (London, 1728)

—— *Observations upon the Prophecies of Daniel and the Apocalypse of St. John* (London, 1733)

Palladio, Andrea, *The Four Books of Architecture* (Dover, New York, 1965)

Picart, Bernard, *Cérémonies et coutumes de tous les peuples du monde, representées par des figures dessinées de la main de B. Picart* (Paris, 1723; translated into English, 1733)

Pococke, Dr Richard, *The Travels through England of Dr. Richard Pococke*, (Camden Society, 1888-9)

Rowlands, Henry, *Mona Antiqua Restaurata* (Dublin, 1723)

Sacheverell, William, *An Account of the Isle of Man . . . to which is added A Dissertation about the MONA of Caesar and Tacitus; and an Account of the Antient Druids, by Mr. Thomas Brown* (J. Harley, 1702)

Shears, Sir Henry, *The History of Polybius* (1693; 2nd ed. 1698)

Smollett, Tobias, *An Essay on the External Use of Water* (1752; reprinted by Johns Hopkins Press, 1935)

—— *The Expedition of Humphry Clinker* (1771)

Stukeley, William, *Itinerarium Curiosum: Centuria I* (London, 1724)

—— *Itinerarium Curiosum: Centuria II* (London, 1776)

—— *Stonehenge a Temple Restor'd to the British Druids* (London, 1740)

—— *Palaeographia Sacra* (London, 1736)

Toland, John, *A Critical History of the Celtic Religion and Learning* (1702)

—— *A History of the Druids* (1726)

Villalpanda, J.B., *Commentaries on Ezekiel* (1604)

Wallis, Revd Stamford, *A Dissertation in Vindication of the Antiquity of Stone Henge*

Warner, Revd Richard, *The History of Bath* (R. Cruttwell, Bath, 1801)

Webb, John, *A Vindication of Stone-Heng Restored* (1665; reissued 1725)

Wither, George, *A Collection of Emblemes, Ancient and Moderne* (1635; Scolar Press Facsimile, 1968)

Wood, John, *A Dissertation Upon the Standard Lineal and Superficial Measures of the Antients* (pamphlet now lost, c.1740)

—— *The Origin of Building, or the Plagiarism of the Heathens Detected* (J. Leake, 1744)

—— *An Essay Towards a Description of Bath* (W. Frederick, 1742-3; revised ed., 1749; 3rd ed., 1765 reprinted by Kingsmead Reprints, 1969)

—— *A Description of the Exchange of Bristol* (J. Leake, 1745; Kingsmead Reprints 1969)

—— *Choir Gaure vulgarly called Stonehenge, Described, Restored and Explained* (Oxford, 1747)

—— *Dissertation Upon the Orders of Columns and their Appendages* (1751)

Wood, John the Younger, *A Series of Plans, for Cottages or Habitations of the Labourer, either in Husbandry or the Mechanic Arts* (1781)

4. Secondary Printed Sources

Ackerman, James S., *Palladio* (Penguin Books, 1966)

Aslet, Clive, *Quinlan Terry: The Revival of Architecture* (Viking, 1986)

Bailey, Bruce A., 'William Brydges and the Rebuilding of Tyberton Church' in *Trans. of the Woolhope Naturalists' Field Club*, vol. xxxvii, part 2 (1962)

Baker, C.H.C. & M.I. *The Life and Circumstances of James Brydges, First Duke of Chandos* (Oxford University Press, 1949)

Binney, Marcus, *Sir Robert Taylor: From Rococo to Neo-Classicism* (George Allen & Unwin, 1984)

Boyce, Benjamin, *The Benevolent Man – A Life of Ralph Allen of Bath* (Harvard University Press, 1967)

Buttress, D.R., 'Llandaff Cathedral in the 18th and 19th centuries' in *Journal of the Hist. Soc. of the Church in Wales* vol.16 (1966)

Clarke, Gillian, *Prior Park: A Compleat Landscape* (Millstream Books, 1987)

Colvin, H.M., *A Biographical Dictionary of British Architects 1600-1840* (John Murray, 1978)

Cotterell, T.S., *Some notes on John Wood the architect and builder of 18th century Bath* (Bath Corporation, 1927)

Cunliffe, Barry, *The City of Bath* (Alan Sutton, 1986)

Drakers, W.S., *John Wood and his Times* (pamphlet, Bath, 1954)

Davies, E.T., 'John Wood's Italianate Temple' in *Journal of the Hist. Soc. of the Church in Wales*, vol.6 (1956)

Dear, L.M., *Whitehaven – The Story of Titan Barrow* (Whitehaven Trust, Bath 1972)

Dobbie, B.M.W., *An English Rural Community: Batheaston with St. Catherine* (Bath University Press, 1969)

Downes, Kerry, *Vanbrugh* (A. Zwemmer, 1977)

—— *Hawksmoor* (A. Zwemmer, 1979)

Edwards, A. Trystan, 'Some Original Drawings by John Wood' in *Architect and Building News*, 4 November 1927

Evans, Joan *A History of the Society of Antiquaries* (Oxford University Press, 1956)

Falconer, J.P.E., 'The Family of John Wood of Bath' in *Notes & Queries*, vol.193 (18 September 1948)

Fisher, Wilfred G., *A History of the Provincial Grand Lodge of Somerset* (The Lodge, Bath, 1962)

Friedman, Terry, *James Gibbs* (Yale University Press, 1984)

Gadd, David, *Georgian Summer: Bath in the Eighteenth Century* (Adams & Dart, 1971; revised ed., Countryside Books, 1987)

Gomme, A.H. & S.M., 'Who Designed Capesthorne Hall?' in *Trans. Historic. Soc. of Lancs. & Cheshire*, vol. cxxi (1969)

Gomme, A, Jenner, M, & Little, B, *Bristol: an architectural history* (Lund Hmphries, 1979)

Green, Mowbray A., *The Eighteenth Century Architecture of Bath* (George Gregory, Bath, 1904)

Hamill, John, *The Craft: A History of English Freemasonry* (Crucible, 1986)

Harris, Eileen, 'Batty Langley: A Tutor to Freemasons (1696-1751)' in *Burlington Magazine*, May 1977

Harris, John, *Sir William Chambers: Knight of the Polar Star* (A. Zwemmer, 1970)

—— *The Palladians* (Trefoil Books, 1981)

—— 'Harley, the Patriot Collector' in *Apollo*, September, 1985

Harris, S.A., 'Sarah Clayton's Letter and John Wood of Bath' in *Trans. Historic. Soc. of Lancs. & Cheshire*, vol.c (1948)

Ison, Walter, *The Georgian Buildings of Bath* (Faber, 1948; 2nd. revised edition by Kingsmead Press, 1980)

—— 'John Wood the Elder' in *Journal of the RIBA*, 3rd series, vol.61 (July 1954)

—— *The Georgian Buildings of Bristol* (Faber, 1952; reprinted by Kingsmead Press, 1978)

Jacob, Margaret C., 'John Toland and the Newtonian Ideologue' in *Journal of the Warburg and Courtauld Institutes*, vol.32 (1969)

Jenkins, Frank, *Architect and Patron* (Oxford University Press, 1961)

Jones, M.G., *The Charity School Movement* (Cambridge University Press, 1938; reprinted by F. Cass, 1964)

Kendrick, T.D., *The Druids* (Methuen, 1927)

Knoop, Douglas & Jones, G.P., *An Introduction to Freemasonry* (Manchester University Press, 1942)

—— *The London Mason in the Seventeenth Century* (Manchester University Press, 1935)

Latimer, John, *The Annals of Bristol in the 18th Century* (William George & Sons, 1893)

Laurence, Godfrey F., *Bathford Past and Present* (Bathford Local History Society, 1985)

Lees-Milne, James, *The Earls of Creation* (Hamish Hamilton, 1962)

—— *English Country Houses: Baroque 1685-1715* (Hamlyn, 1970)

Lees-Milne, J. & Ford, D., *Images of Bath* (St Helena Press, 1982)

Le Fevre, R.A. (ed.), *John Wood and his Times* (Mendip Press, 1954)

Levis, Howard C., *Bladud of Bath* (West Country Editions, Bath, 1973)

Little, Bryan, *The Building of Bath, 47-1947* (Collins, 1947)

Mannel, Frank E., *The Religion of Isaac Newton* (Oxford University Press, 1974)

Mitchell, B. & Penrose, H. (eds.), *Letters from Bath 1766-67 by the Rev. John Penrose* (Alan Sutton, 1983)

Mowl, T. & Earnshaw, B., *Trumpet at a Distant Gate: The Lodge as Prelude to the Country House* (Waterstone, 1985)

Murch, Jerom, *Biographical Sketches of Bath Celebrities* (Isaac Pitman, London, and William Lewis, Bath, 1893)

Neale, R.S., *Bath 1680-1850: A Social History* (Routledge & Kegan Paul, 1981)

Newby, Evelyn, 'The Hoares of Bath' in *Bath History*, vol.1 (Alan Sutton, 1986)

Ollivant, Alfred, *Some Account of the Conditions of the Fabric of Llandaff Cathedral* (London 1857, 2nd ed. 1860)

Owen, A.L., *The Famous Druids: A Survey of Three Centuries of English Literature on Druids* (Oxford University Press, 1962)

Peach, R.E.M., *Historic Houses in Bath and their associations* (Simpkin, Marshall, 1883, 1884)

———— 'Ralph Allen, Prior Park and Bath' in The Antiquary, *vol. 12 (1885)*

———— *Bath Old and New* (Simpkin, Marshall, 1888)

———— *Street-Lore of Bath* (Simpkin, Marshall, 1893)

Pevsner, Nikolaus, 'John Wood at Llandaff' in *Architectural Review*, June 1954

Picton, J.A., *Memorials of Liverpool* (London 1873)

Pigott, Stuart, *The Druids* (Thames & Hudson, 1975)

———— *William Stukeley: An Eighteenth Century Antiquary* (Thames & Hudson, 1985)

The Correspondence of Alexander Pope, ed. by G. Sherburn (Oxford University Press, 1956)

Robertson, C., *Bath: an Architectural Guide* (Faber, 1975)

Roche, Rev. Brother J.S., *A History of Prior Park College and its Founder Bishop Baines* (Burrns Oates & Washbourne, 1931)

Rykwert, Joseph, *The First Moderns: The Architects of the Eighteenth Century* (MIT Press, 1980)

Scott, Maurice, *Discovering Widcombe and Lyncombe, Bath* (Maurice Scott, Bath, 1984)

Shepherd, Monsignor James, *Reminiscences of Prior Park* (Isaac Pitman, 1894)

Sitwell, Edith, *Bath* (Faber, 1932; reprinted by Century Hutchinson 1987)

Smith, E. Baldwin, *The Dome* (Princeton University Press, 1950)

Smith, R.A.L., *Bath* (Batsford, 1944)

Stevenson, Christine, "Solomon 'Engothicked': The Elder John Wood's Restoration of Llandaff Cathedral" in *Art History*, vol.6, no.3 (September 1983)

Stutchbury, Howard E., *The Architecture of Colen Campbell* (Manchester University Press, 1967)

Summerson, John, 'John Wood and the English Town-Planning Tradition' in *Heavenly Mansions* (Cresset Press, 1949)

———— *Georgian London* (Pleiades Books, 1945; Penguin Books 1962)

———— *Inigo Jones* (Penguin Books, 1966)

Sykes, Christopher Simon, *Private Palaces: Life in the Great London Houses* (Chatto & Windus, 1985)

Tunstall, Dr. James, *Rambles about Bath* (Isaac Pitman, London, and William Lewis, Bath, 1899)

Tyte, William, *Bath in the 18th Century* (Chronicle Office, Bath, 1903)

Waylen, James, *Chronicles of the Devizes* (Longman, 1839)

White, George A.H., *Chippenham in Bygone Days* (G. Simpson, Devizes, 1924)

Wilson, Michael I., *William Kent: Architect, Designer, Painter, Gardener, 1685-1748* (Routledge & Kegan Paul, 1984)

Wittkower, Rudolf, *Palladio and English Palladianism* (Thames & Hudson, 1974)

———— 'Federico Zuccari and John Wood of Bath' in *Journal of the Warbur and Courtauld Institutes*, vol.v (1943)

Illustrations

Index